Index
of
North Carolina Bankrupts

Acts *of* 1800, 1841 *and* 1867

Edited By:
William Doub Bennett

Southern Historical Press, Inc.
Greenville, SC   29602

SOUTHERN HISTORICAL PRESS, INC.
PO BOX 1267
Greenville, SC   29601

ISBN #978-1-63914-069-5

Printed in the United States of America

FOREWORD

One of the important cycles in the history of many families, past and present, are the good times and bad times that reflect the economic climate of the United States and around the world. Hard times often caused a family or business to file for bankruptcy. While many bankruptcies were filed in state or local courts, in certain time periods bankruptcy cases were filed in federal courts. These records are in Record Group 21, Records of the U. S. District and Circuit Courts, in the custody of the Regional Archives System of the National Archives.

The United States has had five bankruptcy laws. Those passed in 1800, 1841, 1867, and 1898 were passed in response to severe economic upheavals. The current law, passed in 1976, is a reworking of the 1898 statute to reflect changing business practices and economic realities. The files created under these laws can be a rich source of information about community, business, and family history.

The process for filing for bankruptcy required the petioner to provide the court with information about his or her financial condition. This normally took the form of filing two documents - one showing debts (liabilities) and the other showing assets. The document listing debts is almost always detailed, showing to whom the debt was owed, the nature of the debt, when the debt was assumed, and what security was offered (if any). Because this list may include debts assumed many years before the petition is filed, the debts give the researcher insight into the earlier commercial relationships of the petitioner. The list of debts may also provide unexpected information about occupations, business partners, real estate ownership, or former residences. If the petitioner owed money as the result of court judgment, the researcher may discover clues that will lead to even more detailed information.

The petitioner's list of assets may be very general, listing for example "household goods," or it may be quite detailed, listing each item in the house room by room. The list of assets for a business may include a complete listing of goods, materials, machinery, and buildings, or may simply list "merchandise." The difference seems to depend somewhat on the size of the estate and the complexity of the debts. Assets may also include lists of debts owed to the petitioner, lists of stocks and bonds owned, and insurance policies or memberships in benevolent societies. Certain items were exempt from the bankruptcy proceeding in order to leave the petitioner with enough belongings to start a new life. These items are also listed. A researcher can use these lists to develop an in-depth understanding of the life of the petitioner and his or her family.

Once the financial documents were filed, bankruptcy cases followed a course that produced other documents that may also be of interest to a researcher. A referee was appointed to handle the case; an assignee was appointed to manage the property and pay the debts. The referee was an official of the court, but the assignee might be a friend or neighbor, although usually not a relative. Notices were filed in appropriate newspapers calling for creditors to produce proof of the debt. Once the debts were proved, the name of assignee was responsible for selling the estate, paying court fees, and then paying as much of each debt as possible. For the researcher, the newspaper ads, the assignee, and the sale of the estate may provide further information on the family, business, or community.

As with any source of information it is important for the researcher to understand the limits of the records that are available. The Bankruptcy Act of 1800 applied only to businesses who were forced into involuntary bankruptcy by their creditors. The act was repealed in 1803, making this a very small, narrow, and limited set of records.

The Act of 1841 went into effect in February 1842 and was repealed in March 1843, making it the shortest-lived of the bankruptcy acts. The Bankruptcy Act of 1867 was repealed in 1878. The records from this act are of special interest because they reflect the 1850s through most of the 1870s and allow for some limited comparisons of the periods before and after the Civil War.

In order to be as complete as possible, this index was compiled from both docket books and case files. As a result there are some cases that were listed from docket books where no case files exist. Even in courts where the case files have survived, there are missing or incomplete files. Specific questions about the extent of these records should be addressed to the staff of the National Archives-Southeast Region.

Nineteenth century handwriting can be very difficult to read, so researchers are encouraged to be open-minded about how the names in which they are interested might be spelled. In the same way, the boundaries of the court districts were not rigid. For example, some cases filed under the Act of 1867 from the western part of the state were filed in Wilmington, even though there was a court in Asheville.

Records from the federal bankruptcy acts are an often neglected resource for students of community, business, and family history. The window on the past they provide can help give a context to research that is not possible in most other sources.

Dr. Beverly Watkins
National Archives-Great Lakes Region

INTRODUCTION

Congress was given the power to establish under the constitution "uniform Laws on the subject of Bankruptcies throughout the United States" (Art. I, Sec. 8). Under this authority four national bankruptcy laws have been enacted. Each of these laws was approved shortly after a depression. A business disturbance in 1797 precipitated the first bankruptcy act of 1800; the second bankruptcy act of 1841 was enacted after the Panic of 1837; the depressed economic picture after the Civil War brought on the third bankruptcy act, that of 1867; and the Panic of 1893 with the following years of depression brought on the Act of 1898. Each of the first three acts was repealed after conditions became better. The Act of 1898, however, is still in force although it has been amended many times and rewritten in 1976. Under each of the acts original jurisdiction was assigned by the Congress to the United States district courts, excepting the Act of 1800 whereby jury trials of bankruptcy claims could be had in the United States circuit courts until 29 April 1802, when this function was transferred to the district courts. Appellate jurisdiction in bankruptcy cases under the first three acts was given to the circuit courts. Under the Act of 1898 all appellate jurisdiction was fixed in the United Circuit Court of Appeals.

The first national bankruptcy act, approved 4 April 1800 (2 Stat. 19), provided for an effective period beginning 2 June 1800 and continuing for five years. It applied only to merchants or other persons "residing within the United States, actually using the trade of merchandise, by buying and selling in gross, or by retail, or dealing in exchange, or as a banker, broker, factor, underwriter, or marine insurer." The act provided for compulsory or involuntary bankruptcy, but not for voluntary bankruptcy. It recognized only two acts of bankruptcy: fraudulent conveyance or concealment of a person or his property, and attachments not dissolved within two months. Discharge of the bankrupt from his debts required the consent of creditors having claims of more than $50 each, who together held at least two-thirds of the claims in number and amount. The bankruptcy act was administered under the direction of the district courts by commissioners, who were at first appointed by the district judge, but later, by the President (2 Stat. 164), and assignees, who were elected by the creditors at their first meeting. Because of its limited applicability and for other reasons the act was repealed on 19 December 1803 (2 Stat. 248), months before its expirartion date; although the repealing act provided for the execution of any commission of bankruptcy issued before its passage.

The second national bankruptcy act was passed on 19 August 1841 (5 Stat. 440), and was to take effect on 1 February 1842. The shortest lived of the Federal bankruptrcy laws, it was repealed 3 March 1842 (5 Stat. 614). The law permitted voluntary bankruptcy to all debtors, with involuntary bankruptcy limited to bankers, merchants, factors, traders, and brokers. Consent of creditors for discharge was eliminated but creditors holding a majority in number and amount of claims could block a discharge by written dissent. However, the bankrupt could obtain a discharge by a jury trial if the jury found he had surrendered all property and had complied with the orders of the court. The act was administered by commissioners and assignees, all of whom were appointed by the district judge.

On 2 March 1867, Congress approved the third national bankruptcy act (14 Stat. 517). Under this law involuntary bankruptcy was extended to all classes of debtors. If the bankrupt's assets did not pay fifty per cent of the debts, no discharge was granted without consent of a majority of the creditors. This provision was not to apply to any proceedings begun within a year after the approval of the act. To aid judges administering the law, the act provided for the appointment by the court for registers in bankruptcy who were to hold and preside at the meetings of creditors, take proofs of debts, compute interest and dividends, and to otherwise dispatch the administrative business of the court in bankruptcy matters where there was no opposing interest. In cases where any opposition to an adjudication or discharge arose, the controversy had to be submitted to the court. The act was not popular and in spite of several amendments to correct objectionable features it was repealed 7 June 1878 (20 Stat. 99).

The Act of 13 April 1792 (1 Stat. 252-253) provided for sessions of the district court at New Bern, Wilmington, and Edenton. An Act of 9 June 1794 divided the state into three definite districts based on the judicial districts established for the North Carolina District Superior Courts; the District of Wilmington included all the counties in the state districts of Morgan, Salisbury, Fayetteville, and Wilmington; the District of New Bern included all the counties in the state districts of Hillsborough, Halifax, and New Bern; and the District of Edenton included all the counties of the state district of Edenton. An Act of 4 June 1872 (17 Stat. 215-217) divided North Carolina into Eastern and Western Districts. The Western District was composed of all counties west of, and including, the counties of Person, Orange, Chatham, Moore, and Richmond. District courts were established at Statesville, Asheville, and Greensboro and the Edenton court was moved to Elizabeth City. On 9 June 1878 (20 Stat. 173), a district court was established in Charlotte. These were the district courts which heard cases generated by the first three bankruptcy laws.

Records of only four cases survive from the Act of 1800. These cases are filed with the Elizabeth City (Edenton) Division records. No dockets survive, only case files. There are approximately one hundred case records which have survived from the Act of 1841 found in the Edenton records. These consist of a minute book and loose case files. There are also four cases appealed from the New Bern and Wilmington district courts to the Raleigh circuit court. The case files are found in the mixed case files of the Raleigh circuit court. There are records of nearly five thousand cases generated by the Act of 1867. These are found in the records of the Elizabeth City (Edenton), New Bern, Wilmington, Asheville, Charlotte, Greensboro, Statesville district courts. Case files survive for only about half these cases.

Act of 1800
Elizabeth City Division
Case Files; Arranged alphabetically by surname of bankrupt. Only 4 cases are included. Each case might include creditors petitions for commissions of bankruptcy to issue against debtors; proof of publication of bankruptcy notices; proofs of debt; orders appointing commissioners to inquire into bankruptcy matters; commissioner's oaths of office; memoranda relating to examination of debtors; declarations of the commissioners adjudging the debtors bankrupt; petition for certificate of discharge; certificates of conformity of discharge; and related papers filed in bankruptcy proceedings.

Act of 1841
Elizabeth City Division
Minute Book; Arranged chronologically. Unindexed. A record of proceedings of the district court in bankruptcy cases showing dates of sessions, names of presiding judges, case titles, and orders of the court arising out of the litigation of the cases. The minutes also show the appointments of assignees.
Case Files; Arranged by dates cases were filed. Each case might contain petition for bankruptcy, schedules of creditors, schedules of bankrupt's assets, proofs of publication of bankruptcy notices, proofs of debts submitted by creditors, petitions for and certificates of discharge, reports of commissioners on proofs taken, reports of assignees and orders confirming assignee's reports, and related papers filed in bankruptcy cases

Raleigh Circuit Court
Case Files; Arranged alphabetically with other case files. Each case file might contain the same items found in the above described case files as well as reasons for appealing the judges decision.

INDEX OF NORTH CAROLINA BANKRUPTS

Act of 1867

Elizabeth City Division

Docket Book; Arranged in a single volume by docket numbers 1 - 357 assigned chronologically as cases opened. Indexed by the initial letter of the surname of the alleged bankrupt. The docket provides a record of papers filed and proceedings held in each bankruptcy case from its initiation to its final disposition. Entries for each case show case number, name of the petitioner for bankruptcy, name of the attorney in most cases, and a chronological listing of filings and proceedings.

Case Files: Arranged by case numbers 1 - 607 assigned chronologically as cases opened. Each case might contain petition for bankruptcy, schedules of debts, schedules of creditors, schedules of bankrupt's property, proof of publication of bankruptcy notices, proof of debts, memoranda of meetings of creditors, transcripts of testimony of bankrupts and witnesses, orders of adjudication of bankruptcy, orders of reference on petitions for discharge, and related papers filed in bankruptcy cases.

New Bern Division

Docket Books; Arranged in four volumes. Entries within the volume arranged by docket numbers 1 - 1724 assigned chronologically as cases opened. Each volume is indexed by the name of the alledged bankrupt. The docket provides a record of papers filed and proceedings held in each bankruptcy case from its initiation to its final disposition. Entries for each case show case number, name of the petitioner for bankruptcy, name of the attorney in most cases, and a chronological listing of filings and proceedings.

Discharge Orders; Arranged by date order of discharge was issued. Indexed by name of bankrupt. This volume consists of printed forms on which the clerk entered the district and the state, the name of the bankrupt, his county and state of residence, the date of discharge, and the name of the judge signing the order (but often left blank).

Wilmington Division

Docket Books; Arranged chronologically in two volumes by docket numbers 1 - 884 assigned as the cases opened. Each volume is indexed by the name of the alleged bankrupt. The docket provides a record of papers filed and proceedings held in each bankruptcy case from its initiation to its final disposition. Entries for each case show case number, name of the petitioner for bankruptcy, name of the attorney in most cases, and a chronological listing of filings and proceedings.

Minute Book; Arranged by dates of court sessions. Indexed by name of alledged bankrupt. This volume constitutes a record of proceedings of the court in bankruptcy proceedings, showing dates of court sessions, case titles, and orders of the court arising out of the litigation of bankruptcy cases. Rules of procedure in bankruptcy cases are also included.

Record of Appointment of Registers in Bankruptcy; Arranged chronologically. Unindexed. Each entry includes the name of the register, the congressional district in which he was appointed to serve, and the date he appeared in open court with the nomination and recommendation of the Chief Justice. He then filed a bond and his nomination was certfied to the Chief Justice. A limited number of rules of practice are also included.

Case Files; Arranged by case numbers 2 - 884 assigned chronologically as cases opened. A typical case might contain petition from creditpr or debtor for adjudication of bankruptcy; schedules listing the bankrupt's debts, his creditors, and his assets; memoranda concerning the appointment, notification, and acceptance of assignees; proofs of debt; orders of adjudication of bankruptcy; order of reference to registers on petition to discharge; certificates of the bankrupt's conforming to statutory requirements; assents of creditors to discharge; specifications of creditors objections against discharge; answers to specification against discharge; order of reference to registers on specifications and answers; bankrupt's oath before final discharge, decree of discharge, and other papers filed in bankruptcy proceedings.

INDEX OF NORTH CAROLINA BANKRUPTS

Final Record Book; Arranged by dates cases closed. Unindexed. Entries for each case include copies of petitions for bankruptcy, lists of creditors and assets, reports of registers, orders of the court, and other papers filed in bankruptcy cases.

Asheville Division

Docket Book; Arranged by the dates the cases opened. The volume is indexed alphabetically by the initial letter of the surname of the bankrupts. This volume lists papers filed and proceedings held in these bankruptcy actions, from initiation to conclusion in some, but not all, cases. In most cases the order of discharge is copied in the volume.

Case Files; Arranged by docket numbers 1 - 147 assigned chronologically as cases opened. A typical case file might contain creditor's and debtor's petitions for adjudication of bankruptcy; schedules of petitioner's debts, showing names, place of residence, and sum due each creditor; schedules contain inventories of all real and personal estate of the bankrupt; proofs of publication of bankruptcy notices; memoranda of appointment of assignees; orders of adjudication of bankruptcy; orders of reference on petitions for discharge; bills of cost; and other papers filed in bankruptcy proceedings.

Charlotte Division

Trial Docket; Arranged chronologically. Indexed by the initial letter of the surname of the bankrupt. There are entries for cases numbered 1 to 13 in this volume. This volume lists papers filed and proceedings held in bankruptcy cases. In addition, some orders or decrees are copied into the volume.

Greensboro Division

Docket Books; Arranged chronologically in two volumes. Entries in the volumes are arranged by docket numbers 1 - 704 assigned chronologically as the cases opened. The volumes are labeled Clerk's Dockets, Volume A and Volume B. Each volume is indexed alphabetically by the initial letter of the surname of the bankrupt. This volume lists papers filed and proceedings held in these bankruptcy actions, from initiation to conclusion in some, but not all, cases. In most cases the order of discharge is copied in the volume.

Statesville Division

Docket Book; Arranged chronologically by term. Indexed alphabetically by the initial letter of the surname of the alledged bankrupt. This volume lists papers filed and proceedings held in these bankruptcy actions, from initiation to conclusion in some, but not all, cases. In most cases the order of discharge is copied in the volume.

Case Files; Arranged by case numbers 1 - 333 assigned chronologically as cases were opened. The first several of these cases were transferred from the Eastern District to the Western District upon its creation in 1872. A typical case file might contain creditor's and debtor's petitions for adjudication of bankruptcy; schedules of petitioner's debts, showing names, place of residence, and sum due each creditor; schedules contain inventories of all real and personal estate of the bankrupt; proofs of publication of bankruptcy notices; memoranda of appointment of assignees; orders of adjudication of bankruptcy; orders of reference on petitions for discharge; bills of cost; and other papers filed in bakruptcy proceedings.

This list of bankrupts is taken from a draft list prepared by the staff of the Southeastern Regional Archives Branch at East Point, Georgia. The user should be aware that the list has not been subject to the quality control procedures normally used by the staff in releasing material for publication. For this reason, the user should check carefully for mis-spellings of names. The editor wishes to express appreciation for the cooperation of the staff of the Regional Archives; specifically Dr. Gayle Peters and Dr. Charles Reeves of the National Archives-Southeastern Region at East Point, Georgia, and Dr. Beverly Watkins of the National Archives-Great Lakes Region at Chicago, Illinois.

INDEX OF NORTH CAROLINA BANKRUPTS
ACT OF 1800

Thomas Fitt v. William Rea	October 1801	Murfreesborough
William Wynne v. Jonathan Brickell	December 1801	Hertford County
William Albertson v. John Shaw	October 1802	Pasquotank County
Benjamin Jones v. Henry Baker	November 1803	Halifax County

Comments by Dr. Charles Reeves: I have gone through the four North Carolina bankruptcy cases filed under the 1801 Act to get the names, etc. The cases are very fragile and the handwriting is quite hard to read. Because the cases are so fragile I looked at only a few pages of each. For those reasons I am not at all sure that I got the actual date the cases were filed or the correct city or county of residence for all the cases. I do, however, feel fairly sure that I got the names right.

INDEX OF NORTH CAROLINA BANKRUPTS
ACT OF 1841

The list is basically self explanatory. For those cases where the case number and box number are 0 there is no case file. In these instances, the case was found in the surviving docket or minute book but no case file survives. The box number given is the box in which the case file is stored at the National Archives-Southeast Region.

NAME OF BANKRUPT	RESIDENCE	CASE#	DATE	BOX#
Albertson, Elias	Perquimans	27	01/17/43	4
Alston, William W.	Halifax	2	08/27/42	1
Andrews, Edmund	Martin	0	01/17/43	5
Andrews, William	Martin	6	01/28/43	1
Andrews, William W.	Martin	6	01/28/43	1
Barber, James	Pasquotank	36	09/07/42	4
Barnard, Levin B.	Washington	0	01/17/43	0
Barnard, Levin B.	Washington	0	01/17/43	5
Beasley, Nathaniel	Chowan	10	02/02/43	2
Bell, Bennet H.	Halifax	12	09/12/42	2
Bell, Lorenzo D.	Edgecomb	28	03/03/43	4
Bell, Richard	Halifax	16	12/18/42	3
Bennett, William	Gates	15	02/02/43	3
Betts, Chauncey	Bertie	13	07/05/42	2
Bilbro, William	Northampton	2	10/17/42	1
Bishop, Bryan	Halifax	39	09/08/42	4
Black, J. W. (Adm. for F. L. Shaw)		0	04/01/46	0
Blanchard, Asa	Chowan	12	10/16/43	2
Bland, Theodore	Chowan	1	02/22/42	1
Bond, James C.	Chowan	5	03/05/42	1
Bond, Samuel T.	Chowan	8	03/08/42	2
Bradbury, John T.	Chowan	12	03/15/42	2
Braddy, Isaac	Martin	0	01/17/43	5
Braddy, Isaac B.	Martin	0	01/17/43	0
Brewer, Jesse	Halifax	33	09/03/42	4
Brook, Josiah	Bertie	23	01/17/43	3
Brothers, Andrew M.	Pasquotank	45	09/19/42	4
Brownlow, Lippoo S.	Halifax	3	01/03/43	1
Bryan, Robert	Edgecomb	14	12/10/42	2
Burrows, Stephen	Halifax	11	03/15/42	2
Burrows, Stephen	Halifax	0	10/17/42	0
Burt, Thomas S.	Edgecomb	11	06/25/42	2
Butler, William	Pasquotank	35	09/06/42	4
Butts, Chancy H.	Bertie	0	07/12/42	0
Campbell, John	Halifax	21	02/14/43	3
Casey, Dempsey	Pasquotank	0	04/19/42	0
Casey, Dempsey	Pasquotank	62	04/19/42	5
Casey, Isaac	Pasquotank	57	03/29/42	5
Casey, Isaac	Pasquotank	0	04/19/42	0
Casey, John	Pasquotank	30	09/02/42	4
Charlton, Thomas I.	Chowan	15	03/19/42	3

NAME OF BANKRUPT	RESIDENCE	CASE#	DATE	BOX#
Clark, Samuel D.	Hartford(Hertford)	24	01/17/43	3
Clary, Eldridge	Northampton	9	03/12/42	2
Clary, Willie G.	Bertie	4	10/03/42	1
Cliborn, William	Warren	3	05/02/42	1
Coffied, Thomas R.	Martin	4	03/03/42	1
Capehart, Fredrick M.	Hertford	1	05/09/42	1
Cowper, Joseph G.	Hertford	0	01/17/43	5
Crawford, John	Pasquotank	53	09/19/42	5
Crawford, William	Pasquotank	43	09/20/42	4
Cullipher, Miles G.	Bertie	10	12/03/42	2
Dawson, John	Halifax	8	10/17/42	2
Dean, Stewart	Chowan	7	11/04/42	1
Dortch, James	Nash	0	06/04/42	5
Dozier, William	Nash	15	07/29/42	3
Dozier, Willis	Camden	19	12/14/42	3
Dozier, Wilson B.	Currituck	20	01/17/43	3
Edmondson, John	Halifax	27	08/27/42	4
Evens, George	Nash	5	11/30/42	1
Ferange, Robert H.	Camden	0	10/18/42	5
Frazier, James	Halifax	8	01/26/43	2
Godfrey, Joseph	Perquimans	0	04/19/42	0
Godfrey, Joseph	Pasquotank	56	03/29/42	5
Goodloe, Robert	Franklin	1	04/07/42	1
Green, Constant Sharp	Pasquotank	24	07/13/43	4
Green, Elizabeth	Pasquotank	0	04/01/45	0
Gregory, Nathan	Perquimans	13	12/11/42	2
Gregory, Thomas W.	Halifax	32	09/03/42	4
Hacket, Abraham	Perquimans	0	04/01/45	0
Hardison, William	Washington	8	03/17/42	2
Harnanger, Robert H.	Camden	0	01/17/43	0
Harrison, Leonard	Washington	0	01/17/43	0
Harrison, Leonard	Washington	0	01/17/43	0
Harvey, Nell	Gates	0	01/17/43	0
Harvey, William B.	Gates	13	10/01/42	2
Haskett, Abraham	Perquimans	10	02/21/43	2
Hawkins, Redden	Halifax	11	12/03/42	2
Hearn, Theodore C.	Edgecomb	23	08/22/42	3
Henderson, Alexander	Chowan	18	02/11/43	3
Hill, T. W. (Petitioned G. W. Spiers)	Hertford	0	01/17/43	0
Hodges, N. H.	Hertford	5	01/27/43	1
Holly, James	Bertie	0	04/04/45	0
Hopkins, Bazile (Petitioned H. Williams)	Bal	0	01/17/43	0
Hopkins, J. (with Mr. Heck)		0	04/20/46	0
Howerton, Thomas	Franklin	2	09/21/42	1
Huff, Nathaniel	Franklin	3	09/27/42	1
Hull, Robert (Petitioned H. Williams)	Baltimore	0	01/17/43	0
Hunt, Willis L.	Nash	17	01/17/43	3
Hursey, Jesse	Halifax	38	09/08/42	4
Jackson, Andrew	Franklin	9	02/01/43	2

NAME OF BANKRUPT	RESIDENCE	CASE#	DATE	BOX#
Johnson, Lawrence	Martin	0	04/19/42	0
Johnson, Sam	Martin	0	04/19/42	0
Johnston, Lawrence	Martin	55	03/19/42	5
Johnston, Samuel	Martin	55	03/19/42	5
Jones, Benjamin	Franklin	0	01/17/43	0
Jones, James	Bertie	14	07/04/42	2
Jones, Thomas	Franklin	9	06/17/42	2
Jordon, Mathew O.	Perquimans	61	04/28/42	5
Jordon, Matthew O.	Perquimans	0	04/19/42	0
Kellinger, George N.	Pasquotank	44	09/19/42	4
King, Henry	Edgecomb	51	09/12/42	5
Lamb, Gideon S.	Camden	58	03/31/42	5
Lemite, James R.	Chowan	13	03/15/42	2
Lewis, Daniel	Halifax	17	02/09/43	3
Lillybridge, Clark	Pasquotank	24	08/24/42	3
Long, William	Halifax	7	01/31/43	1
Louise, Benjamin	Franklin	12	02/12/43	2
Mann, William E.	Pasquotank	52	09/20/42	5
McIntosh, Richard	Gates	0	01/17/43	0
Merritt, Robert	Halifax	16	02/09/43	3
Messinger, William	Perquimans	60	04/19/42	5
Milikin, David	Halifax	47	09/19/42	5
Milk, Harry	Halifax	0	04/01/45	0
Miller, Thomas J.	Chowan	2	02/28/42	1
Mitchell, Thomas	Pasquotank	22	04/25/42	3
Moore, Alex	Franklin	10	06/24/42	2
Moore, Charles	Bertie	54	09/12/42	5
Moore, William B.	Halifax	22	08/17/42	3
Mooring, John	Edgecomb	40	09/09/42	4
Nepenger, William	Perquimans	0	04/19/42	0
Norfleet, James E.	Chowan	9	03/08/42	2
Norwood, James H.	Franklin	26	02/21/43	4
Parker, Richard H.	Gates	18	12/14/42	3
Peterson, John W.	Bertie	50	06/11/42	5
Pierce, Abington	Bertie	0	09/21/42	5
Pittman, Blake	Halifax	20	03/15/42	3
Polkinshow, Samuel	Hertford	0	01/17/43	5
Popelston, John	Chowan	17	03/19/42	3
Popelston, John		0		5
Powell, William	Halifax	0		5
Pugh, Thomas T.	Bertie	49	09/12/42	5
Ransom, Robert	Warren	4	05/24/42	1
Eaper, Robert	Pasquotank	34	09/06/42	4
Ricard, John R.	Baltimore	18	08/09/42	3
Richards, Danford	Edgecomb	21	09/19/42	3
Riddick, James	Gates	13	02/06/43	2
Riddick, Thomas	Gates	2	01/02/43	1
Rupell, Augustus V.	Halifax	42	09/10/42	4
Ryan, Marcus	Bertie	11	02/02/43	2
Sallonstall, Chapin	Pasquotank	31	09/02/42	4
Sanal, Gidion	Camden	0	04/19/42	0
Savage, John P.	Halifax	28	09/06/42	4

NORTH CAROLINA BANKRUPTS - ACT OF 1841

NAME OF BANKRUPT	RESIDENCE	CASE#	DATE	BOX#
Shurley, Geraldus	Edgecomb	16	08/02/42	3
Skinner, James B.	Perquimans	25	02/21/43	4
Skinner, Matilda	Chowan	1	12/29/42	1
Spiers, G. W. (Petitioned by T. W. Hill, Lewis Spiers)	Hertford	0	01/17/43	0
Spiers, Lewis T. (Petitioned G. W. Spiers)	Hertford	0	01/17/43	0
Sprucle, Benjamin	Northampton	23	02/21/43	3
Spruill, Benjamin	Halifax	19	02/09/43	3
Staton, Lewelling	Edgecomb	41	09/09/42	4
Taylor, John G.	Halifax	20	09/19/42	3
Tench, Timothy	Nash	0	09/01/44	0
Terrell, Timothy	Nash	4	01/27/42	1
Torksey, William T.	Chowan	59	04/19/42	5
Torsey, William	Chowan	0	04/19/42	0
Vick, Granberry	Nash	7	06/15/42	1
Walker, Richard H.	Halifax	48	09/19/42	5
Weeks, John D.	Halifax	19	08/16/42	3
Whidbee, Thomas C.	Chowan	6	03/05/42	1
Whidler, Thomas	Chowan	0	03/05/42	0
White, Thomas	Pasquotank	29	08/30/42	4
Whitely, Langston	Baltimore	0	08/09/42	0
Wilder, Henry	Chowan	15	12/10/42	2
Wilkes, Henry	Halifax	46	09/09/42	4
Williams, H. (Petitioned by Bazile Hopkins, Rob Hull)	Baltimore	0	01/17/43	0
Williams, Hallowell S.	Currituck	37	09/07/42	4
Williams, Horatio N.	Pasquotank	24	07/13/43	4
Williams, Samuel	Pasquotank	17	08/03/42	3
Wilson, William	Camden	21	12/22/42	3
Wood, John E.	Hertford	3	03/01/42	1
Wright, Townsend	Chowan	15	03/19/42	3
Wright, Wills W.	Pasquotank	8	11/18/42	2
Young, General	Halifax	25	08/23/42	4

BANKRUPTCY CASES APPEALED TO RALEIGH CIRCUIT COURT

There are no case numbers for these files. The box number is the box number in the Mixed Case Files, Raleigh Circuit Court, at the National Archives-Southeast Region.

Casaux, John M.	New Hanover	02/15/42	6
Johnson, Neil		02/02/42	18
Jones, Protheus E. A.	Granville		26
Wilson, Patrick Jefferson	Mecklenburg	04/23/42	17

INDEX OF NORTH CAROLINA BANKRUPTS
ACT OF 1867

NAME OF BANKRUPT	RESIDENCE	CASE NUMBER	CITY OF COURT	DATE FILED
AARON, DAVID J.	DUPLIN	800	WILMINGTON	03/25/76
ABBOT, ALFRED	CAMDEN	180	ELIZABETH CITY	04/18/73
ABBOTT, ALFRED	CAMDEN	364	ELIZABETH CITY	04/17/73
ABBOTT, DELEN H.		322	WILMINGTON	07/16/68
ABBOTT, JAMES D.	CHEROKEE	64	WILMINGTON	02/04/68
ABBOTT, JOSEPH	NEW HANOVER	788	WILMINGTON	12/30/75
ABBOTT, WILL R.	PASQUOTANK	160	ELIZABETH CITY	02/24/68
ABERNATHEY, J. F.	BURKE	168	STATESVILLE	05/28/73
ADAMS, ALBERT	NEW HANOVER	224	WILMINGTON	05/23/68
ADAMS, JESSE P.	WILKES	49	STATESVILLE	02/18/73
ADAMS, JOHN D.	*DOCKET ONLY	1697	NEW BERN	08/23/78
ADAMS, OSCAR F.	*DOCKET ONLY	1541	NEW BERN	12/11/73
ADAMS, STERLING	*DOCKET ONLY	688	GREENSBORO	08/29/78
ADAMS, ZACHARIAH T.	*DOCKET ONLY	955	NEW BERN	11/07/68
ADDERTON, JAMES	*DOCKET ONLY	95	GREENSBORO	02/04/73
ADDERTON, JEN	*DOCKET ONLY	1173	NEW BERN	12/31/68
ADLER & COMPANY,	PHILADELPHIA	768	WILMINGTON	02/19/74
AGOSTINE, J. M.	*DOCKET ONLY	1355	NEW BERN	09/06/71
AGOSTINE, N. B.	*DOCKET ONLY	1633	NEW BERN	10/08/76
ALBEA, WILLIAM	IREDELL	229	WILMINGTON	05/25/68
ALBERTSON, E.W.	PASQUOTANK	77	ELIZABETH CITY	12/05/67
ALBRIGHT, GEORGE W.	*DOCKET ONLY	673	NEW BERN	05/12/68
ALBRIGHT, JAMES W.	*DOCKET ONLY	207	NEW BERN	01/21/68
ALBRIGHT, N. R.	*DOCKET ONLY	582	GREENSBORO	09/26/77
ALBRIGHT, ROBERT H.	*DOCKET ONLY	79	GREENSBORO	01/28/73
ALBRITTON, ELIAS F.	*DOCKET ONLY	1027	NEW BERN	12/22/68
ALCOM, ALFRED S.	*DOCKET ONLY	438	NEW BERN	03/02/68
ALCONN, TEMPLIN R.	*DOCKET ONLY	62	NEW BERN	11/22/67
ALDERMAN, WILLIAM		825	WILMINGTON	04/26/71
ALDERMAN, WILLIAM	CUMBERLAND	666	WILMINGTON	08/14/72
ALEN, Y. C.	*DOCKET ONLY	660	GREENSBORO	08/29/78
ALEPAUGH, SAMUEL	*DOCKET ONLY	1174	NEW BERN	12/31/68
ALEXANDER, B.J.,	BUNCOMBE	28	WILMINGTON	12/01/67
ALEXANDER, J.B	BUNCOMBE	28	WILMINGTON	12/01/67
ALEXANDER, JOHN M.	CLAY	542	WILMINGTON	01/09/69
ALEXANDER, JOHN R.	*DOCKET ONLY	537	GREENSBORO	02/17/76
ALEXANDER, MARY S.	MECKLENBURG	568	WILMINGTON	04/28/70
ALEXANDER, S. P.		572	WILMINGTON	04/19/70
ALEXANDER, S.B.		708	WILMINGTON	05/05/73
ALEXANDER, S.P.		573	WILMINGTON	04/19/70
ALEXANDER, SAMUEL P.		543	WILMINGTON	01/18/69
ALEXANDER, T.S.		627	WILMINGTON	03/29/71
ALFORD, JOHN BRYANT	*DOCKET ONLY	1631	NEW BERN	06/17/76
ALLEN & HARRIS	FRANKLIN	649	ELIZABETH CITY	12/02/72
ALLEN, D.B.	MONTGOMERY	220	WILMINGTON	05/21/68
ALLEN, HARRIS &	*DOCKET ONLY	1341	NEW BERN	04/27/71
ALLEN, JAMES A	*DOCKET ONLY	439	NEW BERN	03/02/68
ALLEN, JOEL R.	HENDERSON	1	ASHEVILLE	01/11/73
ALLEN, JOHN H.	NEW HANOVER	812	WILMINGTON	04/18/78
ALLEN, JUNNIS A.	NORTHAMPTON	386	ELIZABETH CITY	09/20/68
ALLEN, MASON G.	*DOCKET ONLY	592	NEW BERN	03/25/68
ALLEN, T.A.	HENDERSON	579	WILMINGTON	06/21/70
ALLEN, THOMAS C.	*DOCKET ONLY	422	NEW BERN	02/29/68
ALLEN, WILLIAM	*DOCKET ONLY	309	GREENSBORO	06/02/73
ALLEN, WILLIAM N.	*DOCKET ONLY	271	NEW BERN	02/08/68
ALLEN, WILLIAM S.	*DOCKET ONLY	440	NEW BERN	03/02/68
ALLISON, J. H.	CLEVELAND	157	STATESVILLE	05/23/73
ALLISON, T.A.	ROWAN	503	WILMINGTON	01/01/69
ALLISON, THROPHILUS	IREDELL	463	WILMINGTON	12/31/68
ALLISON, W. B.	HENDERSON	3	ASHEVILLE	04/29/73
ALLRED, JAMES	*DOCKET ONLY	228	GREENSBORO	05/12/73
ALPKIN, DURANT	*DOCKET ONLY	1716	NEW BERN	08/29/78

NAME OF BANKRUPT	RESIDENCE	CASE NUMBER	CITY OF COURT	DATE FILE
ALSBROOK, BENJAMIN	HALIFAX	610	ELIZABETH CITY	02/17/73
ALSOP, JOHN T.	HALIFAX	317	ELIZABETH CITY	03/19/77
ALSTON, ALFRED (JR.)	*DOCKET ONLY	1105	NEW BERN	12/29/68
ALSTON, JOHN C.	*DOCKET ONLY	460	NEW BERN	03/04/68
ALSTON, PHILIP G.	*DOCKET ONLY	1058	NEW BERN	12/26/68
ALSTON, ROBERT W.	*DOCKET ONLY	898	NEW BERN	08/19/68
ALSTON, T. M. C.	*DOCKET ONLY	524	NEW BERN	03/17/68
ALSTON, W. F.	*DOCKET ONLY	1710	NEW BERN	08/27/78
AMAN, ANDREW	*DOCKET ONLY	1136	NEW BERN	12/29/68
AMES, WALLACE	*DOCKET ONLY	1164	NEW BERN	12/24/68
ANDERS, ELISHA	SAMPSON	741	WILMINGTON	07/05/73
ANDERSON, ALBERT G.	*DOCKET ONLY	837	NEW BERN	04/18/68
ANDERSON, CHARLES		592	WILMINGTON	10/11/70
ANDERSON, DAVID	CUMBERLAND	451	WILMINGTON	12/30/68
ANDERSON, ESTER	HALIFAX	605	ELIZABETH CITY	07/02/73
ANDERSON, ESTHER J.	HALIFAX	226	ELIZABETH CITY	07/11/73
ANDERSON, JOHN H.	NEW HANOVER	48	WILMINGTON	01/24/68
ANDERSON, JOSEPH	HALIFAX	604	ELIZABETH CITY	07/02/75
ANDERSON, JOSEPH J.	HALIFAX	226	ELIZABETH CITY	07/11/73
ANDERSON, R.R.	HALIFAX	238	ELIZABETH CITY	09/20/73
ANDERSON, WILLIAM B.	MADISON	298	WILMINGTON	05/30/68
ANDREWS, GRANVILLE	*DOCKET ONLY	72	NEW BERN	11/28/67
ANDREWS, MANLY	*DOCKET ONLY	107	NEW BERN	12/14/67
ANDREWS, WILLIAM N.	*DOCKET ONLY	30	NEW BERN	10/12/67
ANTHONY, JOHN [.	LINCOLN	246	STATESVILLE	01/03/74
ANTHONY, JONATHAN	*DOCKET ONLY	442	GREENSBORO	12/18/73
ANTHONY, W.W.	MARTIN	118	ELIZABETH CITY	01/17/68
APPLEWHITE, BARTTEY	BRUNSWICK	725	WILMINGTON	06/19/73
APPLEWHITE, WILLIAM	NEW HANOVER	680	WILMINGTON	06/07/73
AREY, SEBASTIAN S.	CUMBERLAND	332	WILMINGTON	10/02/68
ARLEDGE, JOHN	HENDERSON	2	ASHEVILLE	08/31/78
ARLINE, JAMES	CHOWAN	645	ELIZABETH CITY	12/22/69
ARLINE, NANCY	CHOWAN	645	ELIZABETH CITY	12/22/69
ARMSTRONG, BERRY D.	*DOCKET ONLY	288	NEW BERN	02/10/68
ARMSTRONG, CATHERINE	*DOCKET ONLY	964	NEW BERN	11/18/68
ARMSTRONG, EDWARD	DUPLIN	413	WILMINGTON	12/29/68
ARMSTRONG, J. P	*DOCKET ONLY	1315	NEW BERN	12/31/70
ARMSTRONG, JAMES H.	*DOCKET ONLY	1098	NEW BERN	12/29/68
ARMSTRONG, ROBERT	*DOCKET ONLY	872	NEW BERN	06/23/68
ARNHEIN, A.	*DOCKET ONLY	1639	NEW BERN	01/12/77
ARNOLD, EDWARD	*DOCKET ONLY	671	NEW BERN	05/09/68
ARNOLD, JAMES	*DOCKET ONLY	1096	NEW BERN	12/29/68
ARNOLD, WILLIAM	*DOCKET ONLY	722	NEW BERN	05/28/68
ARTHUR, JOHN A.	*DOCKET ONLY	1050	NEW BERN	12/22/68
ASH, JULIUS	*DOCKET ONLY	1564	NEW BERN	02/09/74
ASHER, MAX	*DOCKET ONLY	18	NEW BERN	09/28/67
ATKINSON & BOWEN	WASHINGTON	262	ELIZABETH CITY	07/14/75
ATKINSON, WILLIAM	WASHINGTON	241	ELIZABETH CITY	11/01/73
ATKINSON, WILLIAM	*DOCKET ONLY	1713	NEW BERN	08/27/78
ATKINSON, WILLIAM A.	BLADEN	834	WILMINGTON	06/07/78
ATWOOD, CHARLES	*DOCKET ONLY	453	GREENSBORO	01/17/74
AUMACK, SAMUEL M.	HERTFORD	137	ELIZABETH CITY	02/10/68
AUSTIN, MARCUS		642	WILMINGTON	06/18/71
AUSTIN, WILLIAM M.	*DOCKET ONLY	298	GREENSBORO	05/29/73
AVENA, WILLIAM H.	*DOCKET ONLY	1625	NEW BERN	02/18/76
AVENT, JAMES H.	*DOCKET ONLY	142	NEW BERN	12/31/67
AVENT, JAMES W.	*DOCKET ONLY	459	NEW BERN	03/04/68
AVENT, THOMAS N.	*DOCKET ONLY	666	NEW BERN	05/02/68
AVERY, W. F.	CATAWBA	252	STATESVILLE	01/20/74
AYCOCKE, JOHN C.	*DOCKET ONLY	1138	NEW BERN	12/30/68
BABB, THOMAS W.	GATES	168	ELIZABETH CITY	02/28/68
BABBITT, F.A.	HALIFAX	249	ELIZABETH CITY	02/15/68
BACON, EDWARD W.	BLADEN	875	WILMINGTON	09/20/78
BAER, KAUFMAN	*DOCKET ONLY	1278	NEW BERN	01/17/70
BAGBY, GEORGE	*DOCKET ONLY	1703	NEW BERN	08/27/78
BAGGETT, A.J. T.	CABARRUS	26	WILMINGTON	12/18/67

NORTH CAROLINA BANKRUPTS - ACT OF 1867

NAME OF BANKRUPT	RESIDENCE	CASE NUMBER	CITY OF COURT	DATE FILED
BAILEOY, SAMUEL	DAVIE	372	WILMINGTON	12/19/68
BAILEY, BRAXTEN	DAVIE	316	WILMINGTON	05/30/68
BAILEY, EZRA H.	MARTIN	611	ELIZABETH CITY	12/16/69
BAILEY, GREEN	DAVIE	91	STATESVILLE	04/30/73
BAILEY, JOHN	DAVIE	621	WILMINGTON	03/23/71
BAILEY, JOHN A.	*DOCKET ONLY	766	NEW BERN	05/30/69
BAILEY, JONATHAN R.	*DOCKET ONLY	167	NEW BERN	01/08/68
BAILEY, RICHMOND	DAVIE	60	STATESVILLE	02/24/73
BAILEY, ROBERT C.	*DOCKET ONLY	291	NEW BERN	02/10/68
BAILEY, W. A.	*DOCKET ONLY	2	GREENSBORO	08/06/72
BAILEY, WILEY	DAVIE	311	WILMINGTON	05/30/68
BAILEY, WILLIAM H.	ROWAN	238	STATESVILLE	10/11/73
BAIRD, J. R. & CO.	GREENVILLE	148	ASHEVILLE	02/18/69
BAIRD, J.R. &	BUNCOMBE	258	WILMINGTON	05/29/68
BAIRD, JOHN	*DOCKET ONLY	554	NEW BERN	03/19/68
BAIRD, JOHN A.	*DOCKET ONLY	553	NEW BERN	03/19/68
BAIRD, THOMAS A.	*DOCKET ONLY	621	NEW BERN	04/09/68
BAIRD, THOMAS A.	*DOCKET ONLY	538	GREENSBORO	02/26/73
BAIRDS, NATHANIEL H.	*DOCKET ONLY	273	NEW BERN	02/08/68
BAKER, ALEXANDER	*DOCKET ONLY	338	NEW BERN	02/24/68
BAKER, GEORGE	HERTFORD	150	ELIZABETH CITY	02/25/68
BAKER, JOHN L.		315	ELIZABETH CITY	12/09/76
BAKER, JOSEPH	*DOCKET ONLY	650	GREENSBORO	08/27/78
BAKER, JOSIAH	*DOCKET ONLY	657	NEW BERN	04/30/68
BAKER, RICHARD G.	*DOCKET ONLY	1458	NEW BERN	05/26/73
BAKER, W.J.		173	ELIZABETH CITY	/ /
BAKER, W.M.	ROWAN	108	WILMINGTON	01/03/68
BAKKLE, JAMES F.	*DOCKET ONLY	1595	NEW BERN	01/26/75
BALL, JAMES L.	PASQUOTANK	15	ELIZABETH CITY	06/21/67
BALL, JAMES R.	*DOCKET ONLY	334	NEW BERN	02/24/68
BALL, JOHN T.	*DOCKET ONLY	947	NEW BERN	10/21/68
BALLANCE, B.B.	PASQUOTANK	43	ELIZABETH CITY	11/04/67
BALLARD, DAVID	BUNCOMBE	5	ASHEVILLE	05/10/73
BALLARD, R. H.	HENDERSON	18	ASHEVILLE	05/06/73
BALLARD, WILLIAM M.	MONTGOMERY	179	WILMINGTON	04/14/68
BALLOW, JOHN	ASHE	186	STATESVILLE	05/27/73
BALTHNOP, JOHN W.	*DOCKET ONLY	1388	NEW BERN	06/24/72
BANK OF CAPE FEAR		645	WILMINGTON	10/13/71
BANK OF MECKLENBURG,	*DOCKET ONLY	536	GREENSBORO	09/18/75
BANK OF NORTH CAR.	*DOCKET ONLY	950	NEW BERN	10/21/68
BANK OF STATESVILLE	*DOCKET ONLY	582	GREENSBORO	07/30/77
BANK OF STATESVILLE,	IREDELL	281	STATESVILLE	06/15/77
BANKS, GEORGE W.	PASQUOTANK	44	ELIZABETH CITY	11/13/67
BANKS, JAMES R.	PASQUOTANK	64	ELIZABETH CITY	11/08/67
BANKS, JOSEPH B.	*DOCKET ONLY	635	NEW BERN	04/17/68
BANKS, THADEUS F.	PERQUIMANS	248	ELIZABETH CITY	04/08/68
BANKS, WILLIAM	PASQUOTANK	283	ELIZABETH CITY	05/29/68
BANNER, BENJAMIN	*DOCKET ONLY	526	GREENSBORO	11/04/72
BANNER, BENJAMINE	FORSYTH	151	WILMINGTON	03/20/69
BANNER, JOHN	*DOCKET ONLY	397	GREENSBORO	09/01/73
BANNER, WILSON C.	*DOCKET ONLY	525	GREENSBORO	11/04/72
BANNERMAN, CHARLES	SAMPSON	734	WILMINGTON	07/04/73
BANNERMAN, CHARLES	SAMPSON	849	WILMINGTON	06/13/78
BANNERMAN, THOMAS	SAMPSON	879	WILMINGTON	08/30/78
BARBEE, G. W.	*DOCKET ONLY	339	NEW BERN	02/24/68
BARBER, DAVID	COLUMBUS	689	WILMINGTON	10/16/72
BARBER, MATHEW	*DOCKET ONLY	42	NEW BERN	10/30/68
BARBOUR, SARAH	CLEVELAND	148	STATESVILLE	05/23/73
BARCO, ALEXANDER G.	CAMDEN	223	ELIZABETH CITY	03/07/68
BARCO, BAILEY	CAMDEN	297	ELIZABETH CITY	04/22/68
BARCO, E.J.	CAMDEN	550	ELIZABETH CITY	02/10/73
BARCO, GIDEON C.	CAMDEN	335	ELIZABETH CITY	08/21/78
BARCO, WILLIAM	CAMDEN	332	ELIZABETH CITY	07/17/78
BARDEN, JAMES W.	*DOCKET ONLY	1705	NEW BERN	08/27/78
BARDEN, WILLIAM	*DOCKET ONLY	1712	NEW BERN	08/27/78
BARDIN, BENJAMIN	*DOCKET ONLY	416	NEW BERN	02/29/68

NORTH CAROLINA BANKRUPTS - ACT OF 1867

NAME OF BANKRUPT	RESIDENCE	CASE NUMBER	CITY OF COURT	DATE FILED
BARHAM, JOSEPH	NORTHAMPTON	205	ELIZABETH CITY	05/26/73
BARHAM, JOSEPH	NORTHAMPTON	584	ELIZABETH CITY	05/23/73
BARID, JAMES D.	IREDELL	147	WILMINGTON	03/14/68
BARID, JAMES M, &	GREENVILLE	148	ASHEVILLE	02/18/69
BARKER, THOMAS A.	*DOCKET ONLY	606	NEW BERN	04/01/68
BARNARD, JOHN, SR.	CURRITUCK	259	ELIZABETH CITY	01/16/74
BARNARD, JOSEPH	BUNCOMBE	12	ASHEVILLE	05/16/73
BARNES, ANSEL H.	*DOCKET ONLY	394	NEW BERN	02/28/68
BARNES, BUNYAN J.	*DOCKET ONLY	1071	NEW BERN	12/26/68
BARNES, DAVID W.	*DOCKET ONLY	1205	NEW BERN	12/31/68
BARNES, JOHN	*DOCKET ONLY	317	NEW BERN	02/21/68
BARNES, JOHN G.	*DOCKET ONLY	1206	NEW BERN	12/31/68
BARNES, JOSHUA B.	*DOCKET ONLY	702	NEW BERN	05/27/68
BARNES. PETER L.	*DOCKET ONLY	1527	NEW BERN	10/27/73
BARNES, STEPHEN H.	*DOCKET ONLY	1801	NEW BERN	01/13/75
BARNES, WILLIE G.	*DOCKET ONLY	1210	NEW BERN	12/31/68
BARNES, WILLIS	ROBESON	777	WILMINGTON	12/26/74
BARNETT, ABASALOM	*DOCKET ONLY	229	NEW BERN	01/29/68
BARNETT, H. J.	HENDERSON	17	ASHEVILLE	12/31/74
BARNETT, JAMES E.	*DOCKET ONLY	881	NEW BERN	05/19/68
BARNETT, JAMES E.	*DOCKET ONLY	839	NEW BERN	09/29/68
BARNETT, JOHN T.	*DOCKET ONLY	1529	NEW BERN	11/01/73
BARNETT, SAMUEL C.	*DOCKET ONLY	272	NEW BERN	02/08/68
BARNETT, WIT J.	HENDERSON	232	WILMINGTON	05/25/68
BARNWELL, WO;;OA, P.	*DOCKET ONLY	684	GREENSBORO	08/31/78
BARRETT, SAMUEL	*DOCKET ONLY	672	GREENSBORO	08/30/78
BARRETT, SYLAVUS	MOORE	802	WILMINGTON	11/22/70
BARRINGTON, STEPHEN	*DOCKET ONLY	374	NEW BERN	02/25/68
BARRON, BOLERO B.	*DOCKET ONLY	719	NEW BERN	05/29/68
BARROW, FRANCUS	HERTFORD.	468	ELIZABETH CITY	12/28/68
BARROW, WILLIAM	FORSYTH	257	WILMINGTON	05/29/68
BARROWS, PITT	*DOCKET ONLY	1548	NEW BERN	12/23/73
BARRY, BASIO	*DOCKET ONLY	1024	NEW BERN	12/22/68
BARTER, J. F.	*DOCKET ONLY	873	GREENSBORO	08/30/78
BARTLEY, MARTIN	*DOCKET ONLY	299	NEW BERN	02/17/68
BARTON, JONES W.	*DOCKET ONLY	1092	NEW BERN	12/29/68
BASHAM, CLAUDIUS A	*DOCKET ONLY	816	NEW BERN	05/30/68
BASHAM, R. G.	*DOCKET ONLY	426	NEW BERN	02/29/68
BASHFORD, JAMES	*DOCKET ONLY	174	NEW BERN	01/09/68
BASNIGHT, B.S.	TYRRELL	132	ELIZABETH CITY	02/17/68
BASNIGHT, BENJAMIN	TYRRELL	613	ELIZABETH CITY	02/06/68
BASON, ISAAC	*DOCKET ONLY	690	GREENSBORO	01/01/90
BASS, WILLIAM R.	*DOCKET ONLY	1075	NEW BERN	12/25/69
BASSETT, WILLIAM A.	*DOCKET ONLY	509	NEW BERN	03/11/68
BAST, ELI	IREDELL	58	STATESVILLE	02/20/73
BASTICK, TRISTAN	*DOCKET ONLY	366	GREENSBORO	07/19/73
BATCHLOR, L.W.	HALIFAX	490	ELIZABETH CITY	12/30/68
BATEMAN, JEROME B.	*DOCKET ONLY	1608	NEW BERN	06/17/75
BATEMAN, JOHN	*DOCKET ONLY	1232	NEW BERN	12/31/68
BATES, JOHN B.	*DOCKET ONLY	526	NEW BERN	03/17/68
BATTLE, LUCIEN N. B.	*DOCKET ONLY	1484	NEW BERN	06/30/73
BATTS, WILLIAM B.	*DOCKET ONLY	419	NEW BERN	02/29/68
BATTS, WILLIE J.	*DOCKET ONLY	1204	NEW BERN	12/31/68
BAUCOM, HENRY	*DOCKET ONLY	47	GREENSBORO	12/16/72
BAUM, ABRAHAM	CURRITUCK	252	ELIZABETH CITY	12/18/73
BAXTER, E.F.	CURRITUCK	236	ELIZABETH CITY	09/15/73
BAXTER, J.W.	CURRITUCK	207	ELIZABETH CITY	06/02/73
BAXTER, JOSEPH W.	*DOCKET ONLY	1128	NEW BERN	12/30/68
BAXTER, JOSHUA W.	CURRITUCK	586	ELIZABETH CITY	06/02/73
BAXTER, PETER Z	LINCOLN	433	WILMINGTON	12/30/68
BAYNES, SIDNEY	*DOCKET ONLY	1142	NEW BERN	12/30/68
BEACH, JOSIAH N.	*DOCKET ONLY	514	GREENSBORO	11/16/75
BEAL, CHRISTOPHER	LINCOLN	209	STATESVILLE	08/27/73
BEAL, J. W.	*DOCKET ONLY	1230	NEW BERN	12/23/68
BEALE, FERDINAND C.	NORTHAMPTON	446	ELIZABETH CITY	12/22/68
BEALE, WILLIS M.	NORTHAMPTON	461	ELIZABETH CITY	12/01/68

NAME OF BANKRUPT	RESIDENCE	CASE NUMBER	CITY OF COURT	DATE FILED
BEAMAN, W.P.	HERTFORD	352	ELIZABETH CITY	08/31/78
BEAMAN, WILLIAM P.	HERTFORD	475	ELIZABETH CITY	12/19/68
BEAR, LEOPOLD	*DOCKET ONLY	654	NEW BERN	04/24/68
BEAR, MEAYER		589	WILMINGTON	10/24/70
BEARD, JAMES	CATAWBA	184	WILMINGTON	04/16/68
BEARD, JOHN	ROWAN	258	STATESVILLE	04/10/74
BEASLY, ROBERT	*DOCKET ONLY	314	NEW BERN	02/21/68
BECKHAM, EDWARD	ALEXANDER	86	STATESVILLE	04/25/73
BECTON, FREDERICK J.	*DOCKET ONLY	813	NEW BERN	05/30/68
BELL & DEAN,	*DOCKET ONLY	575	GREENSBORO	12/22/76
BELL, DAVID W.	*DOCKET ONLY	769	NEW BERN	02/26/68
BELL, J.J		650	ELIZABETH CITY	09/03/68
BELL, J.W	HALIFAX	468	ELIZABETH CITY	12/15/68
BELL, JAMES B.	CLEVELAND	128	WILMINGTON	03/12/68
BELL, JAMES H.	CURRITUCK	153	ELIZABETH CITY	02/24/68
BELL, JASPER N.	BUNCOMBE	15	ASHEVILLE	10/02/72
BELL, JESSE	CAMDEN	308	ELIZABETH CITY	04/25/76
BELL, JOHN & JOHN H. GASTON		160	WILMINGTON	03/28/68
BELL, JOHN B.	CURRITUCK	82	ELIZABETH CITY	12/16/67
BELL, JOHN B.	HALIFAX	211	ELIZABETH CITY	06/11/73
BELL, JOHN B.	HALIFAX	590	ELIZABETH CITY	05/08/73
BELL, JOSEPH J		648	ELIZABETH CITY	09/04/68
BELL, JOSIAH L	*DOCKET ONLY	1308	NEW BERN	12/02/70
BELL, M.L	HALIFAX	491	ELIZABETH CITY	12/15/68
BELL, M.L	HALIFAX	614	ELIZABETH CITY	12/30/68
BELL, PETER H.	*DOCKET ONLY	1321	NEW BERN	01/23/71
BELL, RICHARD C.	*DOCKET ONLY	1184	NEW BERN	12/26/68
BELL, ROBERT	CAMDEN	470	ELIZABETH CITY	12/31/68
BELL, SAMUEL	*DOCKET ONLY	276	GREENSBORO	05/24/73
BELL, SOLOMON H.	*DOCKET ONLY	1185	NEW BERN	12/30/68
BELL, W. F.	*DOCKET ONLY	1709	NEW BERN	08/27/78
BELL, W.H	HALIFAX	492	ELIZABETH CITY	12/15/68
BELL, WILLIAM S.	*DOCKET ONLY	1186	NEW BERN	12/30/68
BELLAMY, WILLIAM E.	HALIFAX	578	ELIZABETH CITY	05/11/73
BELLAMY, WILLIAM E.	HALIFAX	198	ELIZABETH CITY	05/16/73
BENBERRY, LEMUEL C.	CHOWAN	282	ELIZABETH CITY	05/25/68
BENCINI, ANTHONY	ROWAN	466	WILMINGTON	12/31/68
BENCINI, LORENZO D.	ROWAN	39	WILMINGTON	01/13/68
BENDRICK, C.H. &		552	WILMINGTON	08/06/69
BENNETT, BRYANT	WASHINGTON	539	ELIZABETH CITY	03/20/72
BENNETT, C. H.	*DOCKET ONLY	54	NEW BERN	11/15/67
BENNETT, GEORGE W.	RICHMOND	77	WILMINGTON	02/10/68
BENNETT, H. T. &	*DOCKET ONLY	1285	NEW BERN	03/15/70
BENNETT, YOUNG	HAYWOOD	18	ASHEVILLE	05/17/73
BENSON, JOHN C.	ROWAN	465	WILMINGTON	12/21/68
BERIC, NEIL	ROBESON	238	WILMINGTON	05/27/68
BERNARD, SAMUEL A.	BERTIE	288	ELIZABETH CITY	06/01/68
BERNARD, THADDEUS P.	*DOCKET ONLY	1307	NEW BERN	12/18/71
BERNHEIMER, LONG &		656	WILMINGTON	02/21/72
BERRY, JOHN	CLEVELAND	125	STATESVILLE	05/14/73
BERRY, R. T.	*DOCKET ONLY	765	NEW BERN	08/02/68
BERRY, SAMUEL	CURRITUCK	297	ELIZABETH CITY	11/13/75
BESSENT, C.W.	DAVIE	662	WILMINGTON	04/01/72
BEST, COUNCIL (SR.)	*DOCKET ONLY	522	NEW BERN	03/13/68
BEST, HENRY	DUPLIN	683	WILMINGTON	05/13/73
BEST, HENRY H.	*DOCKET ONLY	429	NEW BERN	02/29/68
BEST, JOHN (D/B/A)	*DOCKET ONLY	221	NEW BERN	01/25/68
BEST, NICHOLAS	*DOCKET ONLY	256	NEW BERN	02/05/68
BEST, R. W.	*DOCKET ONLY	1546	NEW BERN	12/22/73
BEST, W. J., C. L.	*DOCKET ONLY	578	GREENSBORO	04/13/77
BIBB, JAMES H.	*DOCKET ONLY	1502	NEW BERN	09/05/73
BIBLE, GEORGE W.	*DOCKET ONLY	1127	NEW BERN	12/30/68
BIBLES, DANIEL P.	*DOCKET ONLY	1231	NEW BERN	12/30/68
BIDDLE, SAMUEL S.	*DOCKET ONLY	727	NEW BERN	05/26/68
BIGGS, ELI C.	HALIFAX	232	ELIZABETH CITY	03/18/68
BIGGS, H.H.	*DOCKET ONLY	1501	NEW BERN	08/04/73

NORTH CAROLINA BANKRUPTS - ACT OF 1867

NAME OF BANKRUPT	RESIDENCE	CASE NUMBER	CITY OF COURT	DATE FILED
BIGGS, HAYWOOD	*DOCKET ONLY	1892	NEW BERN	08/17/78
BILLINGSLEY, JOHN P.	*DOCKET ONLY	315	GREENSBORO	06/03/73
BINGHAM, WILLIAM	*DOCKET ONLY	199	GREENSBORO	05/02/73
BISHOP, ASA	HALIFAX	546	ELIZABETH CITY	10/18/72
BISHOP, WILLIAM M.	HALIFAX	239	ELIZABETH CITY	10/16/73
BISSENT, THOMAS M.	DAVIE	276	STATESVILLE	12/04/75
BISSETT, DANIEL	*DOCKET ONLY	1466	NEW BERN	06/05/73
BITTING, B. L.	*DOCKET ONLY	885	GREENSBORO	08/30/78
BITTING, JOHN W.	ROWAN	860	WILMINGTON	03/20/72
BITTING, JOSEPH	YADKIN	525	WILMINGTON	01/01/69
BIVENS, ROBERT N.	*DOCKET ONLY	377	GREENSBORO	07/10/73
BIZZELL, A. F. &	*DOCKET ONLY	517	GREENSBORO	11/04/73
BIZZELL, MONTRAVIL	*DOCKET ONLY	1401	NEW BERN	11/30/72
BLACK, JEFFERSON	CLEVELAND	3	STATESVILLE	10/12/72
BLACK, JOHN	PASQUOTANK	157	ELIZABETH CITY	02/24/68
BLACK, THOMAS S.	*DOCKET ONLY	570	GREENSBORO	12/07/76
BLACK, THOMAS S. &	*DOCKET ONLY	119	NEW BERN	12/26/67
BLACK, W. J.	*DOCKET ONLY	572	GREENSBORO	01/01/77
BLACK, W. J.	*DOCKET ONLY	692	GREENSBORO	/ /
BLACK, WILLIAM J.	*DOCKET ONLY	885	GREENSBORO	08/29/78
BLACKARD, S. H.	*DOCKET ONLY	407	NEW BERN	02/26/68
BLACKBORN, ROBERT	*DOCKET ONLY	186	GREENSBORO	04/30/73
BLACKBURN, MILTON	*DOCKET ONLY	1141	NEW BERN	12/30/68
BLACKEMORE &		775	WILMINGTON	09/07/74
BLACKNALL, GEORGE W.	*DOCKET ONLY	862	NEW BERN	06/22/68
BLACKNALL, GEORGE W.	*DOCKET ONLY	1201	NEW BERN	12/31/68
BLACKNALL, T. H.	*DOCKET ONLY	1576	NEW BERN	03/26/74
BLACKNALL, THOMAS J.	*DOCKET ONLY	684	NEW BERN	05/19/68
BLACKWELL, C. A.	MCDOWELL	13	ASHEVILLE	05/08/73
BLACKWELL, CASWELL	*DOCKET ONLY	262	GREENSBORO	05/21/73
BLACKWELL, JOSEPH	ROWAN	32	STATESVILLE	01/29/73
BLACKWELL, JOSIAH V.	*DOCKET ONLY	1394	NEW BERN	10/16/72
BLACKWELL, R. &		319	WILMINGTON	06/30/68
BLACKWELL, THOMAS	HENDERSON	14	ASHEVILLE	05/06/73
BLACKWILL, JAMES L.	SURRY	441	WILMINGTON	12/30/68
BLAIR, JAMES M.	*DOCKET ONLY	10	NEW BERN	08/26/67
BLAIR, ROBERT E.	*DOCKET ONLY	245	GREENSBORO	05/12/73
BLAKE, E. C.	*DOCKET ONLY	520	NEW BERN	03/13/68
BLAKENEY, WILLIAM W.	*DOCKET ONLY	572	GREENSBORO	01/25/77
BLAKENY, A., T. C.	*DOCKET ONLY	559	GREENSBORO	05/10/76
BLANCHARD, WILLIAM	*DOCKET ONLY	171	GREENSBORO	04/25/73
BLAND, JOSEPH H.	*DOCKET ONLY	1521	NEW BERN	09/20/73
BLANTON, A. P.	CLEVELAND	310	STATESVILLE	08/18/78
BLEDSOE, MATHIS	ASHE	316	STATESVILLE	08/09/78
BLEVINS, ANDREW F.	WILKES	218	STATESVILLE	07/04/73
BLISS, GEORGE &	CUMBERLAND	17	WILMINGTON	11/07/67
BLOUNT, ELLIAS J.	*DOCKET ONLY	1229	NEW BERN	12/31/68
BLOUNT, JOHN G.	*DOCKET ONLY	389	NEW BERN	02/29/68
BLOUNT, READING	*DOCKET ONLY	1330	NEW BERN	03/06/71
BLOUNT, RICHARD H.	*DOCKET ONLY	259	NEW BERN	02/06/68
BLOUNT, THOMAS	*DOCKET ONLY	179	NEW BERN	01/10/68
BLOUNT, WILLIAM	PASQUOTANK	56	ELIZABETH CITY	11/25/67
BLOUNT, WILLIAM	*DOCKET ONLY	1140	NEW BERN	12/30/68
BLOUNT, WILLLIAM A.	*DOCKET ONLY	1456	NEW BERN	05/27/73
BLUM, DAVID	*DOCKET ONLY	561	GREENSBORO	07/01/78
BLURN, DAVID	*DOCKET ONLY	894	GREENSBORO	/ /
BOBBITE, JOHN J.	*DOCKET ONLY	703	NEW BERN	05/26/68
BOBBITT, JAMES	*DOCKET ONLY	1026	NEW BERN	12/22/68
BODENHAMER, ANDERSON	*DOCKET ONLY	461	GREENSBORO	02/17/74
BODENHAMER, JACOB	*DOCKET ONLY	342	GREENSBORO	06/13/73
BODENHAMER, RANDALL	*DOCKET ONLY	316	NEW BERN	02/21/68
BODFISH, MRS. A. L.	*DOCKET ONLY	589	GREENSBORO	11/21/76
BODSUHASUER, ISAIAH	DAVIDSON	658	WILMINGTON	02/21/72
BOGETT, JOSEPH	*DOCKET ONLY	871	NEW BERN	06/23/68
BOGGAN, JAMES	*DOCKET ONLY	268	GREENSBORO	05/26/73
BOGGAN, PATRICK	*DOCKET ONLY	391	GREENSBORO	07/25/73

NORTH CAROLINA BANKRUPTS - ACT OF 1867

NAME OF BANKRUPT	RESIDENCE	CASE NUMBER	CITY OF COURT	DATE FILED
BOLTON, THOMAS	NORTHAMPTON	382	ELIZABETH CITY	10/08/68
BOND, GEORGE	CHOWAN	358	ELIZABETH CITY	08/22/68
BOND, H.A., JR.	CHOWAN	355	ELIZABETH CITY	08/31/78
BOND, HENRY	HALIFAX	269	ELIZABETH CITY	11/17/75
BOND, J.C.		544	WILMINGTON	02/27/69
BOND, JAMES F.	GATES	167	ELIZABETH CITY	02/28/68
BONEY, DANIEL	SAMPSON	721	WILMINGTON	06/11/73
BONITS, JULIUS A	*DOCKET ONLY	814	NEW BERN	05/30/68
BONNER, JAMES	CHOWAN	378	ELIZABETH CITY	09/09/68
BONNER, WILSON C.	FORSYTH	153	WILMINGTON	03/21/68
BOOE, ALEXANDER M.	DAVIE	504	WILMINGTON	01/01/69
BOOE, WILLIAM E.	DAVIE	655	WILMINGTON	01/31/72
BOON, JAMES	*DOCKET ONLY	1216	NEW BERN	12/31/68
BOON, SPENCER M	*DOCKET ONLY	1718	NEW BERN	09/30/78
BOON, WESLEY F.	NORTHAMPTON	400	ELIZABETH CITY	12/15/68
BOONE, THOMAS A	MECKLENBURG	470	WILMINGTON	12/31/68
BOROUGHS, MATHEW	ANSON	97	WILMINGTON	02/25/68
BOST, JULIUS A. B.	*DOCKET ONLY	1197	NEW BERN	12/31/68
BOSTICK, W. H.	CLEVELAND	249	STATESVILLE	01/15/74
BOSWOOD, G.C.	CURRITUCK	91	ELIZABETH CITY	12/25/67
BOTTS, LAWRENCE A	CLEVELAND	436	WILMINGTON :	12/30/68
BOWEN, ATKINSON &	WASHINGTON	282	ELIZABETH CITY	07/14/75
BOWEN, D.A.	WASHINGTON	260	ELIZABETH CITY	01/16/74
BOWEN, JAMES	*DOCKET ONLY	199	NEW BERN	01/17/68
BOWERS, CANNON	*DOCKET ONLY	79	NEW BERN	11/30/67
BOWERS, WILLIAM J.	*DOCKET ONLY	134	NEW BERN	12/29/67
BOWMAN, CALEB	CALDWELL	133	STATESVILLE	05/21/73
BOWS, WILLIAM B.	*DOCKET ONLY	393	NEW BERN	02/28/68
BOYCE, BAKER F.	CHOWAN	97	ELIZABETH CITY	12/30/67
BOYCE, SAMUEL A	*DOCKET ONLY	243	GREENSBORO	05/13/73
BOYD, CONRAD	*DOCKET ONLY	1106	NEW BERN	12/29/68
BOYD, JOHN C.	*DOCKET ONLY	1365	NEW BERN	11/02/71
BOYD, JOHN E.	*DOCKET ONLY	969	NEW BERN	11/27/68
BOYD, JOHN F.	*DOCKET ONLY	1279	NEW BERN	01/19/70
BOYD, ROBERT J.	*DOCKET ONLY	899	NEW BERN	08/22/68
BOYD, WILLIAM	MECKLENBURG	288	WILMINGTON	05/30/68
BOYD, WILSON	BUNCOMBE	330	WILMINGTON	09/22/68
BOYDEN, NAT. A	SURRY	541	WILMINGTON	01/07/69
BOYDEN, NATHANIEL A	*DOCKET ONLY	93	GREENSBORO	02/03/73
BOYETT, WILLIAM A	*DOCKET ONLY	-1476	NEW BERN	06/20/73
BOYKIN, HARRIS	*DOCKET ONLY	1207	NEW BERN	12/31/68
BOYKIN, JOHN	*DOCKET ONLY	1706	NEW BERN	09/27/78
BOYLE, FRANCIS, A	MARTIN	498	ELIZABETH CITY	03/05/69
BOYLES, F.A	MARTIN	352	ELIZABETH CITY	08/31/78
BOYLES, JOSEPH B.	*DOCKET ONLY	150	GREENSBORO	04/03/73
BOZKIN, LEWIS M.	SAMPSON	714	WILMINGTON	06/11/73
BRACKINS, SAMUEL	ALLEGHANY	231	STATESVILLE	08/14/73
BRACY, ELIAS	NORTHAMPTON	359	ELIZABETH CITY	09/12/68
BRAD, WILLIAMN E.	NORTHAMPTON	347	ELIZABETH CITY	08/29/78
BRADDY, KINCHEM J.	BLADEN	842	WILMINGTON	07/23/78
BRADLEY, CONSTANTINE	HALIFAX	298	ELIZABETH CITY	10/29/73
BRADLEY, J.J.	HALIFAX	311	ELIZABETH CITY	01/25/76
BRADSHAM, WILLIAM T.	*DOCKET ONLY	187	NEW BERN	01/13/68
BRADSHAW, C.W.	MECKLENBURG	280	WILMINGTON	05/29/68
BRADSHAW, JOHN A	ROWAN	492	WILMINGTON	12/31/68
BRADY, RUFUS A	*DOCKET ONLY	511	GREENSBORO	01/21/76
BRANBLEY, HANDY	*DOCKET ONLY	1460	NEW BERN	06/24/73
BRANCH, GEORGE A	HALIFAX	488	ELIZABETH CITY	12/23/68
BRANCH, J. G.	*DOCKET ONLY	848	GREENSBORO	08/27/78
BRANCH, J. H.	*DOCKET ONLY	628	NEW BERN	05/30/68
BRANCH, J.R.	HALIFAX	234	ELIZABETH CITY	03/18/68
BRANCORN, JAMES R.	UNION	464	WILMINGTON	12/31/68
BRAND, ROBERT J.	BUNCOMBE	11	ASHEVILLE	03/22/73
BRANDT, GEORGE	CUMBERLAND	47	WILMINGTON	01/22/68
BRANDT, SIMON	CUMBERLAND	607	WILMINGTON	11/27/77
BRANN, JOHN	*DOCKET ONLY	734	NEW BERN	05/29/68

NORTH CAROLINA BANKRUPTS - ACT OF 1867

NAME OF BANKRUPT	RESIDENCE	CASE NUMBER	CITY OF COURT	DATE FILED
BRANSON, S.	*DOCKET ONLY	966	NEW BERN	11/25/68
BRANTLEY, JOHN	HARNETT	355	WILMINGTON	12/08/68
BRASON, ISAAC	*DOCKET ONLY	189	NEW BERN	01/13/68
BRASWELL, SAMUEL D.	*DOCKET ONLY	1552	NEW BERN	01/03/74
BRAY, ANDREW	CURRITUCK	40	ELIZABETH CITY	11/24/67
BREM & MARTIN	*DOCKET ONLY	691	GREENSBORO	01/01/80
BREWER, R.C.	HALIFAX	221	ELIZABETH CITY	06/30/73
BREWER, ROBERT C.	HALIFAX	599	ELIZABETH CITY	05/19/73
BRIDGES, ALFRED W.	*DOCKET ONLY	1059	NEW BERN	12/26/68
BRIDGES, J. W.	*DOCKET ONLY	423	GREENSBORO	10/28/73
BRIDGES, JOHN	*DOCKET ONLY	677	NEW BERN	05/18/68
BRIDGES, JOHN S.	CLEVELAND	127	STATESVILLE	06/11/73
BRIDGES, N. R	*DOCKET ONLY	145	GREENSBORO	03/21/73
BRIDGES, REDDIN	*DOCKET ONLY	27	NEW BERN	10/08/67
BRIDGES, S. H. J.	*DOCKET ONLY	874	NEW BERN	08/19/68
BRIDGES, THOMAS H.	*DOCKET ONLY	1426	NEW BERN	05/08/73
BRIDGES, THOMAS H.	*DOCKET ONLY	26	NEW BERN	10/08/67
BRIGGS, WILLIAM K.	MADISON	133	WILMINGTON	03/12/68
BRIGHT, ABNER B.	*DOCKET ONLY	1301	NEW BERN	11/11/70
BRIGHT, DAVID	BLADEN	895	WILMINGTON	05/30/73
BRIGHT, JAMES W.	PASQUOTANK	526	ELIZABETH CITY	04/14/71
BRIGHT, JOHN J.	BLADEN	702	WILMINGTON	05/30/73
BRIGHT, JOHN W.	MCDOWELL	108	WILMINGTON	02/27/68
BRINEGER, THOMAS H.	DAVIE	307	WILMINGTON	05/30/68
BRINGHAM, J. (D/B/A/	ROWAN	283	STATESVILLE	07/31/77
BRITE, ANSON H.	*DOCKET ONLY	591	NEW BERN	03/25/68
BRITE, GEORGE W.	PASQUOTANK	92	ELIZABETH CITY	12/25/87
BRITT, JEFFERSON D.	HERTFORD	146	ELIZABETH CITY	02/21/68
BRITTAIN, PHILLIP S.	HENDERSON	10	ASHEVILLE	01/27/73
BRITTIAN, SAMUEL F.	HENDERSON	32	WILMINGTON	01/03/68
BRITTON, JOHN L.	BERTIE	494	ELIZABETH CITY	12/28/68
BRITTON, JOSEPH	BURKE	41	STATESVILLE	02/03/73
BRITTON, ROWAN &	CHEROKEE	198	WILMINGTON	05/06/68
BROCK, DANIEL	SAMPSON	722	WILMINGTON	06/11/73
BRODENHAMER, JACOB	*DOCKET ONLY	25	GREENSBORO	11/22/72
BROOKS, J.T.	HARNETT	779	WILMINGTON	03/13/75
BROOKS, J.T.	HARNETT	779	WILMINGTON	03/13/75
BROOKS, ROBERT		654	WILMINGTON	01/29/72
BROOKSHIRE, WILLLIAM	*DOCKET ONLY	656	GREENSBORO	08/28/78
BROOM, HIRAM	*DOCKET ONLY	447	GREENSBORO	01/07/74
BROWER, ADAM	*DOCKET ONLY	206	GREENSBORO	05/05/73
BROWN & BROTHERS		562	WILMINGTON	10/29/69
BROWN, A. J.	*DOCKET ONLY	036	NEW BERN	12/23/68
BROWN, ABNER	*DOCKET ONLY	901	NEW BERN	08/25/68
BROWN, ANDREW J.	*DOCKET ONLY	449	GREENSBORO	07/08/75
BROWN, ANGUS D.	ROBESON	419	WILMINGTON	12/30/68
BROWN, BURTON	BUNCOMBE	9	ASHEVILLE	04/28/73
BROWN, CALVIN S.	ROWAN	539	WILMINGTON	01/07/69
BROWN, GEORGE	*DOCKET ONLY	390	NEW BERN	02/29/68
BROWN, HENRY N.	*DOCKET ONLY	318	NEW BERN	01/11/71
BROWN, JAMES A.	*DOCKET ONLY	24	GREENSBORO	11/21/72
BROWN, JAMES F.	*DOCKET ONLY	849	GREENSBORO	08/27/78
BROWN, JAMES H.	*DOCKET ONLY	219	GREENSBORO	05/09/73
BROWN, JOHN	CLEVELAND	184	STATESVILLE	06/06/73
BROWN, JOHN D.	ROWAN	274	WILMINGTON	05/30/68
BROWN, JOHN E.	*DOCKET ONLY	609	NEW BERN	04/01/68
BROWN, JOHN L.	*DOCKET ONLY	844	NEW BERN	06/15/68
BROWN, L.B.	CATAWBA	121	STATESVILLE	05/12/73
BROWN, MERRILL W.	DUPLIN	380	WILMINGTON	12/23/68
BROWN, MICHAEL	ROWAN	114	WILMINGTON	03/03/68
BROWN, RIDLEY	*DOCKET ONLY	875	NEW BERN	08/19/68
BROWN, SMILEY	IREDELL	279	STATESVILLE	11/29/76
BROWN, SYLVESTER	*DOCKET ONLY	255	NEW BERN	02/05/68
BROWN, THOMAS B.	*DOCKET ONLY	701	NEW BERN	05/25/68
BROWN, THOMAS J.	DAVIE	502	WILMINGTON	01/01/69
BROWN, THOMAS M.	*DOCKET ONLY	603	GREENSBORO	02/08/78

NAME OF BANKRUPT	RESIDENCE	CASE NUMBER	CITY OF COURT	DATE FILED
BROWN, THOMAS M.	*DOCKET ONLY	603	GREENSBORO	02/08/78
BROWN, THOMAS O	BLADEN	709	WILMINGTON	05/05/73
BROWN, WILLIAM	ROWAN	430	WILMINGTON	12/30/68
BROWN, WILLIAM J.	ROBESON	427	WILMINGTON	12/30/68
BROWN, WILLIAM W.	MARTIN	222	ELIZABETH CITY	03/07/68
BROWNELL, JOSEPH G.	*DOCKET ONLY	21	NEW BERN	10/04/67
BROWNING, WILLIAM P.	*DOCKET ONLY	290	GREENSBORO	05/27/73
BROYLES, WASHINGTON	BUNCOMBE	105	WILMINGTON	02/26/68
BRUNHILD & BROTHERS		770	WILMINGTON	03/14/74
BRYAN, BENJAMIN S.	*DOCKET ONLY	967	NEW BERN	11/25/68
BRYAN, HENRY R.	*DOCKET ONLY	1233	NEW BERN	12/31/68
BRYAN, HUGH B.	*DOCKET ONLY	223	NEW BERN	01/28/68
BRYAN, JAMES	*DOCKET ONLY	1074	NEW BERN	12/25/68
BRYAN, JAMES H.	*DOCKET ONLY	1540	NEW BERN	12/10/73
BRYAN, JAMES H.C.	*DOCKET ONLY	602	NEW BERN	03/27/68
BRYAN, JESSEE	CUMBERLAND	412	WILMINGTON	12/29/68
BRYAN, JOHN S.	*DOCKET ONLY	1107	NEW BERN	12/29/68
BRYAN, JOHNSON H.	*DOCKET ONLY	668	NEW BERN	05/06/68
BRYAN, JOSIAH H.	SAMPSON	626	WILMINGTON	05/14/78
BRYAN, W. C.	*DOCKET ONLY	829	NEW BERN	06/09/68
BRYAN, WILLIAM	*DOCKET ONLY	307	NEW BERN	02/18/68
BRYAN, WILLIAM	*DOCKET ONLY	1228	NEW BERN	12/31/68
BRYAN, WILLIAM G.	BLADEN	685	WILMINGTON	05/17/73
BRYAN, WILLIAM T. &	*DOCKET ONLY	579	NEW BERN	03/19/68
BRYANT, CALVIN O.	*DOCKET ONLY	336	NEW BERN	02/24/68
BRYANT, HENRY H.	*DOCKET ONLY	335	NEW BERN	02/24/68
BRYANT, JAMES	*DOCKET ONLY	183	NEW BERN	01/04/68
BRYANT, JOHN B.	*DOCKET ONLY	923	NEW BERN	09/01/68
BRYANT, WILL D.	HERTFORD	166	ELIZABETH CITY	02/28/68
BRYANT, WILLIAM	*DOCKET ONLY	815	NEW BERN	05/30/68
BRYANT, WILLIAM T.	*DOCKET ONLY	337	NEW BERN	02/24/68
BRYMAN, JOHN WESTLY	*DOCKET ONLY	461	NEW BERN	03/04/68
BRYSON, J.	HENDERSON	529	WILMINGTON	01/04/69
BRZAN, JOSEPH B.	*DOCKET ONLY	385	NEW BERN	02/29/68
BUGRIN, JOHN	BRUNSWICK	83	WILMINGTON	02/13/68
BUICE, WILLIAM A.	MOORE	109	WILMINGTON	03/01/68
BULLA, A. C.	*DOCKET ONLY	39	GREENSBORO	12/07/72
BULLARD, JOHN	SAMPSON	713	WILMINGTON	06/11/73
BULLAS, JAMES R.	*DOCKET ONLY	1175	NEW BERN	12/31/68
BULLOCH, ROBERT	CAMDEN	258	ELIZABETH CITY	05/18/68
BULLOCK, JAMES A.	*DOCKET ONLY	682	NEW BERN	05/19/68
BULLOCK, JOHN	*DOCKET ONLY	552	NEW BERN	03/19/68
BULLOCK, LEONARD H.	*DOCKET ONLY	660	NEW BERN	06/22/68
BULLOCK, RICHARD	*DOCKET ONLY	663	NEW BERN	06/19/68
BULLOCK, RICHARD	*DOCKET ONLY	900	NEW BERN	08/24/68
BULLOCK, WELDON E.	*DOCKET ONLY	661	NEW BERN	06/22/68
BUMPAS, M. D. C.	*DOCKET ONLY	492	NEW BERN	03/07/68
BUNCH, ROBERT C.	*DOCKET ONLY	315	NEW BERN	02/21/68
BUNDY, HARMON	*DOCKET ONLY	51	GREENSBORO	01/04/73
BUNN, ALLISON T.	*DOCKET ONLY	1447	NEW BERN	05/21/73
BUNTING, CHARLES H.	*DOCKET ONLY	340	NEW BERN	02/24/68
BUNTING, JAMES V.	*DOCKET ONLY	333	NEW BERN	02/24/68
BURBANK & GALLAGHER	*DOCKET ONLY	1523	NEW BERN	10/16/73
BURCH, WILLIAM	*DOCKET ONLY	224	NEW BERN	01/28/68
BURGESS, D. L.	*DOCKET ONLY	1550	NEW BERN	12/27/73
BURGESS, FRANCIS M.	*DOCKET ONLY	1591	NEW BERN	11/25/74
BURGESS, JOHN A.	PASQUOTANK	295	ELIZABETH CITY	04/22/68
BURGESS, THOMAS S.	*DOCKET ONLY	659	NEW BERN	06/19/68
BURGESS, WILL B.	PASQUOTANK	29	ELIZABETH CITY	10/04/67
BURGIN, ALMEY	MCDOWELL	95	STATESVILLE	04/30/73
BURGIN, MERRITT	MCDOWELL	254	STATESVILLE	01/02/74
BURGIN, ROBERT	MCDOWELL	161	STATESVILLE	05/26/73
BURGWYN, GEORGE P.	HALIFAX	264	ELIZABETH CITY	02/20/74
BURKE, H.H.	*DOCKET ONLY	773	NEW BERN	08/19/68
BURKE, WILLIAM H.	*DOCKET ONLY	155	GREENSBORO	04/17/73
BURLESON, A. W.	BUNCOMBE	8	ASHEVILLE	05/07/73

NAME OF BANKRUPT	RESIDENCE	CASE NUMBER	CITY OF COURT	DATE FILED
BURLISON, A. (63)	BUNCOMBE	7	ASHEVILLE	05/31/73
BURNETT, BARNET	HENDERSON	608	WILMINGTON	11/30/68
BURNETT, CARRY	RICHMOND	148	WILMINGTON	03/13/68
BURNETT, F. (97)	BUNCOMBE	4	ASHEVILLE	06/06/73
BURNETT, LUCERN	*DOCKET ONLY	216	NEW BERN	01/24/68
BURNETT, OLIVER P.	ANSON	342	WILMINGTON	11/16/68
BURNEY, J.R.	HALIFAX	341	ELIZABETH CITY	08/26/78
BURNHAM, GEORGE W.	CAMDEN	280	ELIZABETH CITY	05/17/75
BURNNETT, W. W.	*DOCKET ONLY	981	NEW BERN	12/08/68
BURNS, ALVIS	*DOCKET ONLY	578	NEW BERN	03/19/68
BURNS, JAMES M.	*DOCKET ONLY	296	GREENSBORO	05/28/73
BURNS, JOHN B. (JR.)	*DOCKET ONLY	297	GREENSBORO	05/28/73
BURNS, LEVI	*DOCKET ONLY	60	NEW BERN	11/21/67
BURNS, WILLIAM	*DOCKET ONLY	525	NEW BERN	03/17/68
BURR, JAMES G.	NEW HANOVER	587	WILMINGTON	02/21/70
BURROUGHS & SPRING		613	WILMINGTON	02/11/71
BURTON, GEORGE W.	*DOCKET ONLY	845	GREENSBORO	08/26/78
BURTON, JOHN O.	HALIFAX	339	ELIZABETH CITY	08/24/78
BURTON, JOSEPH C.	*DOCKET ONLY	313	GREENSBORO	06/02/73
BURTON, R.O.	HALIFAX	340	ELIZABETH CITY	08/24/78
BURTON, ROBERT	HALIFAX	338	ELIZABETH CITY	08/24/78
BURTON, THOMAS	*DOCKET ONLY	223	GREENSBORO	05/10/73
BUSBEE, QUENTIN	*DOCKET ONLY	902	NEW BERN	08/25/68
BUSH & COMPANY,		610	WILMINGTON	01/19/71
BUSH, JAMES P.	BERTIE	297	ELIZABETH CITY	05/27/68
BUTLER, D.M.	COLUMBUS	244	WILMINGTON	05/29/68
BUTLER, JOHN	SAMPSON	836	WILMINGTON	06/17/78
BUTLER, O.	RUTHERFORD	102	STATESVILLE	05/02/73
BUTT, JOHN F.	MECKLENBURG	4	WILMINGTON	09/07/67
BUTTON, LARKIN O.	*DOCKET ONLY	1446	NEW BERN	05/21/73
BUXBAUM, JOSEPH	MECKLENBURG	353	WILMINGTON	11/05/68
BYERS, WILLIAM	HENDERSON	8	ASHEVILLE	04/01/73
BYRD, WILLIAM	ROBESON	736	WILMINGTON	07/05/73
CAIN, ARCHIBALD	*DOCKET ONLY	186	NEW BERN	01/13/68
CAIN, JAMES F.	*DOCKET ONLY	613	GREENSBORO	08/29/77
CALBERTSON, EDWARD	PERQUIMANS	463	ELIZABETH CITY	12/29/68
CALDWELL, JAMES A.		642	WILMINGTON	08/18/71
CALDWELL, JAMES A.		613	WILMINGTON	04/11/71
CALE, D.L.	BERTIE	216	ELIZABETH CITY	06/25/73
CALE, D.L.	BERTIE	595	ELIZABETH CITY	06/24/73
CALE, WILLIAM	*DOCKET ONLY	133	NEW BERN	12/26/67
CALEY, JAMES J.	*DOCKET ONLY	1593	NEW BERN	01/06/75
CALHOUM, R. P.	*DOCKET ONLY	557	GREENSBORO	04/14/76
CALLUM, JAMES R.	*DOCKET ONLY	488	GREENSBORO	04/06/75
CALLUM, N. H.	*DOCKET ONLY	490	GREENSBORO	04/08/75
CALLUM, R. G. & W.	*DOCKET ONLY	487	GREENSBORO	03/29/75
CAMERON, ARCHIBALD	*DOCKET ONLY	1714	NEW BERN	08/27/78
CAMERON, HUGH A.	CUMBERLAND	678	WILMINGTON	05/01/73
CAMERON, NEILL A.	HARNETT	865	WILMINGTON	08/29/78
CAMP, ERSKINE M.	*DOCKET ONLY	986	NEW BERN	12/15/68
CAMPBELL & MCLEAN		772	WILMINGTON	04/27/74
CAMPBELL, A. A.	CHEROKEE	23	ASHEVILLE	03/17/75
CAMPBELL, GEORGE W.	DAVIE	440	WILMINGTON	12/30/68
CAMPBELL, JAMES	*DOCKET ONLY	1594	NEW BERN	01/20/75
CAMPBELL, MATTHEW G.	*DOCKET ONLY	528	NEW BERN	03/17/68
CAMPBELL, MOSES W.	*DOCKET ONLY	1234	NEW BERN	12/31/68
CANBLE, JOHN	ROWAN	129	STATESVILLE	05/16/73
CANBY, RICHARD B.	*DOCKET ONLY	1707	NEW BERN	08/27/78
CANBY, THOMA	*DOCKET ONLY	1708	NEW BERN	08/27/78
CANNON, JOHN	*DOCKET ONLY	669	NEW BERN	05/07/68
CANNON, R.H.		582	WILMINGTON	05/05/70
CANTASPHEN, WILLIAM	TYRRELL	479	ELIZABETH CITY	12/09/68
CAPEHART, C.	CHOWAN	307	ELIZABETH CITY	05/17/76
CAPEL, JOSEPH E.	*DOCKET ONLY	357	GREENSBORO	06/21/73
CARDWELL, JAMES S.	*DOCKET ONLY	1013	NEW BERN	12/19/68
CARDWELL, JOSEPH H.	*DOCKET ONLY	208	NEW BERN	02/12/68

NORTH CAROLINA BANKRUPTS - ACT OF 1867

NAME OF BANKRUPT	RESIDENCE	CASE NUMBER	CITY OF COURT	DATE FILED
CARDWELL, RICHARD H.	*DOCKET ONLY	941	NEW BERN	10/08/68
CARDWELL, RICHARD W.	*DOCKET ONLY	530	GREENSBORO	09/18/73
CARL, G.F.C.		654	WILMINGTON	01/29/72
CARLILE, ERWIN	ROBESON	748	WILMINGTON	08/28/73
CARMADY, W. P	*DOCKET ONLY	95	NEW BERN	12/09/67
CARMAN, EDWARD	*DOCKET ONLY	1057	NEW BERN	12/23/68
CARMER, JOSEPH	*DOCKET ONLY	849	NEW BERN	06/15/68
CARMICHAEL, PETER	RICHMOND	234	WILMINGTON	05/25/68
CARMICHAEL, WILBORNE	WILKES	174	WILMINGTON	04/11/68
CARMICHARL, WILBORNE	WILKES	176	WILMINGTON	04/11/68
CARPENING, THOMAS J.	BURKE	86	WILMINGTON	02/14/68
CARPENING, THOMAS J.	BURKE	135	WILMINGTON	03/12/68
CARPENTER, CHARLES	*DOCKET ONLY	738	NEW BERN	05/29/68
CARPENTER, E.L	STANLY	95	WILMINGTON	04/25/68
CARR, JOHN T.	*DOCKET ONLY	375	NEW BERN	02/25/68
CARRAWAY, JAMES C.	*DOCKET ONLY	221	GREENSBORO	05/10/73
CARRAWAY, WILLIAM W.	*DOCKET ONLY	1413	NEW BERN	02/05/73
CARROLL, HARDY R.	*DOCKET ONLY	562	GREENSBORO	07/13/76
CARROLL, M.L.	GASTON	198	WILMINGTON	05/02/68
CARROWAY, DANIEL T	*DOCKET ONLY	1327	NEW BERN	02/24/71
CARSON, SAMUEL	*DOCKET ONLY	28	NEW BERN	10/09/67
CARSON, W. P.	RUTHERFORD	202	STATESVILLE	01/20/73
CART, G.F.T.		2	STATESVILLE	08/10/72
CARTEN, ALPHA	DAVIE	154	WILMINGTON	03/24/68
CARTER, BENJAMIN F.	*DOCKET ONLY	417	GREENSBORO	10/01/73
CARTER, EDWARD S.	MADISON	26	ASHEVILLE	06/07/73
CARTER, EMSLY	*DOCKET ONLY	282	NEW BERN	02/10/68
CARTER, HENRY	GATES	366	ELIZABETH CITY	11/03/68
CARTER, JESSE	HALIFAX	399	ELIZABETH CITY	12/18/68
CARTER, JOHN C.	*DOCKET ONLY	280	GREENSBORO	05/24/73
CARTER, JOHN R.	ROBESON	402	WILMINGTON	12/26/68
CARTER, ROBERT A.	*DOCKET ONLY	137	GREENSBORO	03/14/73
CARTER, S. S.	*DOCKET ONLY	1060	NEW BERN	12/26/68
CARTER, THOMAS D.	*DOCKET ONLY	6	GREENSBORO	08/12/72
CARTER, THOMAS D.	YANCEY	838	WILMINGTON	06/24/71
CARTER, WADE W. J.	*DOCKET ONLY	341	NEW BERN	02/24/68
CARTER, WILLIAM S.	*DOCKET ONLY	493	NEW BERN	03/07/68
CARTER, WILLIE	BERTIE	187	ELIZABETH CITY	02/28/68
CARTWRIGHT, JAMES S.	PASQUOTANK	59	ELIZABETH CITY	11/25/67
CARTWRIGHT, S.D.	PASQUOTANK	181	ELIZABETH CITY	02/26/68
CARUTHERS, JOHN	*DOCKET ONLY	356	GREENSBORO	06/20/73
CARVEN, JOHN G.	*DOCKET ONLY	431	NEW BERN	03/02/68
CARVIN, T. J.	*DOCKET ONLY	494	NEW BERN	03/07/68
CASE, J. C. (10)	HENDERSON	21	ASHEVILLE	01/27/73
CASE, JESSE (SR.)	HENDERSON	22	ASHEVILLE	06/11/73
CASE, THOMAS	*DOCKET ONLY	524	GREENSBORO	11/04/72
CASE, THOMAS	*DOCKET ONLY	1383	NEW BERN	04/13/72
CASE, WILLIAM (59)	TRANSYLVANIA	31	ASHEVILLE	04/22/74
CASPAR, GEORGE M.	BERTIE	615	ELIZABETH CITY	12/21/68
CASPER, WILLIAM	BERTIE	484	ELIZABETH CITY	12/21/68
CASTOR, P. A.	*DOCKET ONLY	669	GREENSBORO	08/30/78
CATES, THOMAS S.	*DOCKET ONLY	130	NEW BERN	12/28/67
CATES, WIATT	*DOCKET ONLY	126	NEW BERN	12/28/67
CAUDEL, W. M.	*DOCKET ONLY	247	GREENSBORO	05/14/73
CAUDLLE, AMBROSE	*DOCKET ONLY	400	GREENSBORO	09/08/73
CAUSEY, DAVID B.	*DOCKET ONLY	735	NEW BERN	05/29/68
CAUSEY, OLIVER S.	*DOCKET ONLY	1012	NEW BERN	12/19/68
CAUTHON, JOHN C.	*DOCKET ONLY	1444	NEW BERN	06/21/73
CAVANESS, JOHN R.	*DOCKET ONLY	1176	NEW BERN	12/31/68
CAVENEP, ARNOLD E.	MOORE	46	WILMINGTON	01/22/68
CAVNESS, JOHN R.	*DOCKET ONLY	699	GREENSBORO	/ /
CAZAUX, ANTHONY S.	NEW HANOVER	273	WILMINGTON	05/30/68
CECIL, SAMUEL	*DOCKET ONLY	128	GREENSBORO	02/28/73
CHADBOURNE, WILLIAM	NEW HANOVER	884	WILMINGTON	08/31/78
CHADDICK, WILLIAM D.	CURRITUCK	290	ELIZABETH CITY	06/16/68
CHAMBER, P.B.	IREDELL	96	STATESVILLE	04/30/73

NAME OF BANKRUPT	RESIDENCE	CASE NUMBER	CITY OF COURT	DATE FILED
CHAMBERS, E.S.E.	CUMBERLAND	72	WILMINGTON	02/14/68
CHAMBERS, HENRY	WILKES	70	STATESVILLE	03/17/73
CHAMBERS, HESS &	CUMBERLAND	183	WILMINGTON	04/15/68
CHAMBERS, JESSE	*DOCKET ONLY	318	NEW BERN	02/21/68
CHAMBERS, P.B.		15	STATESVILLE	12/12/72
CHAMBERS, PICKNEY R.		570	WILMINGTON	04/01/70
CHAMBERS, W. M.	*DOCKET ONLY	157	NEW BERN	02/03/68
CHANDLER, DANIEL S.	*DOCKET ONLY	158	NEW BERN	01/03/68
CHANDLER, S. B.	*DOCKET ONLY	557	NEW BERN	03/19/68
CHANNEY, WILES &	*DOCKET ONLY	620	GREENSBORO	05/27/78
CHAPIN, ANSEL B.	*DOCKET ONLY	739	NEW BERN	05/29/68
CHAPMAN, LESTER, ET	GREENVILLE	148	ASHEVILLE	02/18/69
CHAPMAN, RICHARD S.	*DOCKET ONLY	1588	NEW BERN	08/25/74
CHAPMAN, ROBERT H.	HENDERSON	415	WILMINGTON	12/30/68
CHARLES, AUSTIN P.	*DOCKET ONLY	191	NEW BERN	01/14/68
CHARLES, ELISHA	*DOCKET ONLY	148	GREENSBORO	04/01/73
CHARLES, F.M.	EDGECOMBE	62	ELIZABETH CITY	11/11/67
CHARLES, JOHN A.	DAVIE	511	WILMINGTON	01/01/68
CHARLES, JOHN N.	DAVIE	275	STATESVILLE	12/04/75
CHAUNCY, RANSOM A.	*DOCKET ONLY	1471	NEW BERN	06/10/73
CHEATHAM & TOWNES	*DOCKET ONLY	890	NEW BERN	08/19/68
CHEEK, JOHN D.	*DOCKET ONLY	335	GREENSBORO	06/10/73
CHERRY, ARCHIBALD	CAMDEN	124	ELIZABETH CITY	01/27/68
CHERRY, GIBSON J.	CAMDEN	284	ELIZABETH CITY	05/30/68
CHERRY, J. J.	*DOCKET ONLY	457	NEW BERN	03/03/68
CHERRY, JOHN E.	MARTIN	417	ELIZABETH CITY	12/22/68
CHERRY, W. S.	*DOCKET ONLY	878	NEW BERN	05/18/68
CHERRY, WILLIAM W.	*DOCKET ONLY	455	NEW BERN	03/03/68
CHESHIRE, JAMES O.A.		31	ELIZABETH CITY	10/15/67
CHESNULT, JAMES P	*DOCKET ONLY	1423	NEW BERN	04/26/73
CHIPLEY, GEORGE.	IREDELL	225	STATESVILLE	07/25/73
CHRISTIAN, J.G.	MONTGOMERY	103	WILMINGTON	02/25/60
CHUK, AUGUSTUS A.	*DOCKET ONLY	1561	NEW BERN	01/30/74
CHUNN, A. B. (123)	BUNCOMBE	29	ASHEVILLE	09/12/73
CHUNN, JSOEPH S.	BUNCOMBE	28	ASHEVILLE	09/12/73
CHUNN, M.L	ROWAN	649	WILMINGTON	01/02/72
CHURCH, RICHARD	*DOCKET ONLY	234	GREENSBORO	05/12/73
CHURCH, THOMAS J.	WILKES	195	STATESVILLE	06/13/73
CILLEY, CHRISTEN A.		569	WILMINGTON	03/02/70
CILLEY, CHRISTEN A.		569	WILMINGTON	03/02/70
CINRAD, JAMES H.	*DOCKET ONLY	240	GREENSBORO	05/12/73
CLAFLIN, H. B. &		321	WILMINGTON	07/06/68
CLAFLIN, H.B. &	MECKLENBURG	611	WILMINGTON	01/17/71
CLAFLIN, H.B.&		387	WILMINGTON	12/25/68
CLAPP, GEORGE W.	*DOCKET ONLY	737	NEW BERN	05/29/68
CLAPP, JOSHUA	*DOCKET ONLY	1274	NEW BERN	06/21/69
CLAPP, JOSHUA	*DOCKET ONLY	35	GREENSBORO	12/02/72
CLAPP, SIMEON R.	*DOCKET ONLY	736	NEW BERN	05/29/68
CLARK, DAVID C.	HALIFAX	120	ELIZABETH CITY	02/07/68
CLARK, DAVID T.	*DOCKET ONLY	203	NEW BERN	01/20/68
CLARK, J. W. & J.M.	*DOCKET ONLY	576	GREENSBORO	07/01/77
CLARK, JAMES W.	ROWAN	319	STATESVILLE	08/18/78
CLARK, JOHN E.	*DOCKET ONLY	1300	NEW BERN	11/07/70
CLARK, JOHN H.	*DOCKET ONLY	1177	NEW BERN	12/31/68
CLARK, JOHN L.	*DOCKET ONLY	73	GREENSBORO	01/25/73
CLARK, JOHN T.		652	WILMINGTON	01/15/72
CLARK, JOSEPH	*DOCKET ONLY	457	GREENSBORO	02/06/74
CLARK, JOSEPH A.	*DOCKET ONLY	1416	NEW BERN	02/11/73
CLARK, SIDNEY P.	*DOCKET ONLY	836	NEW BERN	05/30/68
CLARK, THOMAS C.	*DOCKET ONLY	378	GREENSBORO	07/11/73
CLARK, WILLIAM	*DOCKET ONLY	89	NEW BERN	11/27/67
CLARK, WILLIAM R.		574	WILMINGTON	04/21/70
CLARKE, S. C. (87)	HAYWOOD	20	ASHEVILLE	05/27/73
CLAWSON, H. T.	*DOCKET ONLY	1585	NEW BERN	02/13/74
CLAYTON, JOHN D.	*DOCKET ONLY	787	NEW BERN	05/30/68
CLAYTON, L. S.	*DOCKET ONLY	556	NEW BERN	03/19/68

NAME OF BANKRUPT	RESIDENCE	CASE NUMBER	CITY OF COURT	DATE FILED
CLAYTON, LAMBERT	HENDERSON	527	WILMINGTON	01/04/69
CLAYTON, RICHARD	CHOWAN	10	ELIZABETH CITY	09/09/67
CLEGG, ISAAC N.	*DOCKET ONLY	527	NEW BERN	03/17/68
CLEMENT, GEORGE G.	*DOCKET ONLY	360	GREENSBORO	06/24/73
CLEMENT, S. W.	*DOCKET ONLY	1440	NEW BERN	05/16/73
CLEMENT, SAMUEL	DUPLIN	694	WILMINGTON	05/30/73
CLEMMER, JOHN	GASTON	194	STATESVILLE	06/11/73
CLEMMONS, MARTIN	*DOCKET ONLY	14	GREENSBORO	08/30/72
CLERR, EDWARD	*DOCKET ONLY	397	NEW BERN	02/27/68
CLEVE, WILLIAM	*DOCKET ONLY	156	NEW BERN	01/02/68
CLICK, JESSE D.	IREDELL	348	WILMINGTON	11/21/68
CLINARD, L. N.	*DOCKET ONLY	437	GREENSBORO	11/06/73
CLINGMAN, JOHN P.	DAVIE	16	STATESVILLE	12/13/72
CLOUSE, WILLIAM	DAVIE	198	STATESVILLE	06/18/73
CLOUTS, JAMES	*DOCKET ONLY	398	GREENSBORO	08/04/73
CLOUTZ, ADAM	*DOCKET ONLY	387	GREENSBORO	07/14/73
CLURE, L. E. &	*DOCKET ONLY	1637	NEW BERN	12/09/76
COAT, SION H.	MADISON	31	ASHEVILLE	06/29/78
COATES, THOMAS H.	*DOCKET ONLY	970	NEW BERN	12/05/68
COBB, GARY	*DOCKET ONLY	332	NEW BERN	02/24/68
COBB, HOWELL H.	SAMPSON	712	WILMINGTON	06/11/73
COBB, JOHN C.	*DOCKET ONLY	1530	NEW BERN	11/06/73
COBB, R.A.	BURKE	643	WILMINGTON	09/26/71
COBB, RICHARD G.	*DOCKET ONLY	376	NEW BERN	02/26/68
COBB, T.R. & SON	PASQUOTANK	282	ELIZABETH CITY	05/29/68
COBBS, T.R. & SONS	PASQUOTANK	281	ELIZABETH CITY	05/29/68
COBLE, DAVID	*DOCKET ONLY	788	NEW BERN	05/30/68
COBLE, DAVID S.	*DOCKET ONLY	1193	NEW BERN	12/31/68
COBLE, K. M.	*DOCKET ONLY	338	GREENSBORO	06/11/73
COBLE, ROBERT S.	*DOCKET ONLY	555	NEW BERN	03/19/68
COCHMAN, LEWIS W.	CATAWBA	242	STATESVILLE	11/19/73
COCHRAN & HILL		572	WILMINGTON	04/19/70
COCHRAN, DAVID	POLK	253	WILMINGTON	05/29/68
COCHRAN, MCLEAN &		786	WILMINGTON	12/29/75
COCHRAN, ROBERT	MECKLENBURG	285	WILMINGTON	05/30/68
COCHRANE, THOMAS	CHOWAN	419	ELIZABETH CITY	12/26/68
COCKE, WILLIAM M.	BUNCOMBE	650	WILMINGTON	01/03/72
COE, JOHN P.	*DOCKET ONLY	246	GREENSBORO	05/13/73
COFFIELD, A.H.	MARTIN	243	ELIZABETH CITY	12/02/73
COFFIN, BETHUEL	*DOCKET ONLY	233	GREENSBORO	05/12/73
COFFY, D. S.	*DOCKET ONLY	299	GREENSBORO	05/29/73
COGGINS, GEORGE	*DOCKET ONLY	257	GREENSBORO	05/19/73
COGGINS, JAMES	*DOCKET ONLY	1508	NEW BERN	08/12/73
COGGINS, WILL G.	BERTIE	163	ELIZABETH CITY	02/26/68
COHEN, M.	*DOCKET ONLY	178	NEW BERN	01/09/68
COHEN, NATHAN H.	CUMBERLAND	793	WILMINGTON	01/26/76
COHEN, SAMUEL	*DOCKET ONLY	1348	NEW BERN	05/15/71
COHEN, WILLIAM	*DOCKET ONLY	1390	NEW BERN	08/31/72
COHN, ADOLPH	*DOCKET ONLY	1235	NEW BERN	12/31/68
COHOON, P.A.R.C.	PASQUOTANK	123	ELIZABETH CITY	01/23/68
COKE, GEORGE H.	CHOWAN	6	ELIZABETH CITY	08/03/67
COKER, RICHARD C.	*DOCKET ONLY	855	NEW BERN	06/19/68
COLBERN, ELISHA	*DOCKET ONLY	363	NEW BERN	02/29/68
COLBURN, WILLIAM B.	*DOCKET ONLY	1613	NEW BERN	09/03/75
COLE, B. S.	*DOCKET ONLY	1148	NEW BERN	12/30/68
COLE, GEORGE W.	BUNCOMBE	27	ASHEVILLE	05/07/73
COLE, HENRY	*DOCKET ONLY	106	NEW BERN	12/14/67
COLE, HOWARD, &		563	WILMINGTON	10/29/69
COLE, JOHN B.	*DOCKET ONLY	425	GREENSBORO	11/03/73
COLEMAN, DANIEL	CABARRUS	497	WILMINGTON	12/31/68
COLEMAN, DAVID	CABARRUS	169	WILMINGTON	04/08/68
COLGROVE, O. R. , J.	*DOCKET ONLY	772	NEW BERN	05/30/68
COLLIER, GEORGE W.	*DOCKET ONLY	818	NEW BERN	05/30/68
COLLIER, GEORGE W.	*DOCKET ONLY	6	NEW BERN	07/25/67
COLLINS, THOMAS C.	*DOCKET ONLY	48	NEW BERN	11/06/67
COLLION, WILL H.	NORTHAMPTON	184	ELIZABETH CITY	02/28/68

NAME OF BANKRUPT	RESIDENCE	CASE NUMBER	CITY OF COURT	DATE FILED
COLTON, QUINTEN C.	CURRITUCK	229	ELIZABETH CITY	07/29/73
COLTRANE, ROBERT L.	*DOCKET ONLY	46	NEW BERN	11/06/67
COMER, C.	CLEVELAND	111	STATESVILLE	05/07/73
COMMANADER, JOS. ,SR.	PASQUOTANK	161	ELIZABETH CITY	02/24/68
COMMANDER, JOSEPH	PASQUOTANK	253	ELIZABETH CITY	12/23/73
CONLEY, HARVEY P.	CALDWELL	114	STATESVILLE	05/02/73
CONNATZER, JACOB	DAVIE	55	STATESVILLE	02/18/73
CONNER, JAMES W.	NORTHAMPTON	268	ELIZABETH CITY	05/27/68
CONNOLLY, WILLIAM F.	ALEXANDER	196	STATESVILLE	06/17/73
CONRAD, JOHN C.	YADKIN	185	WILMINGTON	04/16/68
CONRAD, JOHN F.	FORSYTH	113	WILMINGTON	03/01/68
CONRAD, PARKER T.	*DOCKET ONLY	505	GREENSBORO	10/26/75
CONROD, PARKER C.	*DOCKET ONLY	704	GREENSBORO	10/27/75
CONYEARS, LUCURGUS	*DOCKET ONLY	342	NEW BERN	02/24/68
COOK & JOHNSON	CUMBERLAND	818	WILMINGTON	02/01/71
COOK, CALVIN J.	*DOCKET ONLY	345	GREENSBORO	06/14/73
COOK, COLUMBUS	WILKES	616	WILMINGTON	02/21/71
COOK, F.M.	PASQUOTANK	122	ELIZABETH CITY	01/22/68
COOK, F.M.	PERQUIMANS	162	ELIZABETH CITY	02/25/68
COOK, JAMES G.	CUMBERLAND	211	WILMINGTON	05/15/68
COOK, LEMUEL B.	*DOCKET ONLY	28	GREENSBORO	11/28/72
COOK, W. F.	*DOCKET ONLY	574	GREENSBORO	04/17/77
COOKE, GEORGE	*DOCKET ONLY	903	NEW BERN	08/25/68
COOPER, A.W. & T.D.	DAVIDSON	15	WILMINGTON	11/05/67
COOPER, T.D. & A. W.	DAVIDSON	15	WILMINGTON	11/05/67
COOPER, THOMAS N.		592	WILMINGTON	10/11/70
COOPER, W.H.H.	TYRRELL	285	ELIZABETH CITY	10/18/75
COPAGE, WILLIAM A.	PASQUOTANK	68	ELIZABETH CITY	12/04/67
COPE, REDDING	*DOCKET ONLY	234	NEW BERN	01/31/68
CORBETT, C.B.	HALIFAX	517	ELIZABETH CITY	11/23/70
CORBIN, JAMES W.	*DOCKET ONLY	501	GREENSBORO	09/07/75
CORBIN, JAMES W.	*DOCKET ONLY	590	GREENSBORO	07/23/77
CORNWALL, A.C.	CLEVELAND	123	STATESVILLE	05/12/73
CORRELL, PHILLIP A.	*DOCKET ONLY	50	GREENSBORO	12/23/72
COTCHER, ANSON	*DOCKET ONLY	1445	NEW BERN	05/21/73
COTTON, LEWIS	BERTIE	178	ELIZABETH CITY	02/29/68
COUNCIL, A. C.	*DOCKET ONLY	268	NEW BERN	02/07/68
COUNCIL, ENSLEY	*DOCKET ONLY	75	NEW BERN	11/29/67
COUNCIL, JOHN T.	BLADEN	236	WILMINGTON	05/27/68
COUNCIL, W.B.	WATAUGA	56	WILMINGTON	01/17/68
COVINGTON, T.	RICHMOND	80	WILMINGTON	02/11/68
COWAN, ALBERT	ROWAN	391	WILMINGTON	12/26/68
COWAN, JAMES	BUNCOMBE	24	ASHEVILLE	05/31/73
COWAND, D.G.	WASHINGTON	5	ELIZABETH CITY	07/25/67
COWELL, E.T.	CAMDEN	333	ELIZABETH CITY	08/13/78
COWELL, JOSEPH F.	CURRITUCK	235	ELIZABETH CITY	09/02/73
COX, ELI J.	*DOCKET ONLY	1525	NEW BERN	10/24/73
COX, HARRY	*DOCKET ONLY	1289	NEW BERN	06/25/70
COX, IABEZ	CURRITUCK	61	ELIZABETH CITY	11/27/67
COX, JAMES	*DOCKET ONLY	601	NEW BERN	03/26/68
COX, JAMES K.	*DOCKET ONLY	259	GREENSBORO	05/20/73
COX, JOHN	CURRITUCK	60	ELIZABETH CITY	11/28/67
COX, JOHN P.	*DOCKET ONLY	1068	NEW BERN	12/26/68
COX, NATHAN B.	PERQUIMANS	365	ELIZABETH CITY	11/12/68
COX, OLIVER P.	*DOCKET ONLY	202	GREENSBORO	05/05/73
COX, PETER H.	*DOCKET ONLY	838	GREENSBORO	08/17/78
COX, REUBEN N.	*DOCKET ONLY	229	GREENSBORO	05/12/73
COX, ROBERT M.	*DOCKET ONLY	1219	NEW BERN	12/28/68
COX, SHARP K.	CURRITUCK	205	ELIZABETH CITY	03/02/68
COX, WILLIAM A.	*DOCKET ONLY	1187	NEW BERN	12/30/68
COZART, WILLIAM W.	*DOCKET ONLY	1524	NEW BERN	10/22/73
CRAFT, ANDREW J.	*DOCKET ONLY	194	NEW BERN	01/17/68
CRAFTON, BEDFORD A.	*DOCKET ONLY	365	NEW BERN	02/24/68
CRAFTON, GEORGE H.	MARTIN	143	ELIZABETH CITY	02/17/68
CRAFTON, JOHN A.	*DOCKET ONLY	1343	NEW BERN	05/13/71
CRAIGH, JOHN H. &	GASTON	160	WILMINGTON	03/28/68

NAME OF BANKRUPT	RESIDENCE	CASE NUMBER	CITY OF COURT	DATE FILED
CRAMPLER, MARSHALL	SAMPSON	781	WILMINGTON	06/16/75
CRASS, LEONARD	*DOCKET ONLY	104	GREENSBORO	02/05/73
CRAVEN, ENOCH S.	*DOCKET ONLY	34	GREENSBORO	12/02/72
CRAVEN, THOMAS G.	*DOCKET ONLY	232	GREENSBORO	05/12/73
CRAVER, JACOB	*DOCKET ONLY	373	GREENSBORO	07/03/73
CRAWFIELD, W. H.	*DOCKET ONLY	586	GREENSBORO	/ /
CRAWFORD, MALCHUS K.	*DOCKET ONLY	817	NEW BERN	05/30/68
CRAWFORD, TILMAN	ROWAN	307	STATESVILLE	07/02/78
CRAWFORD, W. H.	ROWAN	284	STATESVILLE	08/06/77
CRAWFORD, WILLIAM	*DOCKET ONLY	123	NEW BERN	12/28/67
CREEKMOREN, E.	CAMDEN	350	ELIZABETH CITY	08/31/78
CREEL, JOHN W.	*DOCKET ONLY	58	NEW BERN	11/16/67
CRENSHAW, DAVID M.	DAVIE	186	WILMINGTON	04/03/68
CREW, & MARSH	*DOCKET ONLY	835	GREENSBORO	08/27/78
CREW, THOMAS B.	NORTHAMPTON	443	ELIZABETH CITY	12/21/68
CREWS, JONATHAN	*DOCKET ONLY	53	GREENSBORO	01/06/73
CRIDUP, A.D.	*DOCKET ONLY	876	NEW BERN	08/19/68
CRIGHTON, WILLIAM	CHOWAN	190	ELIZABETH CITY	02/29/68
CRITZ, HARMON	DAVIE	101	STATESVILLE	04/30/73
CROCKER, GEORGE W.	*DOCKET ONLY	172	NEW BERN	01/09/68
CROMARNTIE, A.K.	CUMBERLAND	864	WILMINGTON	10/05/78
CRONLAND, C.R.F.	GASTON	197	WILMINGTON	04/21/69
CROOM, ALLEN	*DOCKET ONLY	1685	NEW BERN	07/05/78
CROOM, CHARLES S.	*DOCKET ONLY	1043	NEW BERN	12/22/68
CROON, SAMUEL M.	*DOCKET ONLY	1047	NEW BERN	12/22/68
CROSCEY, JOHN A.	MCDOWELL	226	STATESVILLE	07/30/73
CROVIN, JOHN A.	*DOCKET ONLY	1143	NEW BERN	12/30/68
CROW, JAMES C.	*DOCKET ONLY	392	GREENSBORO	07/26/73
CROWELL, ANDREW S.	*DOCKET ONLY	33	GREENSBORO	12/02/72
CROWER, BARTEK	CLEVELAND	127	WILMINGTON	03/12/68
CRUDLE, THOMAS F.	*DOCKET ONLY	1351	NEW BERN	07/08/71
CRUMPLER, HENRY C.	*DOCKET ONLY	1533	NEW BERN	11/13/73
CRUMPLER, THOMAS	WILKES	234	STATESVILLE	09/24/73
CRUSE, ALLEN		543	WILMINGTON	01/18/69
CRUSENBERRY, WILLIAM	*DOCKET ONLY	1402	NEW BERN	11/30/72
CRUTCHFIELD, A. A.	*DOCKET ONLY	812	GREENSBORO	05/14/78
CRUTCHFIELD, S.	*DOCKET ONLY	541	GREENSBORO	03/13/74
CRUTCHFIELD, S. H.	*DOCKET ONLY	467	GREENSBORO	03/13/74
CULBERTH, JOHN	*DOCKET ONLY	511	NEW BERN	03/12/68
CULBRETH, GRAY	CUMBERLAND	855	WILMINGTON	08/23/78
CULBRETH, LOVE	CUMBERLAND	740	WILMINGTON	07/05/73
CULPEPPER, M.B.	PASQUOTANK	296	ELIZABETH CITY	05/02/75
CUMMINGHAM, E.H.	BUNCOMBE	261	WILMINGTON	05/29/68
CUNARD, JOHN W.		570	WILMINGTON	04/01/70
CUNNINGHAM, D.C.	MACON	65	WILMINGTON	02/04/68
CUNNINGINS, W. H.	*DOCKET ONLY	904	NEW BERN	08/25/68
CURETON, THOMAS K.	MECKLENBURG	360	WILMINGTON	12/12/68
CURLEE, JOHN W.	STANLY	651	WILMINGTON	01/13/72
CURRICK, WILLIAM J.	ROBESON	810	WILMINGTON	04/12/78
CURTIS, J. D.	CLAY	25	ASHEVILLE	08/28/73
CUTCHIN, J. H.	*DOCKET ONLY	755	NEW BERN	06/02/68
CUTHBURTON, DAVID	UNION	140	WILMINGTON	03/06/68
CUTHBURTSON, JAMES	UNION	526	WILMINGTON	01/04/69
D.G.MAXWELL		573	WILMINGTON	04/19/70
DAILEY, DANIEL	PASQUOTANK	88	ELIZABETH CITY	12/25/67
DALBY, EDWARD	*DOCKET ONLY	1414	NEW BERN	02/02/73
DALLAS, JAMES J.	*DOCKET ONLY	416	GREENSBORO	09/24/73
DALLAS, R. W.	*DOCKET ONLY	643	GREENSBORO	08/21/78
DALTON, JAMES D.	*DOCKET ONLY	790	NEW BERN	05/30/68
DALTON, NICHOLAS	*DOCKET ONLY	437	NEW BERN	03/02/68
DALTON, WILLIAM F.	*DOCKET ONLY	741	NEW BERN	05/29/68
DAMERON, LORENZO L.	SAMPSON	423	WILMINGTON	12/30/68
DANIEL, A. W.	*DOCKET ONLY	558	GREENSBORO	04/14/78
DANIEL, ERASMUS A.	*DOCKET ONLY	1040	NEW BERN	12/30/68
DANIEL, JAMES B.	*DOCKET ONLY	1062	NEW BERN	12/26/68
DANIEL, JOHN B. &	*DOCKET ONLY	726	NEW BERN	05/24/68

NAME OF BANKRUPT	RESIDENCE	CASE NUMBER	CITY OF COURT	DATE FILED
DANIEL, MARY ANN	*DOCKET ONLY	495	NEW BERN	03/07/68
DANIEL, ROMULUS	*DOCKET ONLY	740	NEW BERN	05/29/68
DANIEL, W. C.	*DOCKET ONLY	954	NEW BERN	11/04/68
DANIEL, WATSON L.	HERTFORD	109	ELIZABETH CITY	01/11/68
DANIEL, WILLIAM A.	*DOCKET ONLY	857	NEW BERN	06/19/68
DANIEL, WILLIAM H.	*DOCKET ONLY	905	NEW BERN	08/25/68
DANIEL, THOMAS H.	*DOCKET ONLY	98	GREENSBORO	02/04/73
DANNY, WALTER (JR)	*DOCKET ONLY	1237	NEW BERN	12/31/68
DARDEN, GOODMAN	MARTIN	225	ELIZABETH CITY	03/07/68
DARDEN, J.R.	HERTFORD	474	ELIZABETH CITY	12/02/68
DARDEN, ROBERT M	GATES	457	ELIZABETH CITY	12/29/68
DARDEN, THOMAS E.	MARTIN	235	ELIZABETH CITY	03/20/68
DARDEN, WILL H.	HERTFORD	170	ELIZABETH CITY	02/29/68
DASHIELL, LUTHER C.	PASQUOTANK	13	ELIZABETH CITY	08/13/67
DASHIELL, R.S. &	CHOWAN	616	ELIZABETH CITY	03/25/70
DASHIELL, RUDOLPHUS	PASQUOTANK	12	ELIZABETH CITY	08/13/67
DASHILL, TATUM &	PASQUOTANK	510	ELIZABETH CITY	11/08/70
DAUGHTRY, WILLIAM	SAMPSON	829	WILMINGTON	05/18/78
DAVENPORT, TULLY	TYRRELL	171	ELIZABETH CITY	02/17/68
DAVIDSON, ELIAS	*DOCKET ONLY	1452	NEW BERN	05/23/73
DAVIDSON, J. R.	*DOCKET ONLY	671	GREENSBORO	06/30/78
DAVIDSON, SAMUEL W.	CHEROKEE	243	WILMINGTON	05/26/68
DAVIES, FRANKILN A.	*DOCKET ONLY	389	GREENSBORO	07/24/73
DAVIS, ADAM C.	*DOCKET ONLY	1669	NEW BERN	05/02/78
DAVIS, ALEX L.	*DOCKET ONLY	624	NEW BERN	04/07/68
DAVIS, ALEXANDER B.	*DOCKET ONLY	639	NEW BERN	04/18/68
DAVIS, ARCHIBALD H.	*DOCKET ONLY	1239	NEW BERN	12/26/68
DAVIS, CHARLES	BLADEN	737	WILMINGTON	07/05/73
DAVIS, DAVID (JR.)	*DOCKET ONLY	258	GREENSBORO	05/20/73
DAVIS, EDMOND L.	*DOCKET ONLY	426	GREENSBORO	11/06/73
DAVIS, GAY & (JAMES	*DOCKET ONLY	725	NEW BERN	05/27/68
DAVIS, HALEY	*DOCKET ONLY	376	GREENSBORO	07/09/73
DAVIS, HORACE C.	*DOCKET ONLY	169	GREENSBORO	04/25/73
DAVIS, JAMES M.	*DOCKET ONLY	1421	NEW BERN	04/21/73
DAVIS, JAMES M.	HENDERSON	34	ASHEVILLE	03/31/73
DAVIS, JASPER	*DOCKET ONLY	1670	NEW BERN	06/06/78
DAVIS, JOHN	*DOCKET ONLY	906	NEW BERN	08/25/68
DAVIS, JOHN E.	*DOCKET ONLY	819	NEW BERN	05/30/68
DAVIS, JOHN N., J.	*DOCKET ONLY	506	GREENSBORO	11/19/75
DAVIS, JOHNATHAN	*DOCKET ONLY	1410	NEW BERN	01/30/73
DAVIS, JOSEPH A.	*DOCKET ONLY	617	GREENSBORO	04/29/78
DAVIS, JOSEPH B.	*DOCKET ONLY	664	NEW BERN	04/28/68
DAVIS, JOSHUA N.	*DOCKET ONLY	205	GREENSBORO	05/05/73
DAVIS, MATTHEW B.	*DOCKET ONLY	1612	NEW BERN	08/03/75
DAVIS, MICAJAH	*DOCKET ONLY	204	GREENSBORO	05/05/73
DAVIS, PETER R.	*DOCKET ONLY	1334	NEW BERN	03/22/71
DAVIS, SAMUEL C.	YADKIN	513	WILMINGTON	01/01/69
DAVIS, T. C.	*DOCKET ONLY	723	NEW BERN	05/27/68
DAVIS, T. J.	*DOCKET ONLY	265	NEW BERN	02/07/68
DAVIS, THOMAS W.	*DOCKET ONLY	1061	NEW BERN	12/26/68
DAVIS, W. F.	*DOCKET ONLY	212	GREENSBORO	05/07/73
DAVIS, WILL H.	PASQUOTANK	151	ELIZABETH CITY	02/24/68
DAVIS, WILLIAM	PASQUOTANK	57	ELIZABETH CITY	11/22/67
DAVIS, WILLIAM C.	PASQUOTANK	37	ELIZABETH CITY	11/06/67
DAVIS, WILLIAM H.	*DOCKET ONLY	184	NEW BERN	01/15/68
DAVIS, WILLIAM B.	*DOCKET ONLY	1634	NEW BERN	12/24/78
DAWSON, JOHN W.	*DOCKET ONLY	1437	NEW BERN	05/16/73
DAWSON, JOSEPH	SAMPSON	718	WILMINGTON	06/11/73
DAWSON, L. & H. C.	*DOCKET ONLY	515	GREENSBORO	06/03/74
DAWSON, LEVI	*DOCKET ONLY	874	NEW BERN	05/15/68
DAWSON, WILLIAM	*DOCKET ONLY	1297	NEW BERN	10/25/70
DAY, FRANK	*DOCKET ONLY	559	NEW BERN	03/19/68
DAY, ISAAC W.	*DOCKET ONLY	1108	NEW BERN	12/29/68
DAY, S. S.	*DOCKET ONLY	789	NEW BERN	05/30/68
DAY, WILLIAM B.	HALIFAX	127	ELIZABETH CITY	02/05/67
DEAL, SIDNEY	CALDWELL	318	STATESVILLE	08/12/78

NAME OF BANKRUPT	RESIDENCE	CASE NUMBER	CITY OF COURT	DATE FILED
DEAN, BARTLETT F.	*DOCKET ONLY	1369	NEW BERN	12/13/71
DEAN, BARTLETT Y.	*DOCKET ONLY	527	GREENSBORO	11/04/72
DEAN, JOSHUA	*DOCKET ONLY	1806	NEW BERN	06/04/75
DEAN, MCCUBBINGS.	*DOCKET ONLY	575	GREENSBORO	12/22/76
DEAN, S. F.	*DOCKET ONLY	236	GREENSBORO	05/12/73
DEANS, JACOB	*DOCKET ONLY	1030	NEW BERN	12/23/69
DEARMOND, HUGH K.	MECKLENBURG	197	WILMINGTON	05/05/68
DEBRAM, THOMAS C.	*DOCKET ONLY	529	NEW BERN	03/17/68
DECOSTA, & WEILL		776	WILMINGTON	12/17/74
DEDMAN, THOMAS J.	DAVIE	59	STATESVILLE	02/20/73
DEDMAN, WILLIAM	HENDERSON	33	ASHEVILLE	04/16/73
DELANEY, WILLIAM K.	*DOCKET ONLY	1284	NEW BERN	03/09/70
DELOATCH, AUGUSTUS	*DOCKET ONLY	928	NEW BERN	09/21/68
DELOATCH, D.S.	NORTHAMPTON	209	ELIZABETH CITY	06/03/73
DELOATCH, H.R.	JACKSON	315	ELIZABETH CITY	03/03/77
DENNIS, GEORGE	*DOCKET ONLY	1306	NEW BERN	12/02/70
DENNY, RUFUS K.	*DOCKET ONLY	556	NEW BERN	03/19/68
DENTON, ARCHIBALD H.	*DOCKET ONLY	1296	NEW BERN	10/21/70
DERASSET, LEWIS H.	*DOCKET ONLY	481	GREENSBORO	02/23/75
DERMID, LEMUEL T.	HENDERSON	37	ASHEVILLE	01/06/73
DERMID, MENONY P.	HENDERSON	36	ASHEVILLE .	02/10/73
DETRICK, JOHN	PASQUOTANK	190	ELIZABETH CITY	03/27/76
DEVANE, MILTON K.	DUPLIN	404	WILMINGTON	12/26/68
DEVERAUX, THOMAS P.	*DOCKET ONLY	893	NEW BERN	08/19/68
DEVREAUX, JOHN	*DOCKET ONLY	1270	NEW BERN	05/21/69
DEW, JOHN	*DOCKET ONLY	1629	NEW BERN	04/12/76
DEWEY, F.H.		852	WILMINGTON	03/15/72
DIBBLE, J. H.	*DOCKET ONLY	1238	NEW BERN	12/31/68
DICKENS, BALAAM	HALIFAX	369	ELIZABETH CITY	10/23/68
DICKENS, OSCAR F.	HALIFAX	587	ELIZABETH CITY	05/24/73
DICKENS, OSCAR F.	HALIFAX	208	ELIZABETH CITY	06/03/73
DICKEY, MICHAEL D.	HENDERSON	35	ASHEVILLE	09/07/73
DICKS, ARCHIBALD M.	*DOCKET ONLY	193	GREENSBORO	04/01/73
DICKS, JAMES	*DOCKET ONLY	189	GREENSBORO	04/01/73.
DICKSEN, EDWARD D.	CLEVELAND	548	WILMINGTON	05/22/69
DICKSON, GILBETJ	CLEVELAND	277	WILMINGTON	05/30/68
DICKSON, JAMES	ALLEGHANY	265	STATESVILLE	10/06/74
DICKSON, L. J.	CLEVELAND	149	STATESVILLE	05/23/73
DICKSON, WILLIE J.	YADKIN	351	WILMINGTON	12/04/68
DILL, DAVID H.	*DOCKET ONLY	1380	NEW BERN	04/04/72
DILL, JOSEPH	*DOCKET ONLY	486	GREENSBORO	03/27/75
DILLAHUNT, LAFAYETT	*DOCKET ONLY	1397	NEW BERN	10/30/72
DILLIARD, ISRAEL F.	*DOCKET ONLY	1409	NEW BERN	01/30/73
DILLINGER, HENRY	LINCOLN	94	WILMINGTON	02/22/68
DILLINGER, JOHN	GASTON	58	WILMINGTON	01/10/68
DILLON, JAMES R.	WASHINGTON	34	ELIZABETH CITY	10/21/67
DILWORTH, ARRINGTON	*DOCKET ONLY	680	GREENSBORO	08/31/78
DINKINS, EDWARD	*DOCKET ONLY	1461	NEW BERN	06/01/73
DIXON, BURRILL E.	ONSLOW	744	WILMINGTON	06/27/73
DIXON, GEORGE W.	*DOCKET ONLY	1350	NEW BERN	07/01/71
DIXON, H. C.	*DOCKET ONLY	730	NEW BERN	05/29/68
DIXON, JOSEPH	*DOCKET ONLY	1590	NEW BERN	11/23/74
DIXON, MARTIN C.	*DOCKET ONLY	713	NEW BERN	05/27/68
DIXON, THOMAS G.	*DOCKET ONLY	1004	NEW BERN	12/18/68
DOBBINS, HUGH A.	WATAUGA	282	STATESVILLE	06/22/77
DOBBS, NATHANIEL G.	*DOCKET ONLY	366	NEW BERN	02/24/68
DOBSON, JOHNSON &	BALTIMORE.	627	ELIZABETH CITY	10/19/69
DODSON, THOMAS C.	*DOCKET ONLY	943	NEW BERN	10/19/68
DOGGETT, G.W.	RUTHERFORD	53	WILMINGTON	01/21/68
DOLES, WILLIAM F.	*DOCKET ONLY	343	NEW BERN	02/24/68
DONNELL, VENABLE B.	*DOCKET ONLY	333	GREENSBORO	06/07/73
DONTHIT, WILLIAM	DAVIE	268	STATESVILLE	11/12/74
DORITHEL, JACOB C.	DAVIE	501	WILMINGTON	01/01/69
DORSETT, GEORGE W.	*DOCKET ONLY	838	NEW BERN	04/16/68
DORSETT, HEZEKIAH	*DOCKET ONLY	218	GREENSBORO	05/09/73
DORSETT, J. J.	*DOCKET ONLY	217	GREENSBORO	05/09/73

NORTH CAROLINA BANKRUPTS - ACT OF 1867

NAME OF BANKRUPT	RESIDENCE	CASE NUMBER	CITY OF COURT	DATE FILED
DORSETT, ROBERT	*DOCKET ONLY	90	GREENSBORO	02/01/73
DORTCH, JOHN G.	*DOCKET ONLY	658	NEW BERN	04/30/68
DOSTER, J.P.	UNION	388	WILMINGTON	12/26/68
DOUGAN, W. McK.	*DOCKET ONLY	322	GREENSBORO	05/29/73
DOUGAN, WILLIAM A.	*DOCKET ONLY	263	NEW BERN	02/10/68
DOUGHERTY, WILLIAM	GATES	381	ELIZABETH CITY	11/03/68
DOUGHTRY, HARRISON	NORTHAMPTON	439	ELIZABETH CITY	10/28/68
DOUGHTY, WILLIAM A.	*DOCKET ONLY	345	NEW BERN	02/24/68
DOUGLAS, JOSEPH A.	CHOWAN	617	ELIZABETH CITY	03/22/73
DOWDEN, CALEB	DAVIE	31	STATESVILLE	01/29/73
DOZIER, ABNER	CAMDEN	468	ELIZABETH CITY	12/30/68
DOZIER, AMBROSE A.	CAMDEN	140	ELIZABETH CITY	02/17/68
DOZIER, W.E.	CURRITUCK	344	ELIZABETH CITY	08/29/78
DRAKE, B.F. & W. H.	*DOCKET ONLY	594	NEW BERN	03/25/68
DRAKE, FRANCIS J.	*DOCKET ONLY	623	NEW BERN	04/07/68
DRAKE, JOHN R.	NORTHAMPTON	198	ELIZABETH CITY	05/21/73
DRAKE, JOHN R.	NORTHAMPTON	578	ELIZABETH CITY	05/16/73
DRAKE, N. T.	*DOCKET ONLY	866	NEW BERN	05/02/68
DRAKE, NATHAN (24)	HENDERSON	38	ASHEVILLE	01/28/73
DRAKE, O. P. (23)	HENDERSON	32	ASHEVILLE	01/28/73
DRAKE, WILLIAM C.	*DOCKET ONLY	716	NEW BERN	08/19/68
DRAUGHN, ISAAC	*DOCKET ONLY	309	GREENSBORO	05/31/73
DREW, JOSEPH W.	BERTIE	219	ELIZABETH CITY	03/07/67
DUDLEY, AUGUSTUS	*DOCKET ONLY	260	NEW BERN	02/07/68
DUDLEY, GEORGE J.	*DOCKET ONLY	1702	NEW BERN	08/27/78
DUFFY, FRANCIS S.	*DOCKET ONLY	1264	NEW BERN	12/31/68
DUGGEN, WILLIAM S.	*DOCKET ONLY	388	NEW BERN	02/29/68
DUGIND, EDWARD M.	*DOCKET ONLY	1596	NEW BERN	02/03/75
DUKE, WILLIAM A.		284	ELIZABETH CITY	11/18/75
DULA, BENNETT J.	WILKES	167	STATESVILLE	05/28/73
DULA, S.P.	CALDWELL	483	WILMINGTON	12/31/68
DULA, SARAH H.		240	STATESVILLE	10/17/73
DULA, THOMAS	ALEXANDER	516	WILMINGTON	01/01/69
DUNCAN, JOSEPH	MECKLENBURG	577	WILMINGTON	05/17/70
DUNIGAN, HENRY	*DOCKET ONLY	370	GREENSBORO	07/03/73
DUNN, BENJAMIN F.	*DOCKET ONLY	1129	NEW BERN	12/30/68
DUNN, J.L.	CHOWAN	618	ELIZABETH CITY	03/02/69
DUNN, JAMES L.	*DOCKET ONLY	1236	NEW BERN	12/31/68
DUNN, NATHANIEL	HALIFAX	303	ELIZABETH CITY	04/29/76
DUNN, WILLIAM S.	*DOCKET ONLY	1209	NEW BERN	12/31/68
DUPREE, S.G.	*DOCKET ONLY	173	NEW BERN	01/09/68
DURHAM, ALVIS	*DOCKET ONLY	55	NEW BERN	11/10/67
DURHAM, DOCTOR M.	*DOCKET ONLY	347	GREENSBORO	06/14/73
DURHAM, JAMES M.	*DOCKET ONLY	127	NEW BERN	12/28/67
DYER, BENJAMIN H.	*DOCKET ONLY	594	GREENSBORO	02/08/77
DeGRAFFENRIDT	*DOCKET ONLY	99	GREENSBORO	02/04/73
EAMES & JORDAN		1	ELIZABETH CITY	07/11/67
EAMES, J.S. &		1	ELIZABETH CITY	07/11/67
EARL, JAMES M. (DR.)	*DOCKET ONLY	626	NEW BERN	04/07/68
EARNHARDT, THOMAS T.	ROWAN	92	STATESVILLE	04/30/73
EARNHART, ATBERT S.	ROWAN	382	WILMINGTON	12/25/68
EARNHART, ISAAC W.	ROWAN	245	STATESVILLE	12/06/73
EASON, JOHN	PERQUIMANS	561	ELIZABETH CITY	04/10/73
EASON, JOHN H.	PERQUIMANS	177	ELIZABETH CITY	04/10/73
EASON, JOSIAH	CAMDEN	245	ELIZABETH CITY	04/08/68
EASON, SOLOMON	PERQUIMANS	309	ELIZABETH CITY	04/21/76
EATMAN, ALEXANDER	*DOCKET ONLY	1557	NEW BERN	01/12/74
EATMAN, PETER	*DOCKET ONLY	1652	NEW BERN	11/30/77
EATMAN, RUFFIN	*DOCKET ONLY	1515	NEW BERN	08/22/73
EATON, BUCKNER	*DOCKET ONLY	896	NEW BERN	08/17/68
EBORN, WILLIAM C.	MARTIN	391	ELIZABETH CITY	11/23/68
ECCLES, HENRY C.	IREDELL	90	WILMINGTON	02/20/68
ECKLE, EUGENE	*DOCKET ONLY	583	GREENSBORO	07/13/76
EDGERTON, EXUM	*DOCKET ONLY	1889	NEW BERN	08/02/78
EDGERTON, THOMAS	*DOCKET ONLY	1580	NEW BERN	01/30/68
EDMONDS, ISORN	*DOCKET ONLY	312	GREENSBORO	06/02/73

NAME OF BANKRUPT	RESIDENCE	CASE NUMBER	CITY OF COURT	DATE FILED
EDMUNDS, BENJAMIN	HALIFAX	507	ELIZABETH CITY	10/27/70
EDMUNDS, BENJAMIN C.	HALIFAX	619	ELIZABETH CITY	11/02/70
EDMUNDSON, HUBBARD	*DOCKET ONLY	1489	NEW BERN	07/09/73
EDNEY, L. H. (15)	HENDERSON	40	ASHEVILLE	01/27/73
EDNEY, M. M (146)	HENDERSON	41	ASHEVILLE	08/10/76
EDWARD, SOLOMON O.	ALLEGHANY	76	STATESVILLE	04/02/73
EDWARDS, DANIEL W.	*DOCKET ONLY	1240	NEW BERN	12/31/68
EDWARDS, DAVID L.	LINCOLN	178	STATESVILLE	06/04/73
EDWARDS, ELBERT P.	*DOCKET ONLY	729	NEW BERN	05/29/68
EDWARDS, FRANKLIN,	ROBESON	766	WILMINGTON	01/17/74
EDWARDS, HENDERSON	NORTHAMPTON	220	ELIZABETH CITY	06/30/73
EDWARDS, HENRY H,	*DOCKET ONLY	78	NEW BERN	11/30/67
EDWARDS, JAMES A.	*DOCKET ONLY	1536	NEW BERN	11/26/73
EDWARDS, JESSE	*DOCKET ONLY	388	GREENSBORO	07/21/73
EDWARDS, RICHARD C.	NORTHAMPTON	531	ELIZABETH CITY	08/30/71
EDWARDS, S.W.	HALIFAX	278	ELIZABETH CITY	05/21/75
EDWARDS, SAMUEL H.	*DOCKET ONLY	1241	NEW BERN	12/31/68
EDWARDS, SETH	*DOCKET ONLY	217	NEW BERN	01/24/68
EDWARDS, THEOPHILUS	*DOCKET ONLY	1360	NEW BERN	10/13/71
EDWARDS, WILLIAM	ALLEGHANY	484	WILMINGTON	12/31/68
EDWARDS, WILLIAM C.	*DOCKET ONLY	504	GREENSBORO	10/13/75
EDWARDS, WILLIAM E.	*DOCKET ONLY	791	NEW BERN*	05/20/68
EDWARDS, WILLIAM F.	*DOCKET ONLY	997	NEW BERN	12/11/68
EDWARDS, WILLIAM J.	NORTHAMPTON	218	ELIZABETH CITY	06/30/73
EDWARDS, WILLIAM J.	*DOCKET ONLY	215	NEW BERN	01/24/68
EDWARDS, WILLIAM L.	*DOCKET ONLY	530	NEW BERN	03/17/68
ELDER, JAMES M.	*DOCKET ONLY	628	GREENSBORO	06/04/78
ELDRIGE, DANIEL	FORSYTH	152	WILMINGTON	02/20/68
ELKINS, WILLIAM	*DOCKET ONLY	344	NEW BERN	02/24/68
ELLER, ABSALAL	WILKES	171	STATESVILLE	05/30/73
ELLINGTON, JAMES D.	*DOCKET ONLY	289	NEW BERN	02/11/68
ELLINGTON, WILLIAM	*DOCKET ONLY	441	NEW BERN	03/02/68
ELLINOR, LAWRENCE J.	*DOCKET ONLY	487	NEW BERN	03/05/68
ELLINOR, WILLIAM T.	*DOCKET ONLY	214	NEW BERN	01/24/68
ELLIOT, WILLIAM P.	CUMBERLAND	12	WILMINGTON	10/23/67
ELLIOTT, H.R.	PASQUOTANK	70	ELIZABETH CITY	12/06/67
ELLIOTT, MORDECAI M.	PASQUOTANK	420	ELIZABETH CITY	12/26/68
ELLIOTT, SPENCER D.	*DOCKET ONLY	224	GREENSBORO	05/10/73
ELLIS, E. R	*DOCKET ONLY	1660	NEW BERN	04/08/78
ELLIS, ISAAC W.	DAVIE	72	STATESVILLE	03/24/73
ELLIS, JAMES H.	*DOCKET ONLY	1603	NEW BERN	03/02/75
ELLIS, JEREMIAH B.	DAVIE	43	STATESVILLE	02/07/73
ELLIS, R. A.	*DOCKET ONLY	1528	NEW BERN	11/01/73
ELLIS, RUPELL &	NEW HANOVER	480	WILMINGTON	12/31/68
ELLIS, TARLEY	ROWAN	228	STATESVILLE	07/30/73
ELLIS, WILLIAM M.	*DOCKET ONLY	625	NEW BERN	04/07/68
ELLISON, WILLIAM H.	*DOCKET ONLY	1556	NEW BERN	01/10/74
ELMS, W.W	MECKLENBURG	22	WILMINGTON	11/20/67
ELSON, ABRAHAM	CUMBERLAND	805	WILMINGTON	11/20/76
EMANUEL, H. & B.	*DOCKET ONLY	1344	NEW BERN	05/15/71
EMANUEL, H. & B.	*DOCKET ONLY	1346	NEW BERN	05/15/71
EMERSON, JOHN	*DOCKET ONLY	1359	NEW BERN	09/19/71
EMORY, THOMAS R.	*DOCKET ONLY	80	NEW BERN	11/30/67
EMPIE, WILLIAM R.		326	WILMINGTON	07/03/68
ENERITT, DAVID B.	*DOCKET ONLY	507	NEW BERN	03/10/68
ENERITT, JOHN H.	*DOCKET ONLY	929	NEW BERN	09/21/68
ENLOE, JAMES J.	HENDERSON	39	ASHEVILLE	08/23/76
ENNETT, GEORGE N.	ONSLOW	668	WILMINGTON	08/31/72
ENSLEY, BENNER	*DOCKET ONLY	1025	NEW BERN	12/22/68
EPPLER, ALEX,	*DOCKET ONLY	1278	NEW BERN	01/17/70
ERWIN, A.A	MECKLENBURG	290	WILMINGTON	05/30/68
ERWIN, E.K.	ONSLOW	749	WILMINGTON	09/03/73
ERWIN, L.P.	RUTHERFORD	73	WILMINGTON	02/18/68
ERWIN, WILLIAM C.	BURKE	10	STATESVILLE	11/29/72
ESKRIDGE, R.C.	CLEVELAND	119	STATESVILLE	05/13/73
ESSICK, JACOB	DAVIDSON	255	STATESVILLE	02/20/74

NAME OF BANKRUPT	RESIDENCE	CASE NUMBER	CITY OF COURT	DATE FILED
ESTES, H. B. & T. H.	*DOCKET ONLY	0	NEW BERN	03/25/68
ESTES, JEREMIAH	*DOCKET ONLY	462	NEW BERN	03/04/68
ESTES, LEWIS J.	CALDWELL	183	STATESVILLE	06/04/73
ETHERIDGE, ELIAS	CURRITUCK	85	ELIZABETH CITY	12/03/67
ETHERIDGE, J.W.	DARE	342	ELIZABETH CITY	08/27/76
ETHERIDGE, ROGERS &,		236	ELIZABETH CITY	09/27/73
ETHERIDGE, THOMAS J.	PASQUOTANK	416	ELIZABETH CITY	12/24/68
ETHRIDGE, JASPER	*DOCKET ONLY	1442	NEW BERN	05/21/73
EURE, PETER	GATES	246	ELIZABETH CITY	04/13/68
EVANS, JAMES M.	*DOCKET ONLY	144	GREENSBORO	03/21/73
EVANS, JOHN W.	*DOCKET ONLY	369	GREENSBORO	07/03/73
EVANS, S.B.	*DOCKET ONLY	1137	NEW BERN	12/29/68
EVERETT, JAMES E.	GATES	458	ELIZABETH CITY	12/29/68
EVERETT, SIMON P.	MARTIN	396	ELIZABETH CITY	11/12/68
EVERTON, THOMAS	CURRITUCK	210	ELIZABETH CITY	03/02/68
FAGG, JAMES F.	*DOCKET ONLY	282	GREENSBORO	05/24/73
FAGG, WILLIAM	*DOCKET ONLY	281	GREENSBORO	05/24/73
FAGGART, JOHN	*DOCKET ONLY	18	GREENSBORO	10/07/72
FAIRLELY, JOHN	SCOTLAND	599	WILMINGTON	11/17/70
FAIRLEY, JOHN M.	NEW HANOVER	285	WILMINGTON	05/30/68
FAIRLEY, MARGARET	RICHMOND	333	WILMINGTON	10/02/68
FAIRLEY, ROBERT	RICHMOND	416	WILMINGTON	12/30/68
FAISON, F.S.	NORTHAMPTON	281	ELIZABETH CITY	07/07/75
FAISON, WILLIAM H.	SAMPSON	672	WILMINGTON	12/18/72
FALCON, JAMES A.	HALIFAX	241	ELIZABETH CITY	04/08/68
FALK, SIMON	*DOCKET ONLY	1607	NEW BERN	06/16/75
FALKNER, ASA W. L	*DOCKET ONLY	483	GREENSBORO	03/10/75
FALKS, EMANUEL &	*DOCKET ONLY	1368	NEW BERN	12/09/71
FALLS, DIXON	CLEVELAND	370	WILMINGTON	12/19/68
FALLS, EDWIN	IREDELL	284	WILMINGTON	05/30/68
FALLS, JAMES B.	CLEVELAND	126	STATESVILLE	05/14/73
FALLS, JOHN Z	CLEVELAND	439	WILMINGTON	12/30/68
FARABEE, L.W.		638	WILMINGTON	08/18/71
FARISH, JOHN W.	*DOCKET ONLY	465	NEW BERN	03/04/68
FARLOW, ENOCH	*DOCKET ONLY	633	GREENSBORO	07/06/78
FARLOW, JOSEPH	*DOCKET ONLY	695	GREENSBORO	08/19/78
FARMER, BENJAMIN E.	*DOCKET ONLY	1549	NEW BERN	12/24/73
FARMER, JAMES B.	NORTHAMPTON	325	ELIZABETH CITY	03/23/78
FARMER, JOHN	*DOCKET ONLY	308	NEW BERN	02/18/68
FARMER, JOSE	*DOCKET ONLY	920	NEW BERN	08/28/68
FARMER, WILLIAM D.	*DOCKET ONLY	1073	NEW BERN	12/24/68
FARMER, WILLIAM H.	*DOCKET ONLY	488	NEW BERN	03/05/68
FARNELL, A. F.	*DOCKET ONLY	1352	NEW BERN	07/25/71
FARNELL, EDWARD M.	*DOCKET ONLY	1399	NEW BERN	11/14/72
FARNELL, MACAJAH	*DOCKET ONLY	1338	NEW BERN	04/18/71
FARRABEE, SAMUEL W.	*DOCKET ONLY	26	GREENSBORO	10/15/72
FARRAR, JONATHAN H.	*DOCKET ONLY	100	GREENSBORO	02/04/73
FARRAR, T. B.	*DOCKET ONLY	49	NEW BERN	11/09/67
FARRAR, WILLIAM B.	*DOCKET ONLY	55	GREENSBORO	01/07/73
FARRELL, FRANCIS	*DOCKET ONLY	22	GREENSBORO	11/08/72
FARRIS, CHARLES W.	*DOCKET ONLY	1149	NEW BERN	12/30/68
FARRISON, CHARLES G.	*DOCKET ONLY	395	NEW BERN	02/26/68
FARROW, JOSEPH A	*DOCKET ONLY	1002	NEW BERN	12/15/68
FAUCETT, JAMES R.	*DOCKET ONLY	188	NEW BERN	01/13/68
FAUCETT, ROBERT,	*DOCKET ONLY	177	NEW BERN	01/09/68
FAUCETT, WILLIAM C.	*DOCKET ONLY	564	GREENSBORO	07/26/78
FAUCETT, WILLIAM D.	HALIFAX	404	ELIZABETH CITY	10/29/68
FAUCETT, WILLIAM H.	*DOCKET ONLY	140	NEW BERN	12/30/67
FAULCON, ISAAC	HALIFAX	395	ELIZABETH CITY	11/11/68
FAULCON, JESSE N.	*DOCKET ONLY	774	NEW BERN	08/22/68
FAULK, MALCOM	CUMBERLAND	607	WILMINGTON	12/01/70
FEARING, JOHN B.	PASQUOTANK	23	ELIZABETH CITY	10/07/67
FEARSTON, A. A.	HENDERSON	43	ASHEVILLE	09/18/73
FEARSTON, A. A.	HENDERSON	43	ASHEVILLE	09/16/73
FEATHERSTON, JAMES	*DOCKET ONLY	408	NEW BERN	02/29/68
FEATHERSTON, L.F.	HENDERSON	366	WILMINGTON	12/16/68

NAME OF BANKRUPT	RESIDENCE	CASE NUMBER	CITY OF COURT	DATE FILED
FEATHERTON, WILLIAM	HENDERSON	537	WILMINGTON	01/06/69
FEEZOR, W.A.J.	*DOCKET ONLY	469	GREENSBORO	03/17/74
FEEZOR, WILLIAM A.	*DOCKET ONLY	542	GREENSBORO	03/17/74
FELTON, JOHN	*DOCKET ONLY	1211	NEW BERN	12/31/68
FELTON, NOAH B.	GATES	228	ELIZABETH CITY	04/02/68
FELTON, WILLIAM	PERQUIMANS	465	ELIZABETH CITY	12/16/68
FELTON, WILLIAM	*DOCKET ONLY	1208	NEW BERN	12/31/68
FELZER, JOSEPH H.	*DOCKET ONLY	679	GREENSBORO	08/31/78
FENNER, WILLIAM	HALIFAX	504	ELIZABETH CITY	08/31/70
FENTRESS, DAVID	CURRITUCK	102	ELIZABETH CITY	01/03/68
FERBEE, THOMAS	DAVIE	155	STATESVILLE	05/23/73
FERGUSON, CASWELL C.	HERTFORD	551	ELIZABETH CITY	12/16/68
FERNELL, OWEN, SR.	SAMPSON	847	WILMINGTON	08/05/78
FERREBEE, D.D.		314	ELIZABETH CITY	11/17/76
FERREBEE, D.D., JR.	CAMDEN	351	ELIZABETH CITY	08/31/78
FERREBEE, E.D.	CURRITUCK	199	ELIZABETH CITY	03/02/68
FERREBEE, JAMES M.	CURRITUCK	197	ELIZABETH CITY	03/02/68
FERREBEE, M.S.	CURRITUCK	198	ELIZABETH CITY	03/02/68
FERREBEE, W.B.	CAMDEN	182	ELIZABETH CITY	04/26/73
FERREBEE, WILLIAM B	CAMDEN	565	ELIZABETH CITY	04/26/73
FERRELL, S. D.	*DOCKET ONLY	101	NEW BERN	12/12/67
FERRIS & COMPNAY,		774	WILMINGTON	06/31/74
FESPERMAN, DANIEL	UNION	368	WILMINGTON	12/17/68
FEUTRELL, EXUM	NORTHAMPTON	408	ELIZABETH CITY	12/10/68
FIELDS & SMITH	ROBESON	416	WILMINGTON	12/30/68
FIELDS, CHARLES M.	*DOCKET ONLY	1332	NEW BERN	03/15/71
FIELDS, JAMES	*DOCKET ONLY	1681	NEW BERN	06/13/78
FIELDS, R. H.	*DOCKET ONLY	756	NEW BERN	06/02/68
FIELDS, WILLIAM	*DOCKET ONLY	1679	NEW BERN	06/12/78
FIMBRO, WILLIAM E.	*DOCKET ONLY	700	NEW BERN	05/25/68
FINCHER, BENJAMIN F.	*DOCKET ONLY	353	GREENSBORO	06/19/73
FINCHER, LEROY B.	*DOCKET ONLY	208	GREENSBORO	05/07/73
FINDLAY, ALEXANDER	*DOCKET ONLY	595	NEW BERN	03/25/68
FIRST NATIONAL BANK	MECKLENBURG	549	WILMINGTON	06/01/69
FIRST NATIONAL BANK	NEW HANOVER	561	WILMINGTON	10/22/69
FISHBLATE & BROTHERS	CUMBERLAND	387	WILMINGTON	12/16/68
FISHBLATE, EPHRAIM		797	WILMINGTON	12/29/75
FISHBLATE, S.H. &		387	WILMINGTON	12/25/69
FISHBLATE, S.H. &		610	WILMINGTON	01/19/71
FISHBLATE, SOLOMON &		797	WILMINGTON	12/29/75
FISHER, JOHN H.	SAMPSON	840	WILMINGTON	07/20/78
FITCH, THOMAS	*DOCKET ONLY	330	GREENSBORO	06/06/73
FITTS, FRANCES	*DOCKET ONLY	464	NEW BERN	03/04/68
FITZGERALD & CO.	*DOCKET ONLY	422	GREENSBORO	11/01/73
FITZGERALD, IRA A.	*DOCKET ONLY	659	GREENSBORO	08/28/78
FITZGERALD, JOHN H.	*DOCKET ONLY	640	NEW BERN	04/18/68
FLANAGAN, JOHN	MARTIN	141	ELIZABETH CITY	02/17/68
FLANIGAN, JOHN W.	*DOCKET ONLY	595	GREENSBORO	11/07/77
FLANNER, JOHN D.	*DOCKET ONLY	1408	NEW BERN	01/25/73
FLEETWOOD, GEORGE B	PERQUIMANS	528	ELIZABETH CITY	07/25/71
FLEETWOOD, WILSON M.	PERQUIMANS	191	ELIZABETH CITY	02/29/68
FLEMING, JOHN S.	BURKE	140	STATESVILLE	03/21/73
FLEMMING, J. D. & G.	*DOCKET ONLY	463	NEW BERN	03/04/68
FLOWERS, DAVID F.	BLADEN	479	WILMINGTON	12/31/68
FLOWERS, WILLIE W.	*DOCKET ONLY	417	NEW BERN	02/29/68
FLOYD, GEORGE W.	*DOCKET ONLY	249	GREENSBORO	05/14/73
FLOYD, GILES P.	ROBESON	751	WILMINGTON	11/01/73
FLYN, BURWELL	*DOCKET ONLY	677	GREENSBORO	08/31/78
FLYTHE, BRAXTON	NORTHAMPTON	268	ELIZABETH CITY	05/27/68
FLYTHE, JOHN W.	NORTHAMPTON	380	ELIZABETH CITY	11/11/68
FOARD, JOHN	*DOCKET ONLY	48	GREENSBORO	12/20/72
FOASHEE, WILLIAM F.	*DOCKET ONLY	150	GREENSBORO	04/22/73
FOGLEMAN, PETER	*DOCKET ONLY	87	GREENSBORO	01/22/73
FONVILLE, EDWARD W.	*DOCKET ONLY	1555	NEW BERN	01/10/74
FOOSHEE, JASPER	*DOCKET ONLY	434	GREENSBORO	12/05/73
FORBES, E.R.	CAMDEN	176	ELIZABETH CITY	04/07/73

NAME OF BANKRUPT	RESIDENCE	CASE NUMBER	CITY OF COURT	DATE FILED
FORBES, EVAN R.	CAMDEN	560	ELIZABETH CITY	04/10/73
FORBES, H.J.	CURRITUCK	89	ELIZABETH CITY	12/05/67
FORBES, J.B.	CAMDEN	82	ELIZABETH CITY	12/16/67
FORBES, JAMES H.	*DOCKET ONLY	518	NEW BERN	03/13/68
FORBES, JOSEPH B.	CAMDEN	620	ELIZABETH CITY	10/12/68
FORBES, W.R.	CURRITUCK	93	ELIZABETH CITY	12/23/67
FORD, GEORGE	RUTHERFORD	74	WILMINGTON	02/13/68
FORD, JOHN F.	IREDELL	540	WILMINGTON	01/07/69
FORD, JOHN S.	RUTHERFORD	19	WILMINGTON	11/23/67
FORD, JONATHAN	MACON	44	ASHEVILLE	11/07/72
FORD, O.G.	IREDELL	538	WILMINGTON	01/07/69
FORDHAM, CHRISTOPHER	*DOCKET ONLY	1675	NEW BERN	06/03/78
FORNEY, JAMES H.	RUTHERFORD	34	STATESVILLE	01/31/73
FORREST, JOHN (42)	HENDERSON	42	ASHEVILLE	05/19/73
FORRESTER, WILLIAM	WILKES	108	STATESVILLE	05/02/73
FORT, JOHN	SAMPSON	704	WILMINGTON	05/30/73
FORT, JOHN C.	*DOCKET ONLY	16	NEW BERN	09/30/67
FORTUNE, RICHARD	HENDERSON	46	ASHEVILLE	01/13/73
FORTUNE, WALTER A.	HENDERSON	45	ASHEVILLE	01/28/73
FOSTER, ALBERT H.	*DOCKET ONLY	1242	NEW BERN	12/31/68
FOSTER, AUGUSTUS J.	*DOCKET ONLY	1269	NEW BERN	03/06/69
FOSTER, JOHN M.	*DOCKET ONLY	41	NEW BERN	10/25/67
FOSTER, THOMAS J.		30	STATESVILLE	02/05/73
FOSTER, WILLIAM B.	*DOCKET ONLY	685	NEW BERN	05/19/68
FOSTER,JOHN & JOHN	*DOCKET ONLY	485	GREENSBORO	09/26/75
FOSTESCUE, LEWIS P.	*DOCKET ONLY	1314	NEW BERN	12/24/70
FOULKES, JAMES F.	*DOCKET ONLY	480	GREENSBORO	02/19/75
FOUSBEE, R. J.	*DOCKET ONLY	775	NEW BERN	08/19/68
FOUST, GEORGE K.	*DOCKET ONLY	1271	NEW BERN	05/03/69
FOUST, GEORGE K.	*DOCKET ONLY	421	GREENSBORO	07/19/73
FOWLER, J. W.	CALDWELL	173	STATESVILLE	05/30/73
FOX, GEORGE	PASQUOTANK	198	ELIZABETH CITY	02/28/68
FOX, GEORGE	*DOCKET ONLY	270	GREENSBORO	05/22/73
FOX, HIMER	*DOCKET ONLY	399	GREENSBORO	08/08/73
FOX, S. C.	*DOCKET ONLY	255	GREENSBORO	05/17/73
FOY, BENJAMIN F.	*DOCKET ONLY	432	NEW BERN	03/02/68
FOY, FRANKLIN	*DOCKET ONLY	1500	NEW BERN	07/25/73
FOY, JAMES H.	*DOCKET ONLY	766	NEW BERN	05/29/68
FOY, WILLIAM H.	*DOCKET ONLY	442	NEW BERN	03/02/68
FRANK, ABRAHAM &		786	WILMINGTON	12/29/75
FRANK, MEYER &		786	WILMINGTON	12/29/75
FRANKENTHAL, AMELIA	*DOCKET ONLY	181	GREENSBORO	03/28/73
FRANKINTHALL, HENRY	*DOCKET ONLY	825	GREENSBORO	01/31/77
FRATING, ZENAS	PASQUOTANK	261	ELIZABETH CITY	01/20/74
FRAZEL, JAMES O.	*DOCKET ONLY	1220	NEW BERN	12/31/68
FRAZER, NEHEMIAH	SAMPSON	877	WILMINGTON	08/30/78
FRAZER, PLEASANT	MONTGOMERY	178	WILMINGTON	04/14/68
FRAZIER, C. A.	*DOCKET ONLY	10	GREENSBORO	08/12/72
FRAZIER, CHARLES A.	*DOCKET ONLY	62	GREENSBORO	08/14/72
FRAZIER, CHARLES A.		656	WILMINGTON	02/21/72
FRAZIER, RICHARD G.	*DOCKET ONLY	580	NEW BERN	03/19/68
FRAZIER, SOWELL	*DOCKET ONLY	16	GREENSBORO	09/07/72
FREAINGTON, JOHN J.	*DOCKET ONLY	50	NEW BERN	11/09/67
FREDRICK, JOHN	DUPLIN	689	WILMINGTON	05/29/73
FREDRICK, NORRIS	DUPLIN	204	WILMINGTON	05/06/68
FREEMAN, ARCHIBALD	STANLY	594	WILMINGTON	10/23/70
FREEMAN, ELISHA W.	*DOCKET ONLY	1454	NEW BERN	05/27/73
FREEMAN, FAMES H.	GATES	451	ELIZABETH CITY	12/26/68
FREEMAN, JAMES C.	BERTIE	285	ELIZABETH CITY	06/01/68
FREEMAN, JOEL T.	HENDERSON	47	ASHEVILLE	02/19/73
FREEMAN, SAMUEL	SURRY	598	WILMINGTON	09/21/70
FREEMAN, SAMUEL A.	*DOCKET ONLY	27	GREENSBORO	10/15/72
FRENCH, GEORGE Z.		552	WILMINGTON	07/06/69
FRENCH, GEORGE Z.	NEW HANOVER	794	WILMINGTON	02/22/76
FRENCH, JOHN B.	*DOCKET ONLY	1422	NEW BERN	04/23/73
FRENCH, RUFUS J.	*DOCKET ONLY	51	NEW BERN	11/14/67

NAME OF BANKRUPT	RESIDENCE	CASE NUMBER	CITY OF COURT	DATE FILED
FRESHWATER, JOHN A.	*DOCKET ONLY	1056	NEW BERN	12/26/68
FREY, JOHN	CUMBERLAND	336	WILMINGTON	10/19/68
FRIEDLANDER STICH &		772	WILMINGTON	04/27/74
FRION, JARVIS	*DOCKET ONLY	855	NEW BERN	04/26/68
FRNCH, LEWIS H.	*DOCKET ONLY	1438	NEW BERN	05/16/73
FRONABERGER, D.W.		637	WILMINGTON	08/05/71
FRONEBERGER, D.W.	GASTON	279	WILMINGTON	05/31/68
FRONEBERGER, DAVID	*DOCKET ONLY	3	GREENSBORO	08/08/72
FROST, JAMES F.	DAVIE	99	STATESVILLE	04/20/73
FRY, JONATHAN	ALEXANDER	117	STATESVILLE	05/13/73
FULGHRUM, ROBBINS &	*DOCKET ONLY	1200	NEW BERN	12/30/68
FULLER & WILKERSON	*DOCKET ONLY	11	GREENSBORO	11/04/72
FULLER, ALEX M. &	*DOCKET ONLY	1293	NEW BERN	02/18/70
FULLER, AUGUSTUS	ROBESON	275	WILMINGTON	05/30/68
FULLER, JOSEPH	*DOCKET ONLY	704	NEW BERN	05/26/68
FULLINGS, EDWARD	*DOCKET ONLY	521	GREENSBORO	04/29/73
FULLINGS, EDWARD	MECKLENBURG	276	WILMINGTON	05/30/68
FULP, GASPER S.	*DOCKET ONLY	627	GREENSBORO	05/17/78
FULTON, SAMUEL	*DOCKET ONLY	742	NEW BERN	05/29/68
FURNISS, H.K.	WASHINGTON	255	ELIZABETH CITY	02/26/68
FUTRELL, ANDERSON	NORTHAMPTON	267	ELIZABETH CITY	05/27/68
FUTRILL, ANDREW	NORTHAMPTON	445	ELIZABETH CITY	12/06/68
GADBERRY, LEWIS	YADKIN	445	WILMINGTON	12/30/68
GADDY, ELLIS D.	ANSON	800	WILMINGTON	11/17/70
GAHAGAN, GEORGE W.	MADISON	51	ASHEVILLE	03/13/74
GAINEY, ELIAS	CUMBERLAND	92	WILMINGTON	02/20/68
GAINEY, HOLLY	CUMBERLAND	93	WILMINGTON	02/22/68
GAINEY, JOHN	CUMBERLAND	75	WILMINGTON	02/13/68
GAINEY, WILLIAM	CUMBERLAND	76	WILMINGTON	04/13/68
GAITHER, BURGESS	DAVIE	217	STATESVILLE	07/04/73
GAITHER, THOMAS	*DOCKET ONLY	7	GREENSBORO	08/12/72
GAITHER, THOMAS H.	DAVIE	524	WILMINGTON	01/01/69
GAITHER, THOMAS H.		593	WILMINGTON	10/19/70
GALLAGHER, BURBANK &	*DOCKET ONLY	1523	NEW BERN	10/16/73
GALLAMORE, A.	HENDERSON	53	ASHEVILLE	08/23/78
GALLANT, JOHN F.	MECKLENBURG	551	WILMINGTON	07/01/69
GALLANT, NEAGLE &	GASTON	352	WILMINGTON	12/04/68
GAMBLE, WILLIAM	RUTHERFORD	211	STATESVILLE	06/30/73
GAMMON, JAMES N.	HALIFAX	277	ELIZABETH CITY	04/12/75
GARDNER, BENJAMINE	*DOCKET ONLY	241	GREENSBORO	05/13/73
GARDNER, HENRY B.	*DOCKET ONLY	983	NEW BERN	12/06/68
GARDNER, JAMES	MONTGOMERY	132	WILMINGTON	03/08/68
GARDNER, JOHN L.	*DOCKET ONLY	927	NEW BERN	09/17/68
GARDNER, WILLIAM T.	*DOCKET ONLY	957	NEW BERN	11/09/68
GARMER. LINDSAY	*DOCKET ONLY	105	GREENSBORO	02/04/73
GARNET, R.B.	HALIFAX	218	ELIZABETH CITY	11/20/74
GARRELL, JOHN H.	CHOWAN	821	ELIZABETH CITY	08/18/71
GARREN, J. R. (153)	BUNCOMBE	52	ASHEVILLE	08/26/78
GARRENTON, JAMES F.	CURRITUCK	101	ELIZABETH CITY	12/16/67
GARRETT, E. T.	*DOCKET ONLY	88	GREENSBORO	02/24/73
GARRETT, FRANCIS M.	*DOCKET ONLY	1282	NEW BERN	02/19/70
GARRETT, JOSEPH J.	*DOCKET ONLY	1281	NEW BERN	02/19/70
GARRETT, RICHARD H.	*DOCKET ONLY	1078	NEW BERN	12/26/68
GARRETT, S. A.	*DOCKET ONLY	566	GREENSBORO	09/15/76
GARRINSON, JOSIAH	CURRITUCK	125	ELIZABETH CITY	01/27/68
GARRIS, W.H.	NORTHAMPTON	847	ELIZABETH CITY	01/23/71
GARRIS, WILLIAM H.	NORTHAMPTON	523	ELIZABETH CITY	01/18/71
GARRISON, BLACKEMORE		775	WILMINGTON	09/07/74
GARRISON, HENRY	*DOCKET ONLY	396	NEW BERN	02/28/68
GARRITT, JAMES M.	*DOCKET ONLY	792	NEW BERN	05/30/68
GASKINS, SETH	*DOCKET ONLY	1457	NEW BERN	05/26/73
GASTEN, WILLIAM D.	CUMBERLAND	990	WILMINGTON	08/31/78
GATCHELL, H.T.FRITZ.	BUNCOMBE	626	WILMINGTON	04/26/71
GATES, WILEY P.	*DOCKET ONLY	138	NEW BERN	12/28/67
GATLING, RIDDICK	GATES	242	ELIZABETH CITY	10/23/73
GATON, P.C. &	CHEROKEE	243	WILMINGTON	05/28/68

NORTH CAROLINA BANKRUPTS - ACT OF 1867

NAME OF BANKRUPT	RESIDENCE	CASE NUMBER	CITY OF COURT	DATE FILED
GATTIS, THOMAS M.	*DOCKET ONLY	64	NEW BERN	11/23/67
GATTIS, WILLIAM M.	*DOCKET ONLY	63	GREENSBORO	01/17/73
GAVIN, S.	DUPLIN	711	WILMINGTON	06/11/73
GAY & DAVIS (JAMES	*DOCKET ONLY	724	NEW BERN	05/27/68
GAY, C. H.	*DOCKET ONLY	1063	NEW BERN	12/26/68
GAYLORD, HENRY S.	*DOCKET ONLY	1245	NEW BERN	12/31/68
GAYLORD, JOHN T.	*DOCKET ONLY	1244	NEW BERN	12/31/68
GEER, JOHN	RUTHERFORD	129	WILMINGTON	03/12/68
GENTRY, JOHN W.	*DOCKET ONLY	608	GREENSBORO	05/11/78
GENTRY, WILLIAM H.	*DOCKET ONLY	683	GREENSBORO	08/31/78
GEORGE, P.T. &		799	WILMINGTON	07/15/75
GHEEN, GEORGE H.	ROWAN	33	STATESVILLE	01/28/73
GHES, JOHN	IREDELL	45	STATESVILLE	02/10/73
GIBB, MILL &		771	WILMINGTON	03/28/74
GIBBS, BENJAMIN F.	*DOCKET ONLY	1474	NEW BERN	06/14/73
GIBBS, DAVID G.	*DOCKET ONLY	1485	NEW BERN	07/03/73
GIBSON, JAMES B.	ROWAN	39	STATESVILLE	02/03/73
GIBSON, JAMES K.	CUMBERLAND	762	WILMINGTON	12/25/73
GIBSON, JOHN A.	*DOCKET ONLY	49	GREENSBORO	12/23/72
GIDDENS, JAMES D.	SAMPSON	116	WILMINGTON	03/03/68
GIDDENS, JAMES T.	SAMPSON	778	WILMINGTON	01/18/75
GILBERT, W.W.	BURKE	292	STATESVILLE	05/17/78
GILCHRIST, JAMES D.	*DOCKET ONLY	293	NEW BERN	02/13/68
GILES, JOHN S.	*DOCKET ONLY	410	GREENSBORO	09/03/73
GILLESPIE, JOHN C.	ROWAN	327	WILMINGTON	09/01/68
GILLETT, THOMAS S.	*DOCKET ONLY	1558	NEW BERN	01/14/74
GILLIAM, THOMAS B.	*DOCKET ONLY	521	NEW BERN	03/13/68
GILLIS, DAVID	CUMBERLAND	675	WILMINGTON	03/09/73
GILREATH, A. H.	HENDERSON	50	ASHEVILLE	04/22/73
GLASCOCK, TROY	*DOCKET ONLY	319	NEW BERN	02/21/68
GLASS, ELI	*DOCKET ONLY	512	NEW BERN	03/12/68
GLENN, ELI (66)	BUNCOMBE	49	ASHEVILLE	06/02/73
GLOVER, DAVID K.	*DOCKET ONLY	235	NEW BERN	01/31/68
GLOVER, WILLIAM	PASQUOTANK	256	ELIZABETH CITY	05/11/68
GODFREY, F.M.	PASQUOTANK	415	ELIZABETH CITY	12/24/68
GODWIN, CENDARY	ROBESON	324	WILMINGTON	08/14/68
GODWIN, HAYWOOD W.	*DOCKET ONLY	1578	NEW BERN	04/04/74
GOFORTH, ANDREW	CLEVELAND	260	STATESVILLE	06/14/74
GOLDSMITH, RALPH &	*DOCKET ONLY	513	GREENSBORO	02/08/76
GOLDSTEIN & BROTHERS	*DOCKET ONLY	1644	NEW BERN	03/21/77
GOLDSTON, JOSEPH J.	*DOCKET ONLY	863	NEW BERN	06/22/68
GOOCH & THOMAS	*DOCKET ONLY	452	GREENSBORO	01/16/74
GOODE, JOHN T.	CLEVELAND	13	STATESVILLE	12/07/72
GOODING, STEPHEN	*DOCKET ONLY	770	NEW BERN	05/20/68
GOODMAN, WILL	CURRITUCK	66	ELIZABETH CITY	12/16/67
GOODSON, MELTON	LINCOLN	185	STATESVILLE	05/26/73
GOODWIN, WESLEY	*DOCKET ONLY	149	NEW BERN	12/31/67
GOODWYE, BENJAMIN W.	NORTHAMPTON	444	ELIZABETH CITY	12/28/68
GORDON, JOHN	UNION	137	WILMINGTON	03/12/68
GORDON, JOHN D.	CAMDEN	512	ELIZABETH CITY	11/21/70
GORDON, M.C.	CAMDEN	238	ELIZABETH CITY	03/24/68
GORHAM, RICHARD H.	*DOCKET ONLY	143	NEW BERN	12/31/67
GORNTO, JARROTT	ONSLOW	743	WILMINGTON	06/27/73
GORNTO, SOLOMON	*DOCKET ONLY	1126	NEW BERN	12/30/68
GOSLEY, JOHN	*DOCKET ONLY	641	NEW BERN	04/18/68
GOSLIN, ALEXANDER	*DOCKET ONLY	956	NEW BERN	11/07/68
GOSLIN, WILLIAM	*DOCKET ONLY	1302	NEW BERN	11/11/70
GRACBER, A. F.	ROWAN	241	WILMINGTON	05/28/68
GRAHAM, ALEXANDE	MECKLENBURG	519	WILMINGTON	01/01/69
GRAHAM, ALEXANDER	ROWAN	384	WILMINGTON	12/25/68
GRAHAM, BENJ. G.	MECKLENBURG	21	WILMINGTON	11/20/67
GRAHAM, JOHN C.	ROBESON	755	WILMINGTON	11/01/73
GRAHAM, JOHN K.	ROWAN	4	STATESVILLE	10/12/72
GRAHAM, JOSEPH	*DOCKET ONLY	623	GREENSBORO	05/30/78
GRAHAM, R. FRANK	ROWAN	288	STATESVILLE	04/19/78
GRAHAM, R. FRANK &	*DOCKET ONLY	585	GREENSBORO	01/01/78

NORTH CAROLINA BANKRUPTS - ACT OF 1867

NAME OF BANKRUPT	RESIDENCE	CASE NUMBER	CITY OF COURT	DATE FILED
GRAHAM, THOMAS	*DOCKET ONLY	110	GREENSBORO	02/05/73
GRAHAM, W.P.	ROWAN	469	WILMINGTON	12/31/68
GRAHAM, WILLIAM R.	*DOCKET ONLY	87	NEW BERN	12/04/67
GRAMMER, ROBERT J.	*DOCKET ONLY	909	NEW BERN	08/22/68
GRANBERRY, J.G.	PERQUIMANS	174	ELIZABETH CITY	03/27/73
GRANDY, C.W., JR.	PASQUOTANK	39	ELIZABETH CITY	11/20/67
GRANGER, THADDEUS A.	*DOCKET ONLY	508	NEW BERN	03/10/68
GRASE, SAMUEL	MECKLENBERG	1	STATESVILLE	08/10/72
GRAVES, ALFRED W.	*DOCKET ONLY	109	GREENSBORO	02/05/73
GRAVES, THOMAS W.	*DOCKET ONLY	139	GREENSBORO	02/28/73
GRAY, BENJ. F.	HALIFAX	178	ELIZABETH CITY	04/11/73
GRAY, BENJAMIN D.	*DOCKET ONLY	686	NEW BERN	09/01/68
GRAY, BENJAMIN F	HALIFAX	562	ELIZABETH CITY	04/09/73
GRAY, CHANNCY	*DOCKET ONLY	1586	NEW BERN	07/08/74
GRAY, JOHN F.	CURRITUCK	184	ELIZABETH CITY	02/28/68
GRAY, JOHN S.	*DOCKET ONLY	294	GREENSBORO	05/28/73
GRAY, JOHN W.	DAVIE	189	WILMINGTON	04/21/68
GRAY, JOSEPH	WILKES	617	WILMINGTON	02/25/71
GRAY, NATHANIEL	*DOCKET ONLY	571	GREENSBORO	01/17/77
GRAY, THOMAS C.	CURRITUCK	179	ELIZABETH CITY	02/28/68
GRAY, WILLIAM H.	CHOWAN	648	ELIZABETH CITY	09/04/68
GREEN, AMBROSE G.	HALIFAX	249	ELIZABETH CITY	12/18/73
GREEN, ASA	*DOCKET ONLY	113	NEW BERN	12/19/67
GREEN, C.O. &	POLK	253	WILMINGTON	05/29/68
GREEN, JOHN M.	*DOCKET ONLY	1178	NEW BERN	12/31/69
GREEN, JOSEPH	*DOCKET ONLY	69	GREENSBORO	01/24/73
GREEN, LEONIDAS M.	*DOCKET ONLY	1628	NEW BERN	04/04/78
GREEN, PETER	RUTHERFORD	131	WILMINGTON	03/12/68
GREEN, ROBERT L	*DOCKET ONLY	80	GREENSBORO	01/28/73
GREENE, LAFAYETTE	*DOCKET ONLY	479	GREENSBORO	01/13/75
GREENSBORO MUTUAL	*DOCKET ONLY	1268	NEW BERN	02/23/69
GREENWALD, DAVID &	NEW HANOVER	843	WILMINGTON	07/27/78
GREENSBORO MUTUAL	*DOCKET ONLY	1271	NEW BERN	06/05/69
GREGORY, MAJOR S.	CAMDEN	269	ELIZABETH CITY	08/21/74
GREGORY, RICHARD	*DOCKET ONLY	218	NEW BERN	01/24/68
GREGORY, RICHARD K.	MECKLENBURG	63	WILMINGTON	01/30/68
GREGORY, WILLIAM	MECKLENBURG	283	WILMINGTON	05/30/68
GRIFFIN, JERRY J.	*DOCKET ONLY	929	NEW BERN	09/29/68
GRIFFIN, JESSE G.	*DOCKET ONLY	98	NEW BERN	12/12/67
GRIFFIN, THOMAS A	*DOCKET ONLY	714	NEW BERN	05/27/68
GRIFFIN, WASLEY	*DOCKET ONLY	264	GREENSBORO	05/22/73
GRIFFIN, WILLIAM	DAVIE	210	WILMINGTON	05/15/69
GRIMSLEY, WILLIAM P.	*DOCKET ONLY	1097	NEW BERN	12/29/68
GRINWOLD & KELLOGG		317	WILMINGTON	06/22/68
GRISON, SOLOMON	*DOCKET ONLY	1144	NEW BERN	12/20/68
GRIST, JAMES R.	*DOCKET ONLY	698	NEW BERN	05/25/68
GRIZZARD, JAMES M.	HALIFAX	239	ELIZABETH CITY	03/30/68
GROGAN, JAMES M.	*DOCKET ONLY	840	NEW BERN	05/30/68
GROGAN, JOHN	*DOCKET ONLY	230	NEW BERN	01/29/68
GROGAN, JOHN P.	SURRY	249	WILMINGTON	05/29/68
GROOM, ZACHARIAH	*DOCKET ONLY	318	GREENSBORO	06/03/73
GROSE, SAMUEL		575	WILMINGTON	04/21/70
GROVES, JAMES D.	BERTIE	319	ELIZABETH CITY	07/23/77
GRRE, W. M.	RUTHERFORD	172	STATESVILLE	05/30/73
GRUN, BRIAN W.	*DOCKET ONLY	1674	NEW BERN	05/31/78
GUIRKIN, R.R.	CAMDEN	38	ELIZABETH CITY	11/15/67
GUNN, GEORGE	*DOCKET ONLY	642	NEW BERN	04/18/68
GUNN, W. A.	*DOCKET ONLY	321	GREENSBORO	05/06/73
GUNTER, ANDREW	HALIFAX	506	ELIZABETH CITY	09/28/70
GUNTER, JOHN W.	*DOCKET ONLY	907	NEW BERN	08/25/68
GUPTON, ELIJAH	*DOCKET ONLY	1568	NEW BERN	03/02/74
GURRANT, HUGH L.	*DOCKET ONLY	40	NEW BERN	10/28/67
GUSTAVUS, OBER		326	WILMINGTON	07/03/68
GUTHRIE, CAROLINE E.		119	ASHEVILLE	12/21/78
GUTHRIE, GERMAN B.	*DOCKET ONLY	922	NEW BERN	08/29/68
GUTHRIE, GERMAN B.	CHATHAM	309	WILMINGTON	05/30/68

NAME OF BANKRUPT	RESIDENCE	CASE NUMBER	CITY OF COURT	DATE FILED
GUTHRIE, JAMES C.	*DOCKET ONLY	331	GREENSBORO	06/07/73
GUYER, JOSEPH	*DOCKET ONLY	86	GREENSBORO	01/30/73
GWYN, Z. V.	*DOCKET ONLY	676	GREENSBORO	08/31/78
HAAS, SOLOMAN	WASHINGTON	622	WILMINGTON	03/25/71
HADDOCK, WILLIAM	*DOCKET ONLY	1009	NEW BERN	12/19/68
HADEN, JAMES W.	*DOCKET ONLY	94	GREENSBORO	01/23/73
HAGLER, PAUL	*DOCKET ONLY	210	GREENSBORO	05/07/73
HAInLINE, NATHAN	DAVIE	313	WILMINGTON	05/30/68
HAIR, JACOB F.	IREDELL	467	WILMINGTON	12/31/68
HAITHCOCK, KINTCHEN	*DOCKET ONLY	1459	NEW BERN	05/28/73
HAIZLIP WILLIAM H.	FORSYTH	184	WILMINGTON	04/03/68
HALE, ALONSON	CATAWBA	109	STATESVILLE	05/05/73
HALES, JOSEPH H. &	*DOCKET ONLY	523	NEW BERN	03/16/68
HALEY, SIMON	CUMBERLAND	838	WILMINGTON	06/25/78
HALEY, W. M., W. N.	*DOCKET ONLY	502	GREENSBORO	08/30/75
HALL, A.S.	HALIFAX	199	ELIZABETH CITY	05/24/73
HALL, ALEX E.	SAMPSON	841	WILMINGTON	07/20/78
HALL, ARCHIBALD	HALIFAX	622	ELIZABETH CITY	04/21/73
HALL, DR. J. W.	ROWAN	29	STATESVILLE	01/27/73
HALL, HENRY L.	*DOCKET ONLY	1696	NEW BERN	08/24/78
HALL, JACK	*DOCKET ONLY	701	GREENSBORO	02/12/75
HALL, JACK	ROWAN	197	STATESVILLE	06/18/73
HALL, JAMES	CURRITUCK	66	ELIZABETH CITY	12/04/67
HALL, JAMES H.	*DOCKET ONLY	367	NEW BERN	02/24/68
HALL, JOHN	*DOCKET ONLY	1029	NEW BERN	12/22/68
HALL, JOHN H.	CHOWAN	174	ELIZABETH CITY	04/28/68
HALL, NEWBERRY T.	ROWAN	28	STATESVILLE	01/24/73
HALL, WILBUR G.	CUMBERLAND	784	WILMINGTON	10/13/75
HALSTEAD, GEORGE N.	CURRITUCK	145	ELIZABETH CITY	02/17/68
HALSTEAD, JAMES R.	CURRITUCK	126	ELIZABETH CITY	01/27/68
HALSTEAD, JOHN W.	CAMDEN	320	ELIZABETH CITY	08/29/77
HALSTEAD, LEMUEL H.	CAMDEN	623	ELIZABETH CITY	08/16/71
HALYBURTON, THOMAS	ALEXANDER	88	STATESVILLE	04/25/73
HALYBURTON, THOMAS	BURKE	20	STATESVILLE	01/06/73
HAMELL, JAMES E.	*DOCKET ONLY	77	NEW BERN	11/30/67
HAMILL, A. M.	*DOCKET ONLY	1188	NEW BERN	12/29/68
HAMILL, GEORGE W.	*DOCKET ONLY	1215	NEW BERN	12/31/68
HAMILTON, CHARLES H.	*DOCKET ONLY	168	NEW BERN	01/09/68
HAMILTON, DANIEL H.	*DOCKET ONLY	1015	NEW BERN	12/19/68
HAMILTON, ZERO	CAMDEN	35	ELIZABETH CITY	10/04/67
HAMLETT, JOHN W.	*DOCKET ONLY	745	NEW BERN	05/29/68
HAMLIN, CHARLES	*DOCKET ONLY	446	NEW BERN	03/02/68
HAMLIN, CHESLEY &	*DOCKET ONLY	496	NEW BERN	03/07/68
HAMLIN, JOHN J.	*DOCKET ONLY	20	GREENSBORO	10/25/72
HAMLIN, ROBERT	NORTHAMPTON	223	ELIZABETH CITY	07/03/73
HAMLIN, ROBERT P.	GASTON	624	ELIZABETH CITY	05/01/73
HAMLIN, WILLIS A.	*DOCKET ONLY	411	GREENSBORO	09/05/73
HAMMELL, GEORGE B.	*DOCKET ONLY	97	NEW BERN	12/09/67
HAMMER, ROBERT	*DOCKET ONLY	310	NEW BERN	02/19/68
HAMMOND, COVINGTON	*DOCKET ONLY	1243	NEW BERN	12/31/68
HAMMOND, G. W.	*DOCKET ONLY	1130	NEW BERN	12/30/68
HAMMOND, GILBERT A.	*DOCKET ONLY	1247	NEW BERN	12/21/68
HAMPTON, E.D.	MECKLENBURG	653	WILMINGTON	03/26/72
HAMPTON, J. L &		332	STATESVILLE	10/26/78
HAMPTON, JOHN P.	UNION	141	WILMINGTON	03/12/68
HAMPTON, SAMUEL D.	RUTHERFORD	231	WILMINGTON	05/25/68
HAMPTON, THORNTON P.	*DOCKET ONLY	394	GREENSBORO	07/28/73
HAMPTON, WILLIAMWEST	WILKES	73	STATESVILLE	03/28/73
HAMPTON, ZACHARIAH	*DOCKET ONLY	466	NEW BERN	03/04/68
HANCOCK, E. W.	*DOCKET ONLY	1194	NEW BERN	12/31/68
HAND, M.H.	GASTON	68	WILMINGTON	02/04/68
HAND, PINCKNEY	*DOCKET ONLY	225	NEW BERN	01/29/68
HAND, SAMUEL H.	*DOCKET ONLY	638	GREENSBORO	08/07/78
HAND, SAMUEL P.	NEW HANOVER	81	WILMINGTON	02/12/68
HANDLEY, JAMES	*DOCKET ONLY	820	NEW BERN	05/20/68
HANDY, LEMUEL	*DOCKET ONLY	423	NEW BERN	02/29/68

NAME OF BANKRUPT	RESIDENCE	CASE NUMBER	CITY OF COURT	DATE FILED
HANENS, JONATHAN	*DOCKET ONLY	1407	NEW BERN	01/24/73
HANES, JOHN H.	DAVIE	546	WILMINGTON	03/29/69
HANES, LEWIS	*DOCKET ONLY	4	GREENSBORO	07/10/72
HANFF, JOHN P.	*DOCKET ONLY	1022	NEW BERN	12/21/68
HANNAH, WILLIAM	*DOCKET ONLY	445	NEW BERN	03/02/68
HANNOHAN, JAMES A.	*DOCKET ONLY	711	NEW BERN	05/26/68
HAPPER, WILL H.	TYRRELL	9	ELIZABETH CITY	08/05/67
HARBIN, A.A.	DAVIE	20	WILMINGTON	11/28/67
HARBIN, A.A.		603	WILMINGTON	11/24/70
HARBIN, A.A.		604	WILMINGTON	11/24/70
HARBIN, CASSWILL	DAVIE	389	WILMINGTON	12/26/68
HARDEE, JOSEPH P.	*DOCKET ONLY	968	NEW BERN	11/27/68
HARDIN, J. L.	*DOCKET ONLY	600	GREENSBORO	10/25/77
HARDIN, J. L.	*DOCKET ONLY	600	GREENSBORO	10/25/77
HARDING, GEORGE A.	NORTHAMPTON	265	ELIZABETH CITY	05/27/68
HARDING, S. B.		26	STATESVILLE	12/19/68
HARDING, S.B.	YADKIN	371	WILMINGTON	12/19/68
HARDING, WILLIAN	YADKIN	443	WILMINGTON	12/30/68
HARDY, DAVID	*DOCKET ONLY	1072	NEW BERN	12/26/68
HARDY, JESSE H.	*DOCKET ONLY	1574	NEW BERN	03/06/74
HARDY, JOHN L.	*DOCKET ONLY	1041	NEW BERN	12/22/68
HARDY, STEPHEN P.	*DOCKET ONLY	1042	NEW BERN	12/22/68
HARDY, THOMAS	*DOCKET ONLY	1449	NEW BERN	05/21/73
HARDY, THOMAS E.	NORTHAMPTON	269	ELIZABETH CITY	05/27/68
HARGRAVE, JESSE	*DOCKET ONLY	966	NEW BERN	12/15/68
HARKINS, T. J.	BUNCOMBE	61	ASHEVILLE	12/27/73
HARMAN, JOHN G.	RUTHERFORD	50	WILMINGTON	01/20/68
HARMON, JOSEPH	RUTHERFORD	124	STATESVILLE	05/13/73
HARPER, ELISHA	*DOCKET ONLY	401	GREENSBORO	08/08/73
HARPER, L.D	HALIFAX	483	ELIZABETH CITY	12/16/68
HARPER, LIGMAND D.	HALIFAX	483	ELIZABETH CITY	12/01/68
HARPER, WILLIAM M.	*DOCKET ONLY	555	GREENSBORO	03/22/76
HARPTER, WILLIAM A.	*DOCKET ONLY	396	GREENSBORO	08/01/73
HARRELL, FRILEY	MARTIN	585	ELIZABETH CITY	05/28/73
HARRELL, FRILEY J.	MARTIN	206	ELIZABETH CITY	05/31/73
HARRELL, JACOB	DUPLIN	155	WILMINGTON	05/25/68
HARRELL, JOSEPH H.	GATES	244	ELIZABETH CITY	04/15/68
HARRELL, THOMAS J.	BERTIE	268	ELIZABETH CITY	05/07/74
HARRELL, WILLIAM H.	GATES	243	ELIZABETH CITY	04/15/68
HARRINGTON, JOHN	*DOCKET ONLY	533	NEW BERN	03/17/68
HARRIS & ALLEN	*DOCKET ONLY	1341	NEW BERN	04/27/71
HARRIS & ALLEN	FRANKLIN	649	ELIZABETH CITY	12/02/72
HARRIS, CEBEN L.	*DOCKET ONLY	1348	NEW BERN	06/03/71
HARRIS, EDWARD P.	*DOCKET ONLY	877	NEW BERN	08/19/68
HARRIS, FRANCIS	NORTHAMPTON	234	ELIZABETH CITY	08/27/73
HARRIS, HARVIL	*DOCKET ONLY	1584	NEW BERN	06/05/74
HARRIS, J.A.	RUTHERFORD	534	WILMINGTON	01/06/69
HARRIS, JAMES H.	*DOCKET ONLY	581	NEW BERN	03/19/68
HARRIS, JAMES R.	*DOCKET ONLY	1598	NEW BERN	02/03/75
HARRIS, JASON C.	*DOCKET ONLY	44	GREENSBORO	12/16/72
HARRIS, JILES	MCDOWELL	301	STATESVILLE	05/29/78
HARRIS, JOHN A.	HALIFAX	577	ELIZABETH CITY	12/30/68
HARRIS, JOHN A.	*DOCKET ONLY	1203	NEW BERN	12/31/68
HARRIS, JOHN H.	HALIFAX	197	ELIZABETH CITY	05/20/73
HARRIS, JOHN L.	*DOCKET ONLY	248	NEW BERN	01/31/68
HARRIS, JOHN W.	STANLY	98	WILMINGTON	02/25/69
HARRIS, JOHN W.	*DOCKET ONLY	880	NEW BERN	08/19/68
HARRIS, MARCUS	*DOCKET ONLY	1112	NEW BERN	12/29/68
HARRIS, OSCAR E.	*DOCKET ONLY	1400	NEW BERN	11/20/72
HARRIS, RICHARD	ANSON	181	WILMINGTON	04/15/68
HARRIS, ROBERT H.	*DOCKET ONLY	777	NEW BERN	08/19/68
HARRIS, SIMEON	PASQUOTANK	159	ELIZABETH CITY	02/24/68
HARRIS, WASHINGTON	*DOCKET ONLY	879	NEW BERN	08/19/68
HARRIS, WEST	*DOCKET ONLY	348	NEW BERN	02/24/68
HARRIS, WILLIAM	*DOCKET ONLY	274	NEW BERN	02/08/68
HARRIS, WILLIAM	*DOCKET ONLY	1386	NEW BERN	05/01/74

NAME OF BANKRUPT	RESIDENCE	CASE NUMBER	CITY OF COURT	DATE FILED
HARRIS, WILLIAM G.	*DOCKET ONLY	531	NEW BERN	03/17/68
HARRIS, WILLIAM J.	MECKLENBURG	286	WILMINGTON	05/30/68
HARRIS, WILLIAM R.	*DOCKET ONLY	1113	NEW BERN	12/29/68
HARRISON, CARTER R.	*DOCKET ONLY	1619	NEW BERN	12/23/75
HARRISON, DURANT H.	*DOCKET ONLY	1469	NEW BERN	06/09/73
HARRISON, FRANKLIN	*DOCKET ONLY	1049	NEW BERN	12/23/68
HARRISON, HENRY	*DOCKET ONLY	466	GREENSBORO	03/09/74
HARRISON, HENRY	*DOCKET ONLY	549	GREENSBORO	/ /
HARRISON, JOHN A.	*DOCKET ONLY	1646	NEW BERN	07/05/77
HARRISON, JOHN P.	*DOCKET ONLY	15	NEW BERN	09/30/67
HARRISON, SIDNEY D.	*DOCKET ONLY	1645	NEW BERN	07/27/77
HARRISON, WILLIAM H.	*DOCKET ONLY	1090	NEW BERN	12/26/68
HARRISON, WILLIAM M.	*DOCKET ONLY	444	NEW BERN	03/02/68
HARRISS, HARMMIT J.	*DOCKET ONLY	404	GREENSBORO	08/23/73
HARRISS, W.N.	RUTHERFORD	18	WILMINGTON	11/23/67
HARSHAW, J. N.	CALDWELL	112	STATESVILLE	05/07/73
HART, CHARLES A.	*DOCKET ONLY	1589	NEW BERN	11/03/74
HART, RICHARD H.	NORTHAMPTON	476	ELIZABETH CITY	12/30/68
HARTSELL, ANDREW	*DOCKET ONLY	334	GREENSBORO	06/09/73
HARTSFIELD, J. C.	*DOCKET ONLY	636	NEW BERN	04/17/68
HARTSFIELD, JACOB A.	*DOCKET ONLY	1462	NEW BERN	06/25/73
HARTZ, HERMAN		317	WILMINGTON	06/22/68
HARTZ, HERMAN		321	WILMINGTON	07/06/68
HARVEY, AMOS	*DOCKET ONLY	1000	NEW BERN	12/11/68
HARVEY, JOHN C.	*DOCKET ONLY	264	GREENSBORO	05/23/73
HARVEY, MATTHIAS	*DOCKET ONLY	605	NEW BERN	04/01/68
HASH, JAMES	ASHE	8	STATESVILLE	08/01/73
HASKELL, J. A. &	*DOCKET ONLY	292	NEW BERN	02/13/68
HASKINS, JOHN A.	*DOCKET ONLY	40	GREENSBORO	11/11/72
HASKINS, JOHN R.	*DOCKET ONLY	582	NEW BERN	03/19/68
HASSELL, JOHN W.	TYRRELL	291	ELIZABETH CITY	12/22/75
HASSELL, R.J.	TYRRELL	290	ELIZABETH CITY	12/22/75
HASSHAGAN, CHRISTIAN	*DOCKET ONLY	549	GREENSBORO	03/06/76
HASWELL, EDWARD	*DOCKET ONLY	864	NEW BERN	06/22/68
HATHAWAY, J.R.B.	CHOWAN	354	ELIZABETH CITY	08/31/78
HATHCOCK, WILLIAM	*DOCKET ONLY	663	GREENSBORO	08/29/78
HAUGHTON, EDWARD B.	*DOCKET ONLY	384	NEW BERN	02/29/68
HAUGHTON, JOHN L.,	*DOCKET ONLY	576	GREENSBORO	07/01/77
HAUSTEIN, SAMUEL &	NEW HANOVER	843	WILMINGTON	06/27/78
HAVILAN, RICHARD F.	CUMBERLAND	14	WILMINGTON	11/01/67
HAWKINS, A.M.	HENDERSON	529	WILMINGTON	01/04/69
HAWKINS, DANIEL	BUNCOMBE	104	WILMINGTON	02/25/68
HAWKINS, E.D.	ROWAN	37	STATESVILLE	02/03/73
HAWKINS, GEORGE N.	BUNCOMBE	58	ASHEVILLE	04/14/73
HAWKINS, JOSEPH A.	ROWAN	79	STATESVILLE	04/08/73
HAWKINS, ROBERT	BUNCOMBE	54	ASHEVILLE	05/10/73
HAWLEY, J.T.	CUMBERLAND	628	WILMINGTON	05/22/71
HAWLEY, JOHN	*DOCKET ONLY	1710	NEW BERN	08/27/78
HAWS, HYATT &		628	WILMINGTON	05/22/71
HAYES, HAROLD	WILKES	136	STATESVILLE	05/21/73
HAYES, HORATIO	HERTFORD	74	ELIZABETH CITY	10/18/67
HAYES, JOSEPH M. S.	*DOCKET ONLY	705	NEW BERN	05/26/68
HAYES, PETER	*DOCKET ONLY	707	NEW BERN	05/26/68
HAYES, S.S.	*DOCKET ONLY	865	NEW BERN	06/22/68
HAYES, WILLIAM A.	MOORE	111	WILMINGTON	03/01/68
HAYNES, D. A.	LINCOLN	115	STATESVILLE	05/07/73
HAYNES, F. M. &	*DOCKET ONLY	583	GREENSBORO	01/01/78
HAYNES, THOMAS W. &		295	STATESVILLE	05/21/78
HAYS, H. S.	*DOCKET ONLY	878	NEW BERN	08/19/68
HAYS, JOSEPH D.	*DOCKET ONLY	159	NEW BERN	01/03/68
HAYS, RANDALL D.	*DOCKET ONLY	568	GREENSBORO	10/31/76
HAYS, THOMAS C. &	*DOCKET ONLY	177	NEW BERN	01/09/68
HAYWOOD, JOSEPH A.	*DOCKET ONLY	965	NEW BERN	11/20/68
HEARTT, LEOPOLD E.	*DOCKET ONLY	35	NEW BERN	10/23/67
HEATH, JOHN J.M.	UNION	170	WILMINGTON	04/08/68
HECHT, MARCUS	*DOCKET ONLY	1375	NEW BERN	01/27/72

NORTH CAROLINA BANKRUPTS - ACT OF 1867

NAME OF BANKRUPT	RESIDENCE	CASE NUMBER	CITY OF COURT	DATE FILED
HEDGECOCK, JOHN M.	*DOCKET ONLY	367	GREENSBORO	07/02/73
HEDRICK, DANIEL R.	*DOCKET ONLY	180	GREENSBORO	04/29/73
HEDRICK, JOHN	NEW HANOVER	869	WILMINGTON	08/30/78
HEDRICK, SARAH E.	NEW HANOVER	860	WILMINGTON	08/27/78
HEFLIN, ROBERT L.	*DOCKET ONLY	949	NEW BERN	10/31/68
HEGE BROTHERS	*DOCKET ONLY	475	GREENSBORO	06/10/74
HEGE, GEORGE W.	*DOCKET ONLY	948	NEW BERN	10/21/68
HEIDE, ALEX S.	CUMBERLAND	791	WILMINGTON	01/10/76
HEINANEUM J.	MECKLENBURG	395	WILMINGTON	12/26/68
HEINS, JOHN F.	WASHINGTON	374	WILMINGTON	12/21/68
HELLEN, JOSEPH F.	*DOCKET ONLY	951	NEW BERN	11/02/68
HELMS, C.A.	UNION	396	WILMINGTON	12/26/68
HELMS, LEE	*DOCKET ONLY	185	GREENSBORO	04/22/73
HEMPHILL, JOHN R.	BUNCOMBE	80	ASHEVILLE	03/20/73
HENDERSON, A. R.	*DOCKET ONLY	622	GREENSBORO	05/22/78
HENDERSON, ANDREW J.	HALIFAX	496	ELIZABETH CITY	12/29/68
HENDERSON, EDMONS H.	*DOCKET ONLY	712	NEW BERN	05/27/68
HENDERSON, JOSEHP	ROWAN	584	WILMINGTON	08/15/70
HENDERSON, SIDNEY L.	*DOCKET ONLY	295	GREENSBORO	05/28/73
HENDRICKS, HENRY	DAVIDSON	303	WILMINGTON	05/30/68
HENDRICKS, WILLIAM	DAVIE	27	WILMINGTON	12/07/67
HENDRIX, ALFRED N.	*DOCKET ONLY	299	GREENSBORO	05/26/73
HENDRIX, GEORGE K.	*DOCKET ONLY	324	GREENSBORO	05/27/73
HENLEY, ADDISON	DAVIE	271	STATESVILLE	06/25/75
HENLY, MICAJAH	*DOCKET ONLY	843	NEW BERN	04/18/68
HENRY, ROBERT		582	WILMINGTON	05/05/70
HENRY, ROBERT M.		569	WILMINGTON	03/02/70
HENRY, W. L. (70)	BUNCOMBE	57	ASHEVILLE	05/04/73
HENSON, CHARLES	MECKLENBURG	168	WILMINGTON	04/08/68
HEPTINSTALL, M. C.	*DOCKET ONLY	262	NEW BERN	02/08/68
HERESE, JACOB	CABARRUS	431	WILMINGTON	12/30/68
HERNDON, JOHN J.	*DOCKET ONLY	693	GREENSBORO	06/08/78
HERNDON, MATURINE C.	*DOCKET ONLY	385	GREENSBORO	07/18/73
HERRING, NEDHAM W.	DUPLIN	876	WILMINGTON	04/29/73
HESS, ROGERS &	CUMBERLAND	183	WILMINGTON	04/15/68
HESTER, JOHN H.	*DOCKET ONLY	859	NEW BERN	04/30/68
HESTER, JOHN H.	*DOCKET ONLY	1316	NEW BERN	01/03/71
HESTER, JOSEPH	*DOCKET ONLY	1379	NEW BERN	03/19/72
HESTER, JOSEPH G.	*DOCKET ONLY	529	GREENSBORO	11/04/72
HIATT, GABRIEL	SURRY	251	WILMINGTON	05/29/68
HIATT, JOHN	*DOCKET ONLY	1329	NEW BERN	03/02/71
HIGGIE, JAMES M.	*DOCKET ONLY	532	NEW BERN	03/17/68
HIGGINA, MILLS	BURKE	40	STATESVILLE	02/03/73
HIGGINS, ALBERTO	MCDOWELL	44	STATESVILLE	02/10/73
HIGGINS, BURR	*DOCKET ONLY	448	GREENSBORO	01/08/74
HIGGINS, WILEY F. &	*DOCKET ONLY	491	NEW BERN	03/06/68
HIGGS, GEORGE A.	*DOCKET ONLY	1553	NEW BERN	01/09/74
HIGGS, J.B. & D. P.	*DOCKET ONLY	1559	NEW BERN	01/16/74
HIGGS, JACOB	*DOCKET ONLY	1653	NEW BERN	12/13/77
HIGGS, JOSEPH B.	*DOCKET ONLY	653	NEW BERN	04/22/68
HIGGS, WILLIE J.	*DOCKET ONLY	819	NEW BERN	04/02/68
HIGHT, HARBIRD H.	*DOCKET ONLY	627	NEW BERN	04/07/68
HIGHT, HARTWELL H.	*DOCKET ONLY	629	NEW BERN	04/07/68
HIGHT, THOMAS D.	*DOCKET ONLY	628	NEW BERN	04/07/68
HILDEBRAND, ISREAL	BURKE	2	WILMINGTON	09/14/67
HILDERBRAND, JOHN	BUNCOMBE	297	WILMINGTON	05/30/68
HILDERSHIMER, JOSEPH	*DOCKET ONLY	3	NEW BERN	07/22/67
HILDRETH, AUGUSTUS	*DOCKET ONLY	422	NEW BERN	02/29/68
HILL, CALEB	*DOCKET ONLY	621	GREENSBORO	05/14/78
HILL, G.G.	*DOCKET ONLY	589	GREENSBORO	05/31/77
HILL, HENRY	NORTHAMPTON	583	ELIZABETH CITY	05/23/73
HILL, HENRY J.	NORTHAMPTON	204	ELIZABETH CITY	05/26/73
HILL, ISAAC S.	*DOCKET ONLY	968	NEW BERN	11/02/68
HILL, JAMES S.	STOKES	61	WILMINGTON	01/30/68
HILL, L. H.	LINCOLN	154	STATESVILLE	05/23/73
HILL, L.H.	STOKES	265	WILMINGTON	05/30/68

NAME OF BANKRUPT	RESIDENCE	CASE NUMBER	CITY OF COURT	DATE FILED
HILLARDS, DANDRIDGE	*DOCKET ONLY	1448	NEW BERN	05/21/73
HILLIARD, MICAJAH	*DOCKET ONLY	1468	NEW BERN	06/06/73
HILLIARD, WILLIAM H	*DOCKET ONLY	1293	NEW BERN	10/27/70
HILTON, JOSEPH G.	BURKE	142	STATESVILLE	05/21/73
HILTON, L. G.	DAVIE	321	STATESVILLE	08/23/78
HINES, A. J.	*DOCKET ONLY	297	NEW BERN	02/14/68
HINES, JOHN H.	*DOCKET ONLY	1091	NEW BERN	12/26/68
HINES, LOUIS H. &	*DOCKET ONLY	1082	NEW BERN	12/26/68
HINES, PETER E.	*DOCKET ONLY	1246	NEW BERN	12/31/68
HINES, ROBIN W.	*DOCKET ONLY	427	NEW BERN	02/29/68
HINSHAW, ARLONDO	*DOCKET ONLY	1031	NEW BERN	12/23/68
HINSHAW, MAHEN	*DOCKET ONLY	37	NEW BERN	10/24/67
HINSON, J. E.	*DOCKET ONLY	702	GREENSBORO	03/24/77
HINTON, ALPHEUS	*DOCKET ONLY	1630	NEW BERN	05/25/76
HINTON, E.L.	PASQUOTANK	182	ELIZABETH CITY	02/26/68
HINTON, GEROGE W.	PASQUOTANK	154	ELIZABETH CITY	02/24/68
HINTON, JOHN M.	PASQUOTANK	452	ELIZABETH CITY	12/30/68
HINTON, JOHN W.	GATES	20	ELIZABETH CITY	08/30/67
HOBBS, GUY	GATES	390	ELIZABETH CITY	05/29/68
HOBBS, JAMES A.	MARTIN	318	ELIZABETH CITY	07/03/77
HOBBS, MELTON	DAVIE	67	STATESVILLE	03/05/73
HOBGOOD, ROBERT H.	*DOCKET ONLY	1641	NEW BERN	01/16/77
HOBSON, GEORGE	YADKIN	446	WILMINGTON	12/30/68
HOBSON, JOHN	*DOCKET ONLY	372	GREENSBORO	07/03/73
HOBSON, SAMUEL M.	ROWAN	330	STATESVILLE	08/30/78
HOBSON, W. H.	DAVIE	325	STATESVILLE	08/29/78
HOCHSTADLER, ADOLPH		661	WILMINGTON	02/29/72
HODGES, DAVID	DAVIE	219	STATESVILLE	07/04/73
HODGES, HENRY	*DOCKET ONLY	846	NEW BERN	05/15/68
HODGES, HOLLAND	WATAUGA	312	STATESVILLE	07/25/78
HODGES, L. W.	NEW HANOVER	474	WILMINGTON	12/31/68
HODGES, WILLIAM J.	*DOCKET ONLY	1389	NEW BERN	08/06/72
HODGESN EDWIN G.	*DOCKET ONLY	1053	NEW BERN	12/23/68
HODGIN, ZINNRI	*DOCKET ONLY	192	GREENSBORO	04/01/73
HODSON, STEPHEN	*DOCKET ONLY	513	NEW BERN	03/12/68
HOELL, EDWARD	*DOCKET ONLY	1077	NEW BERN	12/24/68
HOELL, FRANKLIN	*DOCKET ONLY	590	NEW BERN	03/24/68
HOFFLER, JAMES R.	GATES	625	ELIZABETH CITY	12/31/68
HOFFMAN, MALLETT &	NEW HANOVER	118	WILMINGTON	03/02/68
HOFLER, JAMES R.	GATES	449	ELIZABETH CITY	12/30/68
HOGAN, WILLIAM J.	*DOCKET ONLY	924	NEW BERN	09/04/68
HOGGARD, HIXON E.	NORTHAMPTON	411	ELIZABETH CITY	12/16/68
HOGGARD, N.S.	NORTHAMPTON	410	ELIZABETH CITY	12/16/68
HOLBERT, JOSEPH	HENDERSON	56	ASHEVILLE	01/04/73
HOLCOMBE, WILLIAM B.	*DOCKET ONLY	547	GREENSBORO	04/24/74
HOLDEN, ADDISON L.	*DOCKET ONLY	272	GREENSBORO	05/23/73
HOLDEN, E. B.	*DOCKET ONLY	197	NEW BERN	01/17/68
HOLDEN, G. W. (134)	BUNCOMBE	62	ASHEVILLE	02/23/74
HOLDEN, HENRY A.	*DOCKET ONLY	1269	NEW BERN	04/23/70
HOLDER, DAVID M.	*DOCKET ONLY	226	GREENSBORO	05/12/73
HOLDER, NELSON	*DOCKET ONLY	184	GREENSBORO	04/30/73
HOLDERBY, JOSEPH	*DOCKET ONLY	1	GREENSBORO	07/24/72
HOLDERBY, R. A.	*DOCKET ONLY	444	GREENSBORO	12/22/73
HOLDERNEP, JAMES M.	*DOCKET ONLY	177	GREENSBORO	04/26/73
HOLDERNESS, WILLIAM	*DOCKET ONLY	644	NEW BERN	04/17/68
HOLLAND, JESSE	*DOCKET ONLY	1431	NEW BERN	05/13/73
HOLLAND, PHILEMON	*DOCKET ONLY	1520	NEW BERN	09/18/73
HOLLER, DAVID	ALEXANDER	291	STATESVILLE	05/11/78
HOLLERMAN, W. J.	*DOCKET ONLY	467	NEW BERN	03/04/68
HOLLIDAY, ANN &	NORTHAMPTON	376	ELIZABETH CITY	09/14/68
HOLLIDAY, JESSE &	NORTHAMPTON	376	ELIZABETH CITY	09/14/68
HOLLINGSWORTH, ISAAC	CUMBERLAND	33	WILMINGTON	01/03/68
HOLLINGSWORTH, S. C.	*DOCKET ONLY	687	NEW BERN	05/19/68
HOLLOWAY, JAMES	*DOCKET ONLY	794	NEW BERN	05/30/68
HOLLOWAY, JAMES	*DOCKET ONLY	237	NEW BERN	01/31/68
HOLLOWAY, ROBERT	*DOCKET ONLY	795	NEW BERN	05/30/68

NAME OF BANKRUPT	RESIDENCE	CASE NUMBER	CITY OF COURT	DATE FILED
HOLLOWAY, WILLIAM F.	*DOCKET ONLY	359	GREENSBORO	06/24/73
HOLLOWAY, WILLIAM S.	*DOCKET ONLY	560	NEW BERN	03/19/68
HOLLOWAY, WILLIAMSON	*DOCKET ONLY	238	NEW BERN	01/31/68
HOLM & WIATT		581	WILMINGTON	06/22/68
HOLMAN, CHARLES	*DOCKET ONLY	1587	NEW BERN	08/19/74
HOLMES, ALLMOND	SAMPSON	457	WILMINGTON	12/31/68
HOLMES, ARCHIBALD	CUMBERLAND	623	WILMINGTON	04/01/71
HOLMES, H.H.	TYRRELL	276	ELIZABETH CITY	03/19/75
HOLMES, J. B.	*DOCKET ONLY	515	NEW BERN	03/12/68
HOLOMB, W. B.	*DOCKET ONLY	472	GREENSBORO	04/24/74
HOLT, EDWIN M.	*DOCKET ONLY	982	NEW BERN	11/13/68
HOLT, JOHN A.	ROWAN	9	STATESVILLE	11/02/72
HOLT, S. P.	*DOCKET ONLY	597	GREENSBORO	11/23/77
HOLT, W. N. & W. M.	*DOCKET ONLY	502	GREENSBORO	08/30/75
HOLT, WILLIAM D.	*DOCKET ONLY	633	NEW BERN	04/15/68
HOLTEN, ABNER S.	*DOCKET ONLY	1180	NEW BERN	12/31/68
HOLTON, ALEXANDER H.	*DOCKET ONLY	1618	NEW BERN	12/22/75
HOLYFIELD, C. C.	*DOCKET ONLY	374	GREENSBORO	07/03/73
HOMES, AMOS		7	STATESVILLE	06/06/72
HONEYCUTT, JAMES	*DOCKET ONLY	239	NEW BERN	01/31/68
HONEYCUTT, S.	UNION	397	WILMINGTON	12/26/68
HOOD, SAMUEL H.	*DOCKET ONLY	1150	NEW BERN	12/30/68
HOOPER, R. G	*DOCKET ONLY	496	GREENSBORO	06/28/75
HOOVER, BENJAMIN F.	*DOCKET ONLY	174	GREENSBORO	04/25/73
HOOVER, CHARLES	*DOCKET ONLY	71	GREENSBORO	01/24/73
HOOVER, EDMUND D.	*DOCKET ONLY	1054	NEW BERN	12/23/68
HOOVER, JOHN T.	*DOCKET ONLY	1572	NEW BERN	03/10/74
HOOVER, PETER	DAVIDSON	14	STATESVILLE	12/07/72
HOOVER, PLEASANT A.	*DOCKET ONLY	70	GREENSBORO	01/24/73
HOOVER, S.S.	MECKLENBURG	551	WILMINGTON	07/01/69
HOOVER, VALENTINE	*DOCKET ONLY	163	GREENSBORO	04/22/73
HOPKINS, L. G.	*DOCKET ONLY	320	NEW BERN	02/21/68
HOPKINS, MARTIN P.	*DOCKET ONLY	744	NEW BERN	05/29/68
HOPKINS, PLEASANT	*DOCKET ONLY	409	NEW BERN	02/28/68
HORAH, JOHN M. &	*DOCKET ONLY	485	GREENSBORO	09/26/75
HORN, AZARIAH	DAVIE	299	WILMINGTON	05/30/68
HORNESLY, ALBERT R.	CLEVELAND	428	WILMINGTON	12/30/68
HORTON, H. C.	*DOCKET ONLY	776	NEW BERN	08/19/68
HORTON, JOHN	WATAUGA	311	STATESVILLE	08/23/76
HORTON, SAMUEL P.	*DOCKET ONLY	1064	NEW BERN	12/26/68
HOSKINS, JOHN A.	*DOCKET ONLY	1382	NEW BERN	04/13/72
HOSKINS, THOMAS J.	BUNCOMBE	257	WILMINGTON	05/29/68
HOULDER, RUFFIN J.	*DOCKET ONLY	1109	NEW BERN	12/29/68
HOUSE, LEONARD	*DOCKET ONLY	610	NEW BERN	04/01/68
HOUSE, N.O.	HALIFAX	202	ELIZABETH CITY	05/24/73
HOUSE, W. O.	HALIFAX	629	ELIZABETH CITY	04/22/73
HOUSTON, GEORGE E.	DUPLIN	693	WILMINGTON	05/30/73
HOUSTON, GOERGE E.	*DOCKET ONLY	1429	NEW BERN	05/08/73
HOUSTON, W.M. H.	*DOCKET ONLY	551	GREENSBORO	10/07/74
HOUSTON, WILLIAM H.	UNION	87	WILMINGTON	01/18/67
HOWARD, COLE &		583	WILMINGTON	10/29/69
HOWELL, BENJAMIN N.	*DOCKET ONLY	680	NEW BERN	04/30/68
HOWELL, CHARLES W.	DAVIE	181	STATESVILLE	06/04/73
HOWELL, GIDEON F.	DAVIE	523	WILMINGTON	01/01/69
HOWELL, HENRY K.	ROBESON	452	WILMINGTON	12/31/68
HOWELL, J.W.	MARTIN	626	ELIZABETH CITY	03/10/74
HOWELL, JAMES A.	HERTFORD	175	ELIZABETH CITY	02/26/68
HOWELL, JAMES E.	*DOCKET ONLY	1110	NEW BERN	12/29/68
HOWELL, JAMES M.	*DOCKET ONLY	314	GREENSBORO	06/03/73
HOWELL, JAMES P.	HERTFORD	629	ELIZABETH CITY	02/12/73
HOWELL, JOHN C.	DAVIE	209	WILMINGTON	05/15/68
HOWELL, LEVI D.	*DOCKET ONLY	837	NEW BERN	05/30/68
HOWELL, MARMADUKE	ROBESON	835	WILMINGTON	06/10/78
HOWELL, S.L.	ALEXANDER	514	WILMINGTON	01/01/69
HOWELL, SHADRACK	ROBESON	846	WILMINGTON	07/30/78
HOWERTON, WILLIAM H.	ROWAN	18	STATESVILLE	12/20/72

NORTH CAROLINA BANKRUPTS - ACT OF 1867

NAME OF BANKRUPT	RESIDENCE	CASE NUMBER	CITY OF COURT	DATE FILED
HOWES, AMOS	ROWAN	865	WILMINGTON	06/06/72
HOWES, AMOS	*DOCKET ONLY	8	GREENSBORO	08/12/72
HOWEY, JOSEPH W.	*DOCKET ONLY	402	GREENSBORO	08/09/73
HOWIE, ROBERT J.	*DOCKET ONLY	30	GREENSBORO	12/02/72
HOYT J.B. & COMPANY		657	WILMINGTON	02/21/72
HUBBBS & BROTHERS	*DOCKET ONLY	1325	NEW BERN	02/15/71
HUDSON	DAVIE	297	STATESVILLE	05/24/78
HUDSON, JAMES	ROWAN	385	WILMINGTON	12/25/68
HUFFINES, WILLIAM	*DOCKET ONLY	76	GREENSBORO	01/27/73
HUFFMAN, JOHN R.	*DOCKET ONLY	92	GREENSBORO	02/01/73
HUGGINS, WILLIAM F.	*DOCKET ONLY	1398	NEW BERN	11/12/72
HUGHES, A. J.	*DOCKET ONLY	397	NEW BERN	02/28/68
HUGHES, GEORGE	*DOCKET ONLY	971	NEW BERN	11/28/68
HUGHES, JOSEPH G.	CAMDEN	52	ELIZABETH CITY	11/18/67
HUGHES, THOMAS C.	*DOCKET ONLY	204	NEW BERN	01/20/68
HUGHES, WILLIAM H.		630	ELIZABETH CITY	03/12/69
HUGHES, WILLIAM H.	*DOCKET ONLY	23	NEW BERN	10/07/67
HUGHES, WILLIAM P.	*DOCKET ONLY	492	GREENSBORO	04/21/75
HUGHEY, R. N.	BUNCOMBE	63	ASHEVILLE	04/17/73
HULZLER, JOSEPH &	*DOCKET ONLY	1388	NEW BERN	12/09/71
HUMBER, OLIVER	*DOCKET ONLY	830	NEW BERN	05/30/68
HUMPHRIES, THOMAS C.	CURRITUCK	87	ELIZABETH CITY	12/16/67
HUMPHRIES, WILLIAM	CURRITUCK	53	ELIZABETH CITY	11/27/67
HUMPHRY, LOUIS E.	*DOCKET ONLY	1424	NEW BERN	04/30/74
HUNEYCUTT, DEMPSEY	UNION	138	WILMINGTON	03/12/68
HUNNINGTON, JESSE &		3	ELIZABETH CITY	07/24/67
HUNSUCKER, JOHN	CATAWBA	259	STATESVILLE	05/14/74
HUNT, ELIJAH M.	*DOCKET ONLY	266	NEW BERN	02/07/68
HUNT, JAMES A. G.	*DOCKET ONLY	469	GREENSBORO	03/24/74
HUNT, JAMES A. G.	*DOCKET ONLY	543	GREENSBORO	03/24/74
HUNT, JAMES P.	*DOCKET ONLY	1111	NEW BERN	12/29/68
HUNT, JOHN A.	*DOCKET ONLY	606	GREENSBORO	04/29/78
HUNT, JOHN L.	*DOCKET ONLY	706	NEW BERN	05/26/68
HUNT, JOHN W.	*DOCKET ONLY	496	NEW BERN	03/07/68
HUNT, NATT	*DOCKET ONLY	839	GREENSBORO	06/17/78
HUNT, RICHARD H.	*DOCKET ONLY	236	NEW BERN	01/31/68
HUNT, SAMUEL R.	*DOCKET ONLY	596	NEW BERN	03/25/68
HUNT, WILLIAM J.	*DOCKET ONLY	534	NEW BERN	03/17/68
HUNTER, ALEXANDER	*DOCKET ONLY	86	NEW BERN	12/04/67
HUNTER, CHARLEY	DAVIE	110	WILMINGTON	03/01/68
HUNTER, H. F.	ALEXANDER	77	STATESVILLE	04/04/73
HUNTER, JOHN H.	*DOCKET ONLY	1620	NEW BERN	01/22/76
HUNTER, NICHOLAS	*DOCKET ONLY	1682	NEW BERN	06/14/78
HUNTER, TIMOTHY	PASQUOTANK	269	ELIZABETH CITY	05/23/68
HUNTLEY, R.S.	UNION	256	WILMINGTON	05/29/68
HUNTS, DAMIEL W.	*DOCKET ONLY	728	NEW BERN	05/29/68
HUNTTING & WESSON		320	WILMINGTON	06/30/68
HUNTTING, WESSON &		320	WILMINGTON	06/30/68
HURDLE, BEDFORD &	*DOCKET ONLY	793	NEW BERN	05/30/68
HURDLE, HENRY C.	*DOCKET ONLY	1179	NEW BERN	12/31/68
HURLEY, NIXON	*DOCKET ONLY	284	NEW BERN	02/10/68
HUTCHINGS, JOHN W.	HERTFORD	387	ELIZABETH CITY	11/18/68
HUTCHINS, GILES	YADKIN	5	WILMINGTON	09/21/67
HUTCHINS, JAMES T.	*DOCKET ONLY	337	GREENSBORO	06/10/73
HUTCHINSON, E. NYE	*DOCKET ONLY	2	NEW BERN	10/03/67
HYATT, J.H.	PERQUIMANS	414	ELIZABETH CITY	12/23/68
HYDE, THOMAS C.	ROWAN	46	STATESVILLE	07/12/73
HYDEN, WILLIAM D.	BUNCOMBE	55	ASHEVILLE	03/27/73
HYMAN, AQUILLA P.	HALIFAX	544	ELIZABETH CITY	09/04/72
INGRAM, E.D.	ANSON	219	WILMINGTON	05/21/68
INGRAM, LEWIS (101)	BUNCOMBE	87	ASHEVILLE	06/02/73
INGRAM, THOMAS N.	*DOCKET ONLY	111	NEW BERN	12/19/67
INGRAM, URIAH	*DOCKET ONLY	112	NEW BERN	12/19/67
INGRAM, WILLIAM B.	*DOCKET ONLY	831	GREENSBORO	06/12/78
IRAIL, B.J.	HENDERSON	531	WILMINGTON	01/04/69
IRWIN, H. C. & L.	*DOCKET ONLY	515	GREENSBORO	06/03/76

NAME OF BANKRUPT	RESIDENCE	CASE NUMBER	CITY OF COURT	DATE FILED
ISBY, J. K. (114)	HENDERSON	64	ASHEVILLE	06/26/73
ISENHOUR, DANIEL	ROWAN	75	STATESVILLE	03/28/73
ISLEY, DANIEL	*DOCKET ONLY	268	GREENSBORO	05/21/73
ISLEY, LEVI	*DOCKET ONLY	267	GREENSBORO	05/22/73
ISRAEL, F. J. (116)	HENDERSON	65	ASHEVILLE	06/14/73
ISRAEL, J. M. (140)	BUNCOMBE	69	ASHEVILLE	06/05/73
ISRAEL, JULIUS	*DOCKET ONLY	122	GREENSBORO	02/25/73
ISRAEL, P. J. (77)	BUNCOMBE	66	ASHEVILLE	05/17/73
ISRAEL, S. M. (84)	HENDERSON	68	ASHEVILLE	01/22/73
J. LAGOWITZ &		758	WILMINGTON	12/17/73
JACKSON & PEARCE	CUMBERLAND	13	WILMINGTON	10/26/87
JACKSON, ALFORD W.	*DOCKET ONLY	347	NEW BERN	02/24/68
JACKSON, ALFRED	CUMBERLAND	667	WILMINGTON	08/14/72
JACKSON, ANDREW L.	ANSON	216	WILMINGTON	05/21/68
JACKSON, HENRY	SAMPSON	719	WILMINGTON	06/11/73
JACKSON, JACOB	*DOCKET ONLY	1686	NEW BERN	04/30/78
JACKSON, JAMES J.	*DOCKET ONLY	348	NEW BERN	02/24/68
JACKSON, JEPA B.	*DOCKET ONLY	1691	NEW BERN	08/10/78
JACKSON, JOHN W.	*DOCKET ONLY	1169	NEW BERN	12/31/68
JACKSON, MOSES	PASQUOTANK	505	ELIZABETH CITY	12/02/70
JACKSON, SAMUEL F.	*DOCKET ONLY	291	GREENSBORO	05/28/73
JACKSON, SHADE	*DOCKET ONLY	1592	NEW BERN	12/15/74
JACKSON, WILLIAM	PASQUOTANK	234	ELIZABETH CITY	03/24/68
JACKSON, WILLIAM D.	*DOCKET ONLY	349	NEW BERN	02/24/68
JACOBS, A.E.	CURRITUCK	133	ELIZABETH CITY	02/10/68
JACOBS, B. & N. F.	*DOCKET ONLY	500	GREENSBORO	08/26/75
JACOBS, NATHANIEL	NEW HANOVER	845	WILMINGTON	07/29/78
JAMES, JOHN G.	GATES	95	ELIZABETH CITY	12/27/67
JAMES, THOMAS B.	*DOCKET ONLY	694	NEW BERN	08/07/68
JARMAM, THOMAS J.	ONSLOW	759	WILMINGTON	12/19/73
JARMAN, F.H.	*DOCKET ONLY	831	NEW BERN	05/30/68
JARMAN, HENRY	*DOCKET ONLY	1391	NEW BERN	09/20/72
JARRATT, I. A.	*DOCKET ONLY	412	GREENSBORO	09/06/73
JASKINS, THOMAS H.	*DOCKET ONLY	1294	NEW BERN	10/03/70
JAY, J.V.	RUTHERFORD	59	WILMINGTON	01/20/68
JEFFRAYS, LITTLETON	*DOCKET ONLY	535	NEW BERN	03/17/68
JENKINS, A. T.	*DOCKET ONLY	536	NEW BERN	03/17/68
JENKINS, ALONZO T.	*DOCKET ONLY	142	GREENSBORO	03/24/73
JENKINS, BENJAMIN	HALIFAX	397	ELIZABETH CITY	12/18/69
JENKINS, BENJAMIN F.	*DOCKET ONLY	1538	NEW BERN	12/06/73
JENKINS, COLEMAN	YADKIN	447	WILMINGTON	12/30/69
JENKINS, J.W.	NORTHAMPTON	356	ELIZABETH CITY	08/31/78
JENKINS, JOHN C. C.	*DOCKET ONLY	1202	NEW BERN	12/31/68
JENKINS, NELSON E.	HALIFAX	251	ELIZABETH CITY	12/19/73
JENKINS, PAUL	*DOCKET ONLY	93	NEW BERN	12/04/67
JENKINS, THOMAS	*DOCKET ONLY	1720	NEW BERN	08/30/78
JENKINS, WILLIAM A.	*DOCKET ONLY	59	NEW BERN	11/21/67
JENKINS, WILSON T.	*DOCKET ONLY	688	NEW BERN	09/01/68
JENNETT, THOMAS	*DOCKET ONLY	1477	NEW BERN	06/22/73
JENNINGS, FEORGE	PASQUOTANK	592	ELIZABETH CITY	06/14/73
JENNINGS, FREDERICK	PASQUOTANK	106	ELIZABETH CITY	01/10/68
JENNINGS, GEORGE	PASQUOTANK	212	ELIZABETH CITY	06/14/73
JENNINGS, JOHN M.	PASQUOTANK	55	ELIZABETH CITY	11/18/67
JINKINS, BELLFIELD	*DOCKET ONLY	66	NEW BERN	11/23/67
JOHN C. PACE (55)	HENDERSON	111	ASHEVILLE	04/19/73
JOHN, ADLER &	PHILADELPHIA	788	WILMINGTON	02/19/74
JOHNSON & DOBSON	BALTIMORE	627	ELIZABETH CITY	10/19/69
JOHNSON & WARRAN	*DOCKET ONLY	505	GREENSBORO	08/26/75
JOHNSON, ALBERT	*DOCKET ONLY	1381	NEW BERN	04/13/72
JOHNSON, ALEX., JR.	NEW HANOVER	670	WILMINGTON	10/23/72
JOHNSON, BENJAMIN S.	LINCOLN	410	WILMINGTON	12/29/69
JOHNSON, COOK &	CUMBERLAND	618	WILMINGTON	03/01/71
JOHNSON, EVAN	BLADEN	764	WILMINGTON	01/06/74
JOHNSON, HUGH	*DOCKET ONLY	446	GREENSBORO	12/29/73
JOHNSON, HUGH (118)	HENDERSON	77	ASHEVILLE	08/23/73
JOHNSON, ISHAM P.	*DOCKET ONLY	213	GREENSBORO	05/07/73

NAME OF BANKRUPT	RESIDENCE	CASE NUMBER	CITY OF COURT	DATE FILED
JOHNSON, J.H.	YADKIN	550	WILMINGTON	06/05/69
JOHNSON, J.J.		831	ELIZABETH CITY	09/11/69
JOHNSON, JACKON	CUMBERLAND	177	WILMINGTON	04/14/68
JOHNSON, JAMES	DAVIE	315	WILMINGTON	05/30/68
JOHNSON, JAMES H.	MARTIN	230	ELIZABETH CITY	07/14/73
JOHNSON, JOHN	*DOCKET ONLY	329	GREENSBORO	08/06/73
JOHNSON, JOHN	*DOCKET ONLY	1080	NEW BERN	12/26/68
JOHNSON, JOHN A.	CURRITUCK	98	ELIZABETH CITY	12/30/67
JOHNSON, JOHN S.	*DOCKET ONLY	368	NEW BERN	02/24/68
JOHNSON, M. H. (22)	HENDERSON	75	ASHEVILLE	05/22/73
JOHNSON, PETER H.	WILKES	51	STATESVILLE	02/18/73
JOHNSON, RAWLEY G.	*DOCKET ONLY	514	NEW BERN	02/12/68
JOHNSON, RICHARD	*DOCKET ONLY	1093	NEW BERN	12/29/68
JOHNSON, ROBERT A.	*DOCKET ONLY	622	NEW BERN	04/03/68
JOHNSON, TARLTON	*DOCKET ONLY	135	GREENSBORO	03/14/73
JOHNSON, THOMAS J.		320	WILMINGTON	06/30/68
JOHNSON, THOMAS M.	*DOCKET ONLY	160	NEW BERN	01/03/68
JOHNSON, WALTER B.	*DOCKET ONLY	187	GREENSBORO	04/30/73
JOHNSON, WASHINGTON	ROBESON	831	WILMINGTON	05/21/78
JOHNSTON, JAMES C.	CHOWAN	42	ELIZABETH CITY	11/04/67
JOHNSTON, JOHN D.	ROWAN	110	STATESVILLE	05/04/73
JOHNSTON, JOHN W.	*DOCKET ONLY	655	NEW BERN	06/19/68
JOHNSTON, ROBERT D.	*DOCKET ONLY	1037	NEW BERN	12/23/68
JOHNSTON, ROBERT F.	DAVIE	306	WILMINGTON	05/30/68
JOHNSTON, S.C.	GASTON	390	WILMINGTON	12/26/68
JOHNSTON, WILLIAM H.	TYRRELL	257	ELIZABETH CITY	03/08/74
JOINER, LEWIS W.	*DOCKET ONLY	48	GREENSBORO	12/18/72
JOLLEY, J.B.	CLEVELAND	134	WILMINGTON	03/12/68
JOLLEY, MERIDITH	RUTHERFORD	236	STATESVILLE	10/08/73
JONES & BROTHERS	DAVIDSON	657	WILMINGTON	02/21/72
JONES BROTHER	*DOCKET ONLY	9	GREENSBORO	08/12/72
JONES, A. H.	*DOCKET ONLY	588	NEW BERN	03/19/68
JONES, ALLEN W.	MOORE	112	WILMINGTON	03/01/68
JONES, BALDY H.	*DOCKET ONLY	1280	NEW BERN	01/20/70
JONES, BENJAMIN W.	GATES	448	ELIZABETH CITY	12/29/68
JONES, CHARLEY R.	IREDELL	328	WILMINGTON	09/01/68
JONES, CLAYTON	*DOCKET ONLY	647	GREENSBORO	08/27/78
JONES, DAN M. (156)	HENDERSON	76	ASHEVILLE	08/31/78
JONES, DUNCAN	RICHMOND	78	WILMINGTON	04/10/68
JONES, EDMOND W.	CURRITUCK	186	ELIZABETH CITY	02/28/68
JONES, EDMUND D.	*DOCKET ONLY	44	NEW BERN	11/04/67
JONES, EZEKIEL P.	*DOCKET ONLY	141	GREENSBORO	03/04/73
JONES, EZEKIEL P.	*DOCKET ONLY	1378	NEW BERN	02/19/72
JONES, FRIDAY	*DOCKET ONLY	161	NEW BERN	01/03/68
JONES, GEORGE	*DOCKET ONLY	1678	NEW BERN	06/10/78
JONES, GEORGE W.	*DOCKET ONLY	1677	NEW BERN	06/08/78
JONES, ISAAC W.	ROWAN	493	WILMINGTON	12/31/68
JONES, J.L.	NORTHAMPTON	282	ELIZABETH CITY	09/03/75
JONES, JAMES A.	*DOCKET ONLY	275	NEW BERN	02/08/68
JONES, JAMES M.	*DOCKET ONLY	290	NEW BERN	02/11/68
JONES, JAMES M.	ROWAN	357	WILMINGTON	12/10/68
JONES, JAMES W.	*DOCKET ONLY	1418	NEW BERN	03/03/73
JONES, JOHN	GATES	358	ELIZABETH CITY	12/28/68
JONES, JOHN E.	*DOCKET ONLY	1167	NEW BERN	12/31/68
JONES, JOHN M.	CHOWAN	297	ELIZABETH CITY	04/19/76
JONES, JOHN W.	*DOCKET ONLY	497	NEW BERN	03/07/68
JONES, JOHNSON B.	MECKLENBURG	282	WILMINGTON	05/30/68
JONES, JOSEPH	PASQUOTANK	27	ELIZABETH CITY	11/16/67
JONES, JOSEPH JOHN	*DOCKET ONLY	689	NEW BERN	05/19/68
JONES, JOSEPH S.	*DOCKET ONLY	1168	NEW BERN	12/31/68
JONES, JOSEPH S.	PASQUOTANK	54	ELIZABETH CITY	11/18/67
JONES, LEVI. (5)	HENDERSON	71	ASHEVILLE	03/25/73
JONES, M. M. (49)	BUNCOMBE	70	ASHEVILLE	05/10/73
JONES, NOEL	SAMPSON	830	WILMINGTON	05/18/78
JONES, O. R. (46)	BUNCOMBE	79	ASHEVILLE	03/22/73
JONES, RICHARD M.	*DOCKET ONLY	166	GREENSBORO	12/16/72

NORTH CAROLINA BANKRUPTS - ACT OF 1867

NAME OF BANKRUPT	RESIDENCE	CASE NUMBER	CITY OF COURT	DATE FILED
JONES, ROBERT	*DOCKET ONLY	321	NEW BERN	02/21/68
JONES, ROBERT (JR)	HENDERSON	72	ASHEVILLE	07/01/73
JONES, ROBERT B.	*DOCKET ONLY	203	GREENSBORO	05/05/73
JONES, RUFFIN W.	*DOCKET ONLY	919	NEW BERN	08/27/68
JONES, SAMUEL , H.	*DOCKET ONLY	1295	NEW BERN	03/15/68
JONES, SAMUEL T.	*DOCKET ONLY	1340	NEW BERN	04/28/71
JONES, THOMAS	MARTIN	563	ELIZABETH CITY	04/08/73
JONES, THOMAS	MARTIN	179	ELIZABETH CITY	04/14/73
JONES, THOMAS	HENDERSON	74	ASHEVILLE	06/11/73
JONES, TIMOTHY JR.	TYRRELL	322	ELIZABETH CITY	12/19/77
JONES, W. H. &	*DOCKET ONLY	1543	NEW BERN	11/22/73
JONES, WILLIAM A.	*DOCKET ONLY	415	NEW BERN	02/29/68
JONES, WILLIAM H.	*DOCKET ONLY	858	NEW BERN	06/19/68
JONES, WILLIAM N.	*DOCKET ONLY	796	NEW BERN	05/30/68
JONES, WILLIAM P.	MARTIN	321	ELIZABETH CITY	11/18/77
JONES, YANCEY	*DOCKET ONLY	319	GREENSBORO	06/04/73
JONUS, ANDREW J.	*DOCKET ONLY	1654	NEW BERN	03/02/78
JORDAN, A.S.	PASQUOTANK	11	ELIZABETH CITY	08/08/67
JORDAN, ALFRED	MARTIN	429	ELIZABETH CITY	12/24/68
JORDAN, C. H.	*DOCKET ONLY	300	NEW BERN	02/17/68
JORDAN, JOHN V.	*DOCKET ONLY	995	NEW BERN	12/12/68
JORDAN, L. M.	*DOCKET ONLY	263	NEW BERN	02/07/68
JORDAN, STEPHEN D.	TRANSYLVANIA	78	ASHEVILLE	01/27/73
JORDAN, THOMAS LEROY	*DOCKET ONLY	195	NEW BERN	01/17/68
JORDAN, THOMAS W.	NORTHAMPTON	224	ELIZABETH CITY	07/02/73
JORDAN, WILLIAM B.	*DOCKET ONLY	757	NEW BERN	06/02/68
JORDAN, WILLIAM G.	*DOCKET ONLY	307	NEW BERN	02/15/68
JORDAN, WILLIAM G.	*DOCKET ONLY	25	NEW BERN	10/07/67
JOSEPH, THEODORE	*DOCKET ONLY	1277	NEW BERN	10/25/69
JOSEY, NAPOLEON B.	NORTHAMPTON	520	ELIZABETH CITY	12/30/70
JOSEY, MARTIN	ROWAN	232	STATESVILLE	08/20/73
JOSLIN, ISAAC R.	*DOCKET ONLY	380	NEW BERN	02/29/68
JOYCE, JOHN (SR)	*DOCKET ONLY	278	GREENSBORO	05/24/73
JOYCE, THOMAS H.	*DOCKET ONLY	293	GREENSBORO	05/28/73
JOYNER, GEORGE	*DOCKET ONLY	456	NEW BERN	03/03/68
JOYNER, JAMES	*DOCKET ONLY	1543	NEW BERN	12/13/73
JOYNER, MOSES	*DOCKET ONLY	1248	NEW BERN	12/31/68
JOYNER, PETER H.	*DOCKET ONLY	1151	NEW BERN	12/30/68
JUDD, WILLIAM J.	*DOCKET ONLY	1114	NEW BERN	12/29/68
JUDKINS, JOHN L	HALIFAX	336	ELIZABETH CITY	08/23/78
JULIAN, HORNGILL	*DOCKET ONLY	285	NEW BERN	02/10/68
JULIAN, JOHN F. S.	*DOCKET ONLY	176	GREENSBORO	04/25/73
JULIAN, PETER	*DOCKET ONLY	175	GREENSBORO	04/25/73
JUSTICE, WILLIAM D.	HENDERSON	73	ASHEVILLE	03/01/73
JUSTUS, W.D.	RUTHERFORD	532	WILMINGTON	01/04/69
KAHNWEILER & BROTHER	NEW HANOVER	10	WILMINGTON	09/07/67
KAKSTRAW, JOHN F.	*DOCKET ONLY	1032	NEW BERN	12/23/68
KALE, POLSER	CATAWBA	131	STATESVILLE	05/16/73
KALLAM, JAMES M.	*DOCKET ONLY	276	NEW BERN	02/08/68
KASSMOWICZ, WILLARD	NEW HANOVER	667	WILMINGTON	08/29/78
KATZ, MORRIS M.	NEW HANOVER	792	WILMINGTON	01/21/78
KEA & NEWELL	DUPLIN	477	WILMINGTON	12/31/68
KEATON, B.F.	PASQUOTANK	16	ELIZABETH CITY	08/22/67
KEATON, SILAS	IREDELL	189	STATESVILLE	06/09/73
KEATON, WILL F.	PASQUOTANK	30	ELIZABETH CITY	10/14/67
KEE, WILL F.	NORTHAMPTON	149	ELIZABETH CITY	02/21/68
KEELING, JOHN L.	*DOCKET ONLY	561	GREENSBORO	06/26/76
KEEN & KENNEDY	ROWAN	278	STATESVILLE	11/02/76
KEEN, JOHN R.	*DOCKET ONLY	870	NEW BERN	05/07/68
KEEN, SOLOMON	HERTFORD	134	ELIZABETH CITY	02/10/68
KEHR, AUGUSST	NEW HANOVER	186	WILMINGTON	04/18/69
KELLAM, BRYAN	*DOCKET ONLY	1439	NEW BERN	05/16/73
KELLER, JACOB	BURKE	139	STATESVILLE	05/21/73
KELLEY, GEORGE H.	ROBESON	266	WILMINGTON	05/30/68
KELLOGG, MOSES	*DOCKET ONLY	7	NEW BERN	08/09/67
KELLOGG, TIFT,		317	WILMINGTON	06/22/68

NORTH CAROLINA BANKRUPTS - ACT OF 1867

NAME OF BANKRUPT	RESIDENCE	CASE NUMBER	CITY OF COURT	DATE FILED
KELLY, A.C.	DAVIE	150	STATESVILLE	05/31/73
KELLY, JAMES A.	DAVIE	507	WILMINGTON	01/01/69
KELLY, JOHN O.	CAMDEN	105	ELIZABETH CITY	01/10/68
KENDRICK, JAMES M.	*DOCKET ONLY	698	GREENSBORO	08/31/78
KENDRICK, L. H.	CLEVELAND	146	STATESVILLE	05/23/73
KENNEDY, DOUGLAS	CUMBERLAND	824	WILMINGTON	05/09/78
KENNEDY, KEEN &	ROWAN	278	STATESVILLE	11/02/76
KENNEDY, RUFFIN	WILKES	71	STATESVILLE	03/21/73
KENNODLE, RUFUS W.	*DOCKET ONLY	433	NEW BERN	03/02/68
KEOUGH, RICHARD	CHOWAN	18	ELIZABETH CITY	08/27/67
KERCHNER, F.M.		544	WILMINGTON	02/27/69
KERNODLE, JOHN R.	*DOCKET ONLY	91	GREENSBORO	02/01/73
KERNS, & KERNS	*DOCKET ONLY	516	GREENSBORO	11/24/76
KERNS, JOHN P. &		266	STATESVILLE	10/10/74
KERR, J.W.A.	IREDELL	7	WILMINGTON	01/14/67
KERR, JAMES WIT	IREDELL	363	WILMINGTON	12/14/68
KIMBELL, JOSEPH W.	*DOCKET ONLY	1575	NEW BERN	03/20/74
KIMBRO, A. J.	*DOCKET ONLY	368	GREENSBORO	07/30/73
KIMRAY, N.R.	*DOCKET ONLY	185	GREENSBORO	05/02/73
KINBALL, WILLIAM J.	*DOCKET ONLY	537	NEW BERN	03/17/68
KINCEY, JESSE W.	*DOCKET ONLY	1717	NEW BERN	08/29/78
KINETT, S. W.	*DOCKET ONLY	436	GREENSBORO	11/05/73
KING, B. S.	*DOCKET ONLY	151	NEW BERN	12/31/67
KING, BARNABAS	RUTHERFORD	103	STATESVILLE	05/02/73
KING, BENJAMIN K.	HENDERSON	80	ASHEVILLE	01/28/73
KING, HENRY & JOSEPH	*DOCKET ONLY	523	NEW BERN	03/16/68
KING, JOHN	*DOCKET ONLY	277	NEW BERN	02/08/68
KINGSBERRY, RUSSELL	*DOCKET ONLY	1406	NEW BERN	01/14/73
KINGSMON, RICHARD S.	*DOCKET ONLY	1221	NEW BERN	12/26/68
KINSEY, JOB L.	*DOCKET ONLY	1217	NEW BERN	12/26/68
KINSEY, WILLIAM C.	*DOCKET ONLY	1473	NEW BERN	06/12/73
KINYON, DAVID W.	DAVIE	214	STATESVILLE	07/02/73
KINYONN, JOHN	YADKIN	82	WILMINGTON	02/13/68
KINYOUN, LEMUEL G.	DAVIE	317	STATESVILLE	08/09/78
KINZEY, ELIJAH W.	HENDERSON	81	ASHEVILLE	01/15/73
KIRKMAN, JOHN C.	*DOCKET ONLY	268	GREENSBORO	05/22/73
KIRKPATRICK, HUGH	*DOCKET ONLY	240	NEW BERN	01/31/68
KIRKPATRICK,	*DOCKET ONLY	508	GREENSBORO	12/19/75
KIRKSEY, ELIJAH J.	MCDOWELL	210	STATESVILLE	06/30/73
KISNEL, DAVID C.	*DOCKET ONLY	140	GREENSBORO	03/25/73
KITTRELL, EATON H.	*DOCKET ONLY	881	NEW BERN	08/19/68
KITTRELL, G. W.	*DOCKET ONLY	866	NEW BERN	06/22/68
KITTRELL, JOHN	GATES	96	ELIZABETH CITY	12/27/67
KIX, R. L.	WILKES	303	STATESVILLE	06/06/78
KLEINE, DANIEL	*DOCKET ONLY	580	GREENSBORO	05/18/77
KLUTTS, ROBSON	ROWAN	488	WILMINGTON	12/31/68
KLUTTS, SOLOMON	ROWAN	185	STATESVILLE	06/06/73
KLUTTTS, MICHAEL	ROWAN	324	STATESVILLE	08/29/78
KLYE, HENRY		578	WILMINGTON	06/06/70
KNIGHT, CHARLES E.	HERTFORD	525	ELIZABETH CITY	01/11/71
KNIGHT, JAMES W.	*DOCKET ONLY	425	NEW BERN	02/29/68
KNIGHT, JOHN L.	MARTIN	522	ELIZABETH CITY	01/24/71
KNIGHT, THOMAS W.	TYRRELL	8	ELIZABETH CITY	08/05/67
KNOX, R.R.	ROWAN	190	STATESVILLE	06/11/73
KNOX, WILLIAM	IREDELL	369	WILMINGTON	12/18/68
KOONCE, PHILIP	*DOCKET ONLY	1326	NEW BERN	02/16/71
KOOPMAN, BERNARD	MECKLENBURG	611	WILMINGTON	01/17/71
KOOPMAN, BERNHARD	*DOCKET ONLY	533	GREENSBORO	02/12/74
KOOPMAN, BERNHARD &	*DOCKET ONLY	493	GREENSBORO	06/07/75
KOSMINSKI, WILLIAM	*DOCKET ONLY	1665	NEW BERN	04/27/78
KRABEN, HENRY	CHOWAN	256	ELIZABETH CITY	01/03/74
KYLE, JESSP J.	CUMBERLAND	871	WILMINGTON	08/30/78
KYLE, JOHN	BUNCOMBE	194	WILMINGTON	04/29/68
LABARBE, AMOS P.	*DOCKET ONLY	519	NEW BERN	03/15/68
LACK, GEORGE	*DOCKET ONLY	597	NEW BERN	03/25/68
LACKEY, EDWARD	CLEVELAND	204	STATESVILLE	06/20/73

NAME OF BANKRUPT	RESIDENCE	CASE NUMBER	CITY OF COURT	DATE FILED
LAMB, LEMUEL W.	CAMDEN	193	ELIZABETH CITY	05/14/73
LAMB, WILSON G.	MARTIN	535	ELIZABETH CITY	08/19/71
LAMBERT, DUGALD A.	BLADEN	687	WILMINGTON	05/23/73
LAMN, WILLIE	WILSON	343	WILMINGTON	11/14/68
LAMOND, JAMES F. A.	*DOCKET ONLY	630	NEW BERN	04/07/68
LAMONT, MALCOLM C.	CUMBERLAND	269	WILMINGTON	05/30/68
LANAE, WILLIAM K.	*DOCKET ONLY	430	NEW BERN	02/29/68
LANCASTER, B. J.	*DOCKET ONLY	1249	NEW BERN	12/31/68
LANCASTIRE, JAMES W.	CUMBERLAND	615	WILMINGTON	04/30/78
LAND, WILLIAMSON H.	*DOCKET ONLY	436	NEW BERN	03/02/68
LANDEN, WILLIAM	ONSLOW	733	WILMINGTON	06/27/73
LANDLIN, HENRY H.	*DOCKET ONLY	1395	NEW BERN	10/17/72
LANE, B.B.	*DOCKET ONLY	1507	NEW BERN	09/09/73
LANE, ENOCH H.	*DOCKET ONLY	1426	NEW BERN	04/29/73
LANE, FRANK D	*DOCKET ONLY	144	NEW BERN	12/31/67
LANE, HENBY J.	PASQUOTANK	633	ELIZABETH CITY	02/19/71
LANE, W.W.	NEW HANOVER	43	WILMINGTON	01/22/68
LANE, WILLIAM A.	*DOCKET ONLY	1542	NEW BERN	12/17/03
LANE, WILLIAM F.	*DOCKET ONLY	748	NEW BERN	05/29/68
LANE, WILLIAM K.	*DOCKET ONLY	821	NEW BERN	05/30/68
LANEY, ARCHIBALD B.	LINCOLN	361	WILMINGTON	12/14/68
LANEY, CALVIN	*DOCKET ONLY	152	GREENSBORO	04/09/73
LANG, ISAAC	*DOCKET ONLY	264	NEW BERN	02/07/68
LANGEENOUR, LEWIS C.	*DOCKET ONLY	1335	NEW BERN	03/23/71
LANGFORD, JAMES	NORTHAMPTON	572	ELIZABETH CITY	05/07/73
LANGFORD, JAMES	NORTHAMPTON	199	ELIZABETH CITY	05/13/73
LANGLEY, WILLIAM A.	*DOCKET ONLY	708	NEW BERN	05/26/68
LANGSTON, THOMAS B.	GATES	543	ELIZABETH CITY	12/10/68
LANIER, JAMES	MECKLENBURG	586	WILMINGTON	09/29/70
LANIER, ROBERT M.	STANLY	229	WILMINGTON	05/25/68
LANNIER, THOMAS A.	NORTHAMPTON	367	ELIZABETH CITY	04/17/68
LAPLIN, BYNON	*DOCKET ONLY	1337	NEW BERN	04/18/71
LASSITER, BRYANT	NORTHAMPTON	375	ELIZABETH CITY	09/12/68
LASSITER, CALEB	NORTHAMPTON	365	ELIZABETH CITY	10/02/68
LASSITER, H.E.	PASQUOTANK	343	ELIZABETH CITY	08/28/78
LASSITER, JAMES L.	NORTHAMPTON	212	ELIZABETH CITY	06/11/73
LASSITER, JAMES P.	NORTHAMPTON	372	ELIZABETH CITY	10/02/68
LASSITER, JAMES S.	NORTHAMPTON	591	ELIZABETH CITY	06/09/72
LASSITER, MOSES M.	HERTFORD	128	ELIZABETH CITY	02/05/68
LASSITER, ROBERT	*DOCKET ONLY	1635	NEW BERN	11/29/76
LASSITER, ROBERT W.	*DOCKET ONLY	1396	NEW BERN	10/19/72
LASSITER, S.M.	NORTHAMPTON	302	ELIZABETH CITY	03/29/76
LATHAM, ALEXANDER C.	*DOCKET ONLY	188	NEW BERN	01/08/68
LATHAM, AUGUSTUS	*DOCKET ONLY	1331	NEW BERN	03/12/71
LATHAM, DEMPREY, H.	*DOCKET ONLY	1051	NEW BERN	12/23/68
LATHAM, EDGAR R.	WASHINGTON	543	ELIZABETH CITY	06/21/72
LATHAM, NORFLEET F.	*DOCKET ONLY	1124	NEW BERN	12/30/68
LATON, JOHN H.	*DOCKET ONLY	942	NEW BERN	10/12/68
LATTA, JAMES C.	*DOCKET ONLY	132	NEW BERN	12/28/67
LATTA, JOSEPH	*DOCKET ONLY	125	NEW BERN	12/28/67
LAUGHTER, J. J.	HENDERSON	91	ASHEVILLE	04/12/73
LAUGHLIN, DANIEL M.	*DOCKET ONLY	1045	NEW BERN	12/24/68
LAUGHTER, S. L. (88)	HENDERSON	92	ASHEVILLE	06/02/73
LAURANCE, JACOB	RUTHERFORD	71	WILMINGTON	02/10/69
LAURIN, DUNCAN	CUMBERLAND	454	WILMINGTON	12/31/68
LAWRENCE, BENNETT B.	*DOCKET ONLY	141	NEW BERN	12/31/67
LAWRENCE, GEORGE W.	CUMBERLAND	14	WILMINGTON	11/01/67
LAWRENCE, GEORGE W.	CUMBERLAND	17	WILMINGTON	11/07/67
LAWRENCE, J. J.	*DOCKET ONLY	1614	NEW BERN	10/21/75
LAWRENCE, JAMES H.	*DOCKET ONLY	1039	NEW BERN	12/22/68
LAWRENCE, THOMAS N.	*DOCKET ONLY	1451	NEW BERN	05/21/73
LAWRENCE, WILLIAM	*DOCKET ONLY	201	GREENSBORO	05/05/73
LAWREY, DABUEY L.	DAVIE	277	STATESVILLE	05/13/76
LAWRY, JAMES M.	BUNCOMBE	82	ASHEVILLE	05/06/73
LAWS, ROBERT	*DOCKET ONLY	688	GREENSBORO	06/01/78
LAWSON, J. J.	*DOCKET ONLY	745	NEW BERN	05/29/68

NORTH CAROLINA BANKRUPTS - ACT OF 1867

NAME OF BANKRUPT	RESIDENCE	CASE NUMBER	CITY OF COURT	DATE FILED
LAY, WILLIAM, H.	*DOCKET ONLY	654	GREENSBORO	08/27/78
LEA, AVILLA	*DOCKET ONLY	499	NEW BERN	03/07/69
LEA, JAMES	*DOCKET ONLY	324	NEW BERN	02/21/69
LEACH, J. Q. A.	*DOCKET ONLY	667	NEW BERN	06/22/68
LEACH, JOHN &	ROBESON	610	WILMINGTON	04/12/78
LEAK, JAMES H.	*DOCKET ONLY	670	GREENSBORO	08/30/78
LEAK, JAMES R.	NORTHAMPTON	373	ELIZABETH CITY	09/29/68
LEARY & BROTHERS	CHOWAN	635	ELIZABETH CITY	05/19/76
LEARY, JOSEPH	BERTIE	258	ELIZABETH CITY	01/09/74
LEARY, SAMUEL	CAMDEN	75	ELIZABETH CITY	12/11/67
LEARY, WALTER J.	CHOWAN	185	ELIZABETH CITY	05/19/76
LEARY, WEST	CHOWAN	442	ELIZABETH CITY	12/28/68
LEARY, WEST R.	CHOWAN	481	ELIZABETH CITY	12/29/68
LEATHERS, JAMES S.	*DOCKET ONLY	539	NEW BERN	03/17/68
LEATHERS, JOHN	*DOCKET ONLY	351	NEW BERN	02/24/68
LEATHERS, JOHN B.	*DOCKET ONLY	538	NEW BERN	03/17/68
LEAVISTER, GEORGE T.	*DOCKET ONLY	611	NEW BERN	04/01/68
LEDBETTER, DAVID T.	HENDERSON	87	ASHEVILLE	06/19/73
LEDBETTER, GEORGE W.	HENDERSON	89	ASHEVILLE	06/19/73
LEDBETTER, THOMAS	HENDERSON	90	ASHEVILLE	08/22/78
LEDBETTER, WILLIAM	HENDERSON	63	ASHEVILLE	01/10/73
LEE, D.M.	CHOWAN	254	ELIZABETH CITY	01/03/73
LEE, JAMES R.		625	WILMINGTON	04/26/71
LEE, R. H.	*DOCKET ONLY	57	NEW BERN	11/10/67
LEE, WILL H.	GATES	169	ELIZABETH CITY	02/28/68
LEGGETT, ALFRED	*DOCKET ONLY	1356	NEW BERN	09/06/71
LEGGETT, BENJAMIN F.	*DOCKET ONLY	1495	NEW BERN	07/19/73
LEGGETT, BLOUNT	*DOCKET ONLY	1509	NEW BERN	08/14/73
LEGGETT, JOHN	NEW HANOVER	409	WILMINGTON	12/28/68
LEHMAN, BERTHA		661	WILMINGTON	03/29/71
LEHMAN, H. R.	*DOCKET ONLY	238	GREENSBORO	05/12/73
LEIGH, JOHN H.	*DOCKET ONLY	758	NEW BERN	06/02/68
LELAND, JERMSON A.	*DOCKET ONLY	8	NEW BERN	08/28/67
LEMMOND, JOHN Q.	*DOCKET ONLY	390	GREENSBORO	07/24/73
LEMMOND, CYRUS Q	*DOCKET ONLY	31	GREENSBORO	12/02/72
LENELEY, W.A.		603	WILMINGTON	11/24/70
LENNON, JOHN P.	BRUNSWICK	742	WILMINGTON	07/17/73
LENTON, JAMES C.	*DOCKET ONLY	115	NEW BERN	12/20/67
LENTZ, ABRAM	ROWAN	302	STATESVILLE	05/31/78
LENTZ, ADAM	ROWAN	320	STATESVILLE	08/23/78
LEOG, SOLOMON	NEW HANOVER	768	WILMINGTON	02/19/74
LEOG, SOLOMON	NEW HANOVER	769	WILMINGTON	04/23/74
LEONARD, DANIEL	*DOCKET ONLY	39	GREENSBORO	12/06/72
LEONARD, DAVID	*DOCKET ONLY	130	GREENSBORO	03/06/73
LEONARD, ELI	*DOCKET ONLY	52	GREENSBORO	11/04/73
LESTER, THOMAS J.	HENDERSON	535	WILMINGTON	01/06/69
LEVY, LEOPOLD	*DOCKET ONLY	1704	NEW BERN	08/27/78
LEWIS, ABNER	*DOCKET ONLY	185	NEW BERN	01/13/68
LEWIS, CULLEN	*DOCKET ONLY	583	NEW BERN	01/19/68
LEWIS, DURHAM	ROBESON	732	WILMINGTON	06/27/73
LEWIS, HOLDEN	HARNETT	679	WILMINGTON	05/03/73
LEWIS, JOHN G.	GASTON	193	STATESVILLE	06/11/73
LEWIS, JOHN L	*DOCKET ONLY	1724	NEW BERN	08/31/78
LEWIS, JOHN W.	HERTFORD	148	ELIZABETH CITY	02/21/68
LEWIS, N. M.	*DOCKET ONLY	151	GREENSBORO	04/08/73
LEWIS, RICHARD	BLADEN	674	WILMINGTON	02/12/72
LEWIS, SPENCER C.	*DOCKET ONLY	564	NEW BERN	03/19/68
LEWIS, WATSON	BERTIE	323	ELIZABETH CITY	01/12/78
LEWIS, WILLIAM	*DOCKET ONLY	822	NEW BERN	05/30/68
LEWIS, WILLIAM F.	*DOCKET ONLY	194	GREENSBORO	05/02/73
LIDDLE, W. J. F.	*DOCKET ONLY	568	GREENSBORO	11/28/77
LIGEN, ELIAS L	DAVIDSON	214	WILMINGTON	05/19/69
LILES & MEACHUM	ANSON	136	WILMINGTON	03/12/68
LILES, D N.	*DOCKET ONLY	132	GREENSBORO	03/10/73
LILES, EDWARD R.	ANSON	217	WILMINGTON	05/21/68
LILLARD, JAMES W.	*DOCKET ONLY	482	GREENSBORO	03/16/75

NORTH CAROLINA BANKRUPTS - ACT OF 1867

NAME OF BANKRUPT	RESIDENCE	CASE NUMBER	CITY OF COURT	DATE FILED
LILLEY, EDMOND	ROBESON	233	WILMINGTON	05/25/68
LILLY, CALVIN J.	*DOCKET ONLY	470	GREENSBORO	03/28/74
LILLY, CALVIN J.	*DOCKET ONLY	544	GREENSBORO	03/28/74
LINCOLN IRON COMPANY		580	WILMINGTON	07/07/70
LINDLEY, FRANKLIN D	*DOCKET ONLY	778	NEW BERN	08/19/68
LINDLEY, OWEN	*DOCKET ONLY	111	GREENSBORO	02/06/73
LINDSAY, LEWIS	*DOCKET ONLY	469	NEW BERN	03/04/68
LINDSAY, WILLIAM A.	*DOCKET ONLY	85	GREENSBORO	01/30/73
LINDSEY, CHARLEY B.	ANSON	182	WILMINGTON	04/15/68
LINDSEY, D. MCD.	CURRITUCK	90	ELIZABETH CITY	12/25/67
LINDSY, ALEXANDER H.	*DOCKET ONLY	554	GREENSBORO	03/04/78
LINEBERG, ELWOOD B.	*DOCKET ONLY	369	NEW BERN	02/24/68
LINEBERRY, WILLIAM	*DOCKET ONLY	301	GREENSBORO	05/29/73
LINEBERY, ZECHIRRAH	*DOCKET ONLY	52	NEW BERN	11/14/67
LINEBURGER, JONAS R.	GASTON	267	STATESVILLE	11/05/74
LINGLE, T. C. & A.	*DOCKET ONLY	559	GREENSBORO	05/10/78
LINKER, ISAAC S.	*DOCKET ONLY	66	GREENSBORO	01/20/73
LINN, DAVID M.	ROWAN	99	WILMINGTON	02/25/68
LINSTER, FRED F.	ROWAN	521	WILMINGTON	01/01/69
LIPE, LEVI	*DOCKET ONLY	460	GREENSBORO	02/14/74
LIPPARD, J. H. A	ROWAN	25	STATESVILLE	01/12/73
LIPSCOMB, OSWALD	*DOCKET ONLY	759	NEW BERN	05/29/68
LISSNER, MARCUS	CUMBERLAND	35	WILMINGTON	01/10/68
LISTER, J.S.	PASQUOTANK	277	ELIZABETH CITY	05/29/68
LITLE, WILLIAM P.		635	WILMINGTON	06/15/71
LITTLE & COMPANY	*DOCKET ONLY	1673	NEW BERN	05/25/78
LITTLE, GEORGE E.	*DOCKET ONLY	1605	NEW BERN	05/15/75
LITTLE, JACOB S.	*DOCKET ONLY	364	GREENSBORO	06/30/73
LITTLE, JOHN G. A.	*DOCKET ONLY	134	GREENSBORO	03/12/73
LITTLE, LEONIDAS	*DOCKET ONLY	1673	NEW BERN	05/25/78
LITTLE, WILLIAM P.		627	WILMINGTON	03/29/71
LITTLE, WILLIAM W.	*DOCKET ONLY	1518	NEW BERN	08/23/73
LITTLEFIELD, MILTON	*DOCKET ONLY	1266	NEW BERN	03/14/70
LIVINGSTON, JOSEPH	HENDERSON	93	ASHEVILLE	01/16/73
LLOYD, SATTIE	BLADEN	478	WILMINGTON	12/31/68
LLOYD, THOMAS M.	*DOCKET ONLY	129	NEW BERN	12/28/67
LLOYD, WILLIAM	*DOCKET ONLY	129	NEW BERN	12/28/67
LOADER, ROBERT	*DOCKET ONLY	96	NEW BERN	12/09/67
LOCKANEY, NATHAN	SAMPSON	697	WILMINGTON	05/30/73
LOCKANEY, WILLIAM	SAMPSON	701	WILMINGTON	05/30/73
LOCKANEY, WILSON	SAMPSON	705	WILMINGTON	05/30/73
LOCKHART, JOSEPH G.	*DOCKET ONLY	350	NEW BERN	02/24/68
LOCKHART, WILLIAM	*DOCKET ONLY	581	NEW BERN	03/19/68
LOEB, ADOLPH & JACOB	NEW HANOVER	854	WILMINGTON	08/21/78
LOFTEN, WILLIAM F.	*DOCKET ONLY	1683	NEW BERN	07/02/78
LOFTIS, A. A.	*DOCKET ONLY	797	NEW BERN	05/30/68
LOFTIS, A. J. (125)	TRANSYLVANIA	94	ASHEVILLE	06/12/74
LONDON, HENRY A.	*DOCKET ONLY	992	NEW BERN	12/09/68
LONDON, MANGER	NEW HANOVER	833	WILMINGTON	05/29/78
LONG & BERNHEIMER		656	WILMINGTON	02/21/72
LONG, ALFRED	*DOCKET ONLY	455	GREENSBORO	02/05/74
LONG, DAVID	*DOCKET ONLY	648	GREENSBORO	08/27/78
LONG, EDWIN	*DOCKET ONLY	669	NEW BERN	06/22/68
LONG, HENRY	UNION	175	WILMINGTON	03/13/68
LONG, ISAAC (JR)	*DOCKET ONLY	406	GREENSBORO	08/25/73
LONG, J. D.	*DOCKET ONLY	945	NEW BERN	10/20/68
LONG, JAMES K	NORTHAMPTON	368	ELIZABETH CITY	08/17/68
LONG, JOHN	*DOCKET ONLY	399	NEW BERN	02/28/68
LONG, LAWSON H.	*DOCKET ONLY	153	GREENSBORO	04/14/73
LONG, NEWTON J.	CLEVELAND	104	STATESVILLE	05/02/73
LONG, RICHMOND	RICHMOND	337	WILMINGTON	11/02/68
LONG, THOMAS B.	ROWAN	327	STATESVILLE	08/29/78
LONG, THOMAS B.	*DOCKET ONLY	908	NEW BERN	08/25/68
LONG, THOMAS, DOCTOR	YADKIN	349	WILMINGTON	11/28/68
LONG, W.W.	YADKIN	312	WILMINGTON	05/30/68
LORNE, CARNADY	*DOCKET ONLY	94	NEW BERN	12/06/67

NAME OF BANKRUPT	RESIDENCE	CASE NUMBER	CITY OF COURT	DATE FILED
LOUDERMILK, RANSON	*DOCKET ONLY	398	NEW BERN	02/28/68
LOUGENOUR, ANDREW L.	*DOCKET ONLY	112	GREENSBORO	02/07/73
LOUGENOUR, LEWIS C.	*DOCKET ONLY	520	GREENSBORO	04/25/73
LOVE & OVENBAUGH	CUMBERLAND	571	WILMINGTON	04/09/70
LOVE, ROBERT (17)	HENDERSON	84	ASHEVILLE	08/22/73
LOVELACE, P.M.	ASHE	496	WILMINGTON	12/31/68
LOVIN, SQUIRE B.	RICHMOND	150	WILMINGTON	03/17/68
LOVINGGOOD, H.	CHEROKEE	225	WILMINGTON	05/23/68
LOVINGGOOD, HARMON	CHEROKEE	86	ASHEVILLE	03/27/75
LOWD, C. L. & C. G.	*DOCKET ONLY	587	GREENSBORO	12/14/76
LOWE, JACKSON	MARTIN	273	ELIZABETH CITY	05/29/68
LOWE, RICHARD N.	*DOCKET ONLY	323	NEW BERN	02/21/68
LOWE, STEPHEN	*DOCKET ONLY	99	NEW BERN	12/12/67
LOWE, THOMAS O.	PASQUOTANK	299	ELIZABETH CITY	06/01/68
LOWE, W. M.	*DOCKET ONLY	116	NEW BERN	12/25/67
LOWENBERG, CHARLES &	*DOCKET ONLY	1292	NEW BERN	09/09/70
LOWRY, ALLEN	*DOCKET ONLY	117	GREENSBORO	02/12/73
LOWRY, S. P.	*DOCKET ONLY	468	NEW BERN	03/04/68
LOWTHEN, SAMUEL J.	GATES	313	ELIZABETH CITY	10/24/76
LOY, G. H.	*DOCKET ONLY	322	NEW BERN	02/21/68
LOYD, ANDREW G. R.	*DOCKET ONLY	68	NEW BERN	11/04/67
LOYD, GREEN	*DOCKET ONLY	121	NEW BERN	12/28/67
LOYNS, A. W.	*DOCKET ONLY	698	GREENSBORO	05/28/78
LUCA, DAVID	*DOCKET ONLY	1580	NEW BERN	05/08/74
LUCAS, JOHN J.D.	BLADEN	797	WILMINGTON	03/10/76
LUCK, WILLIAM	*DOCKET ONLY	197	GREENSBORO	05/02/73
LUDEWICK	ROWAN	309	STATESVILLE	08/15/78
LUMSFORD, JAMES N.	*DOCKET ONLY	269	NEW BERN	02/07/68
LUNSFORD, COLLEY	*DOCKET ONLY	226	NEW BERN	01/28/68
LUNSFORD, J. A. & A.	*DOCKET ONLY	607	NEW BERN	04/01/68
LUNSFORD, JAMES N.	*DOCKET ONLY	353	NEW BERN	02/24/68
LUNSFORD, WALTER H.	*DOCKET ONLY	196	NEW BERN	01/17/68
LUSH, J.G		604	WILMINGTON	11/24/70
LUSK, JOSEPH	GASTON	435	WILMINGTON	12/30/68
LYDA, DAVID M. (35)	HENDERSON	85	ASHEVILLE	04/07/73
LYNCH, ADOLPHAS B.	*DOCKET ONLY	352	NEW BERN	02/24/68
LYNCH, LEMON	*DOCKET ONLY	470	NEW BERN	03/04/68
LYON, ELKANAH E.	*DOCKET ONLY	1310	NEW BERN	12/05/70
LYON, JACOB		775	WILMINGTON	09/07/74
LYON, JOEL	DAVIE	174	STATESVILLE	05/30/73
LYON, THOMAS B.	*DOCKET ONLY	1309	NEW BERN	12/05/70
LYON, WILLIAM H.	PASQUOTANK	252	ELIZABETH CITY	05/11/68
LYTLE, JOHN	MCDOWELL	227	STATESVILLE	07/20/73
LYTLE, MILLINGTON	BUNCOMBE	88	ASHEVILLE	05/10/73
LYTTE, JAMES	HENDERSON	364	WILMINGTON	12/16/68
MABRY, JOHN P.	*DOCKET ONLY	170	NEW BERN	01/09/68
MACK, JACOB &		789	WILMINGTON	12/31/75
MACKS, ISAAC &		632	ELIZABETH CITY	01/29/76
MACKS, JACOB & ISAAC		632	ELIZABETH CITY	01/29/76
MACNAIR, COLIN	*DOCKET ONLY	510	NEW BERN	03/11/68
MACNAIR, R. E.	*DOCKET ONLY	180	NEW BERN	01/10/68
MACNAIR, W. T.	*DOCKET ONLY	687	NEW BERN	05/06/68
MACON, THOMAS B.	*DOCKET ONLY	911	NEW BERN	08/22/68
MACRAE, JAMES C.		645	WILMINGTON	11/23/71
MADISON, LEWIS F.	IREDELL	90	STATESVILLE	04/30/73
MAGET, JAMES H.	HERTFORD	472	ELIZABETH CITY	12/21/68
MAGET, JAMES H.	NORTHAMPTON	636	ELIZABETH CITY	12/31/68
MALLARD, JOHN C.	DUPLIN	612	WILMINGTON	01/21/71
MALLETT & HOFFMAN	NEW HANOVER	117	WILMINGTON	03/02/68
MALLETT, CHARLEY B.	CUMBERLAND	40	WILMINGTON	01/17/68
MALLETT, WILLIAM	*DOCKET ONLY	4	NEW BERN	07/23/67
MALLONY, FRANCIE	HALIFAX	423	ELIZABETH CITY	12/21/68
MALLONY, JOHN T.	*DOCKET ONLY	137	NEW BERN	12/28/67
MALLORY, WILLIAM	*DOCKET ONLY	993	NEW BERN	12/15/68
MALLOY, DAVID M.	*DOCKET ONLY	370	NEW BERN	02/24/68
MANARD, W. C.	*DOCKET ONLY	135	NEW BERN	12/28/67

NAME OF BANKRUPT	RESIDENCE	CASE NUMBER	CITY OF COURT	DATE FILED
MANCH, JOHN A.	*DOCKET ONLY	169	NEW BERN	01/09/68
MANER, JOHN	*DOCKET ONLY	120	NEW BERN	12/28/67
MANGUM, WESLEY B.	MARTIN	233	ELIZABETH CITY	08/14/73
MANGUM, WILLIAM C.	*DOCKET ONLY	354	NEW BERN	02/24/68
MANLEY, RUFUS R.	*DOCKET ONLY	381	GREENSBORO	07/14/73
MANN, ROBERT N.	*DOCKET ONLY	64	GREENSBORO	01/17/73
MANN, SAMUEL	DARE	193	ELIZABETH CITY	05/14/73
MANN, WILLIAM S.	*DOCKET ONLY	1518	NEW BERN	09/06/73
MANNEY, E. & SON		665	WILMINGTON	06/06/72
MANNING, WILLIAN H.	GATES	427	ELIZABETH CITY	12/24/68
MANTLSBY, WILLIAM	BLADEN	884	WILMINGTON	05/17/73
MANWELL, JAMES	*DOCKET ONLY	1863	NEW BERN	04/22/78
MARABLE, JOHN R.	SAMPSON	190	WILMINGTON	04/21/68
MARCUS & COHEN	*DOCKET ONLY	1854	NEW BERN	01/20/78
MARCUS, HERMAN		325	WILMINGTON	06/25/68
MARCUS, HERMAN	NEW HANOVER	449	WILMINGTON	12/30/68
MARKETT, FREDERICK	*DOCKET ONLY	1587	NEW BERN	02/16/74
MARKHAM, THOMAS	PASQUOTANK	292	ELIZABETH CITY	06/01/69
MARKS, JSOEPH	*DOCKET ONLY	1850	NEW BERN	11/15/77
MARKS, O.	*DOCKET ONLY	926	NEW BERN	09/14/68
MARLEY, WILLIAM B.	*DOCKET ONLY	1166	NEW BERN	12/31/68
MARLIN, WILLIAM F.	ROWAN	335	WILMINGTON	10/16/69
MARROW, T. H. & H.	*DOCKET ONLY	598	NEW BERN	03/25/68
MARSALL, ZAPHARRIAH	*DOCKET ONLY	1430	NEW BERN	05/12/73
MARSH, ABNER B.	*DOCKET ONLY	307	GREENSBORO	05/29/73
MARSH, CREW &	*DOCKET ONLY	635	GREENSBORO	08/27/78
MARSH, JOHN ROBIN	*DOCKET ONLY	910	NEW BERN	08/25/68
MARTIN, BREM &	*DOCKET ONLY	691	GREENSBORO	01/01/80
MARTIN, D.L.		250	ELIZABETH CITY	12/26/73
MARTIN, E.A.	NORTHAMPTON	370	ELIZABETH CITY	11/11/68
MARTIN, HENRY	*DOCKET ONLY	1212	NEW BERN	12/31/68
MARTIN, JAMES	*DOCKET ONLY	222	GREENSBORO	05/11/73
MARTIN, JOHN W.	*DOCKET ONLY	497	GREENSBORO	07/09/75
MARTIN, LELAND	WILKES	596	WILMINGTON	12/31/70
MARTIN, NICHOLAS	*DOCKET ONLY	478	GREENSBORO	01/01/75
MARTIN, P. R.	DAVIE	272	STATESVILLE	06/25/75
MARTIN, P.H.	*DOCKET ONLY	678	GREENSBORO	08/31/78
MARTIN, RICHARD	*DOCKET ONLY	651	GREENSBORO	08/27/78
MARTIN, THOMAS J.	YADKIN	314	WILMINGTON	05/30/68
MARTIN, WILLIAM F.	*DOCKET ONLY	118	GREENSBORO	02/13/73
MARTINDALE &	CHOWAN	627	ELIZABETH CITY	10/19/69
MASER, SIMON	*DOCKET ONLY	261	GREENSBORO	05/21/73
MASON, G.G.	DAVIE	78	STATESVILLE	04/04/73
MASON, JOHN E.	*DOCKET ONLY	81	NEW BERN	11/30/67
MASSENBERG, W. P.	*DOCKET ONLY	1365	NEW BERN	11/21/71
MASSEY, JAMES	*DOCKET ONLY	21	GREENSBORO	11/04/72
MASSEY, RUFUS H.	*DOCKET ONLY	747	NEW BERN	05/29/68
MASSEY, RUFUS N.	*DOCKET ONLY	532	GREENSBORO	04/02/74
MASTEN; WILLIAM	WILKES	215	STATESVILLE	07/02/73
MATEER, JAMES M.	*DOCKET ONLY	124	GREENSBORO	02/26/73
MATHERSON, NATHAN	HALIFAX	231	ELIZABETH CITY	07/14/73
MATHEWS, JAMES E.	STOKES	250	WILMINGTON	05/29/68
MATHEWS, W.G.	CUMBERLAND	799	WILMINGTON	07/15/75
MATHWES, THOMAS W.	*DOCKET ONLY	472	NEW BERN	03/04/68
MATTHESON	MECKLENBURG	508	WILMINGTON	01/01/69
MATTHEW; JAMES M.	CUMBERLAND	782	WILMINGTON	08/19/75
MATTHEWS, DAVIS M.	*DOCKET ONLY	748	NEW BERN	05/29/68
MATTHEWS, GEORGE S.	FORSYTH	263	WILMINGTON	05/30/68
MATTHEWS, H. M. P.	*DOCKET ONLY	320	GREENSBORO	06/05/73
MATTHEWS, MARTINDALE	CHOWAN	627	ELIZABETH CITY	10/19/69
MATTHEWS, W. W.	*DOCKET ONLY	138	GREENSBORO	03/13/73
MATTOCKS, E, W & W.	*DOCKET ONLY	634	NEW BERN	04/17/68
MATTOCKS, JAMES A.	*DOCKET ONLY	1069	NEW BERN	12/26/68
MAULTSBY, THOMAS N.	BLADEN	757	WILMINGTON	11/28/73
MAXWELL, ALFORD	*DOCKET ONLY	371	NEW BERN	02/24/68
MAXWELL, JOHN S.	DAVIE	241	STATESVILLE	10/24/73

NORTH CAROLINA BANKRUPTS - ACT OF 1867

NAME OF BANKRUPT	RESIDENCE	CASE NUMBER	CITY OF COURT	DATE FILED
MAXWELL, R.H.	MECKLENBURG	522	WILMINGTON	01/01/69
MAXWELL, SAMUEL	HENDERSON	365	WILMINGTON	12/16/68
MAY, ANDREW JACKSON	*DOCKET ONLY	1597	NEW BERN	02/03/75
MAY, G. W.	*DOCKET ONLY	143	GREENSBORO	03/27/73
MAY, G. W.	*DOCKET ONLY	242	NEW BERN	01/31/68
MAY, WILLIAM H.	*DOCKET ONLY	376	NEW BERN	02/25/68
MAYBERRY, ABRAHAM	ALEXANDER	144	STATESVILLE	05/22/73
MAYBERRY, FRANKLIN	ALEXANDER	145	STATESVILLE	05/22/73
MAYER, FEIST	NEW HANOVER	293	WILMINGTON	05/30/68
MAYER, NATHAN	CUMBERLAND	852	WILMINGTON	08/19/78
MAYERS, W. W.	*DOCKET ONLY	1688	NEW BERN	05/01/78
MAYNARD, RICHARD	*DOCKET ONLY	211	GREENSBORO	05/07/73
MAYNARDS, ROBERT	*DOCKET ONLY	562	NEW BERN	03/19/68
MCADAMS, JAMES	*DOCKET ONLY	435	NEW BERN	03/02/68
MCALL, ALEXANDER	TRANSYLVANIA	107	ASHEVILLE	06/11/73
MCBRAYER, ELISHA	CLEVELAND	438	WILMINGTON	12/30/68
MCCAIN, DAVID	*DOCKET ONLY	1189	NEW BERN	12/30/68
MCCAIN, HUGH	*DOCKET ONLY	249	NEW BERN	01/31/68
MCCALL, J. A. (85)	TRANSYLVANIA	106	ASHEVILLE	06/02/73
MCCALL, JAMES N.	TRANSYLVANIA	102	ASHEVILLE	06/02/73
MCCALL, JOHN N.		754	WILMINGTON	10/29/73
MCCALL, SOLOMAN D.	ROBESON	354	WILMINGTON	12/07/68
MCCAULEY, STEUHOUSE	*DOCKET ONLY	615	GREENSBORO	04/26/78
MCCLAIN, JOEL M.	CUMBERLAND	641	WILMINGTON	09/18/71
MCCLOER, JAMES G.	*DOCKET ONLY	448	NEW BERN	03/02/68
MCCLUMB, THOMAS	SAMPSON	706	WILMINGTON	05/31/73
MCCLUSE, CHARLES	TYRRELL	178	ELIZABETH CITY	04/29/68
MCCOLLUM, JOHN Y.	*DOCKET ONLY	301	NEW BERN	02/17/68
MCCONNAGHEY, J.G.	ROWAN	394	WILMINGTON	12/26/68
MCCONNAUGHEY, JOHN	ROWAN	206	STATESVILLE	05/25/73
MCCORMIC, DANIEL M.	ROBESON	329	WILMINGTON	09/14/68
MCCORMICK, JAMES	NEW HANOVER	45	WILMINGTON	01/22/68
MCCOY, JAMES C.	CHOWAN	272	ELIZABETH CITY	05/30/68
MCCRARY, SPENCER W.	*DOCKET ONLY	325	NEW BERN	02/21/68
MCCRAW, A. P.	CLEVELAND	200	STATESVILLE	06/20/73
MCCRAY, DOLPHUS	HENDERSON	109	ASHEVILLE	03/27/75
MCCUBBING, BELL &	*DOCKET ONLY	575	GREENSBORO	12/22/76
MCCUBBINS, JOHN A	DAVIE	331	STATESVILLE	08/31/78
MCCULLEN, B.	*DOCKET ONLY	1686	NEW BERN	07/18/78
MCCULLOCH, CALVIN	*DOCKET ONLY	447	NEW BERN	03/02/68
MCCULLOCH, JOHN	*DOCKET ONLY	241	NEW BERN	01/31/68
MCCURDY, JOHN R.	CHOWAN	447	ELIZABETH CITY	12/29/68
MCDADE, PATTERSON H.	*DOCKET ONLY	87	NEW BERN	11/23/67
MCDANIEL, FURNIFOLD	*DOCKET ONLY	1427	NEW BERN	05/02/73
MCDANIEL, JAMES W.	*DOCKET ONLY	209	NEW BERN	01/21/68
MCDANIEL, PETER	NORTHAMPTON	409	ELIZABETH CITY	12/17/68
MCDANIEL, STARKEY	*DOCKET ONLY	1532	NEW BERN	11/11/73
MCDANIEL, WILLIAM	*DOCKET ONLY	192	NEW BERN	01/17/68
MCDONALD, ANDREW	MACON	344	WILMINGTON	11/20/68
MCDOUGALD, AKEX	ROBESON	590	WILMINGTON	10/05/70
MCDOUGALD, JOHN	MCDOWELL	328	STATESVILLE	08/30/78
MCDOWELL, ELISHA C.	HALIFAX	383	ELIZABETH CITY	11/16/68
MCDOWELL, JOHN N.	*DOCKET ONLY	1152	NEW BERN	12/30/68
MCDOWELL, JOSEPH A	BUNCOMBE	254	WILMINGTON	05/29/68
MCDUFFIE, GEORGE	NEW HANOVER	476	WILMINGTON	12/31/68
MCEACHIN, JOHN	ROBESON	828	WILMINGTON	05/17/78
MCEASTMAN, WILLIAM	*DOCKET ONLY	1497	NEW BERN	07/23/73
MCELRUTH, JOHN W.	BUNCOMBE	405	WILMINGTON	12/26/68
MCENTIRE, WILLIAM P.	RUTHERFORD	222	STATESVILLE	07/14/73
MCENTYRE, JOHN Y.	RUTHERFORD	47	STATESVILLE	02/18/73
MCERATH, ROBERT J.	BURKE	158	STATESVILLE	05/26/73
MCFALLS, ARTHUR	HAYWOOD	100	ASHEVILLE	12/29/74
MCGEE, DANIEL D.	CATAWBA	132	STATESVILLE	05/19/73
MCGEE, W. H.	*DOCKET ONLY	355	NEW BERN	02/24/68
MCGIBBONY, JOHN	*DOCKET ONLY	443	NEW BERN	03/02/68
MCGILL, ARCHIBALD D.	CUMBERLAND	820	WILMINGTON	05/02/78

NAME OF BANKRUPT	RESIDENCE	CASE NUMBER	CITY OF COURT	DATE FILED
MCGILL, NEIL	BLADEN	698	WILMINGTON	05/30/73
MCGILL, THOMAS R.	UNION	171	WILMINGTON	04/08/68
MCGLAWHORN, JERRY	*DOCKET ONLY	1470	NEW BERN	06/10/73
MCGOWAN, JOAMES W.	*DOCKET ONLY	850	NEW BERN	04/20/68
MCGREGOR, DANIEL	RICHMOND	203	WILMINGTON	05/08/68
MCGUIRE, JAMES	DAVIE	547	WILMINGTON	02/16/69
MCGUIRE, JOHN	WATAUGA	304	STATESVILLE	06/08/78
MCHORNEY, B.F.	CURRITUCK	267	ELIZABETH CITY	05/29/74
MCINTIRE, ROBERT M.	NEW HANOVER	208	WILMINGTON	05/14/68
MCINTOCH, MITTEN M.	ROBESON	122	WILMINGTON	03/07/68
MCINTYRE, ANDREW J.	*DOCKET ONLY	977	NEW BERN	12/07/68
MCKAY, WILLIAM A.	RICHMOND	341	WILMINGTON	11/11/68
MCKENZIE, CHARLES H.	ROWAN	285	STATESVILLE	10/02/77
MCKESSON, WILLIAM F.	*DOCKET ONLY	1	NEW BERN	06/04/67
MCKIMMON, ARTHUR &	*DOCKET ONLY	220	NEW BERN	01/24/68
MCKINNEY, F. B.	*DOCKET ONLY	948	NEW BERN	10/28/68
MCKINNEY, JOSEPH	BUNCOMBE	101	ASHEVILLE	10/05/72
MCKINNIE, DAVID	*DOCKET ONLY	823	NEW BERN	05/30/68
MCKINNON, MURDOCK M.	RICHMOND	200	WILMINGTON	05/08/69
MCKNIGHT, DAVID	*DOCKET ONLY	808	NEW BERN	04/01/68
MCLAIN, RUFUS T.	HENDERSON	103	ASHEVILLE	06/19/73
MCLANROCK, JULIS L.	DAVIE	215	WILMINGTON	05/21/68
MCLAUGHLIN, J. B.	*DOCKET ONLY	254	GREENSBORO	05/17/73
MCLAURIN, DAVID M.	RICHMOND	144	WILMINGTON	03/10/68
MCLAURIN, JOHN C.	RICHMOND	409	WILMINGTON	12/28/68
MCLEAN & COMPANY	*DOCKET ONLY	1290	NEW BERN	07/25/70
MCLEAN & COMPANY,		786	WILMINGTON	12/29/75
MCLEAN, ARCHIBALD	HARNETT	100	WILMINGTON	01/15/68
MCLEAN, CAMPBELL &		772	WILMINGTON	04/27/74
MCLEAN, HUGH	HARNETT	465	WILMINGTON	12/31/68
MCLEAN, JAMES S.	ALEXANDER	128	STATESVILLE	05/15/73
MCLEAN, ROBIN S.	*DOCKET ONLY	593	NEW BERN	03/25/68
MCLEAN, THOMAS G.	*DOCKET ONLY	312	NEW BERN	02/19/68
MCLEAN, W. S.	*DOCKET ONLY	1185	NEW BERN	12/31/68
MCLEOD, DANIEL	ROBESON	724	WILMINGTON	06/17/73
MCLEOD, J.W.	WATAUGA	313	STATESVILLE	07/25/78
MCLEODE, M.D.L.	MECKLENBURG	518	WILMINGTON	01/01/69
MCLLHENNY, THOMAS C.	NEW HANOVER	866	WILMINGTON	11/03/78
MCMAHON, WILLIAM F.	DAVIDSON	91	WILMINGTON	04/20/68
MCMAHON, J.H.	HALIFAX	329	ELIZABETH CITY	04/30/78
MCMAHON, MICHAEL	HALIFAX	548	ELIZABETH CITY	02/04/73
MCMARKS, W. R.	*DOCKET ONLY	953	NEW BERN	11/04/68
MCMICHAEL, OBED	*DOCKET ONLY	200	GREENSBORO	05/02/73
MCMILLAN, ALEX	ROBESON	760	WILMINGTON	12/23/73
MCMILLAN, HECTOR	CUMBERLAND	631	WILMINGTON	06/01/71
MCMILLAN, HECTOR	CUMBERLAND	631	WILMINGTON	06/01/71
MCMILLAN, HECTOR		632	WILMINGTON	05/17/71
MCMILLAN, HECTOR	CUMBERLAND	70	WILMINGTON	01/29/68
MCMINN, GEORGE &	HENDERSON	104	ASHEVILLE	12/01/74
MCMINN, JAMES N.	HENDERSON	105	ASHEVILLE	06/03/73
MCMURRAY, J. W &	*DOCKET ONLY	508	GREENSBORO	11/19/75
MCMURRAY, JOSEPH H.	MECKLENBERG	269	STATESVILLE	04/19/78
MCNAIR, ED. D.	*DOCKET ONLY	114	NEW BERN	12/20/67
MCNAIR, JOHN F.	RICHMOND	202	WILMINGTON	05/06/68
MCNAIR, MATHEW W.	RICHMOND	201	WILMINGTON	05/08/68
MCNAIR, NEIL A.	RICHMOND	124	WILMINGTON	03/12/68
MCNAIR, THOMAS L.	*DOCKET ONLY	428	GREENSBORO	11/26/73
MCNEELEY & YOUNG	ROWAN	107	WILMINGTON	03/01/68
MCNEELEY, JAMES A.	*DOCKET ONLY	149	GREENSBORO	04/02/73
MCNEELY, JULIUS D.	ROWAN	27	WILMINGTON	01/13/68
MCNEIL, A.S.	ROBESON	400	WILMINGTON	12/26/68
MCNEIL, DR. W.M.	HARNETT	268	WILMINGTON	05/30/68
MCNEIL, ELI	ASHE	322	STATESVILLE	08/26/78
MCNEIL, NEIL	ROBESON	424	WILMINGTON	12/30/68
MCNEILL, A.D.	ROBESON	459	WILMINGTON	12/31/68
MCNEILL, ALEX	CUMBERLAND	746	WILMINGTON	09/02/73

NAME OF BANKRUPT	RESIDENCE	CASE NUMBER	CITY OF COURT	DATE FILED
MCNEILL, DANIEL	ROBESON	460	WILMINGTON	12/31/68
MCNEILL, HECTOR	ROBESON	461	WILMINGTON	12/31/68
MCNEILL, MALCOM D.	*DOCKET ONLY	327	GREENSBORO	06/06/73
MCPHAIL, NEILL	HARNETT	839	WILMINGTON	07/15/78
MCPHERSON, JAMES I	*DOCKET ONLY	191	GREENSBORO	04/01/73
MCPHERSON, JOSEPH	CAMDEN	236	ELIZABETH CITY	03/24/68
MCPHERSON, NOAH	CAMDEN	201	ELIZABETH CITY	03/02/68
MCPHERSON, WILLIAM	CAMDEN	226	ELIZABETH CITY	03/09/68
MCQUIN, JAMES S.	ROBESON	421	WILMINGTON	12/30/68
MCRAE & TURRENTINE		771	WILMINGTON	03/28/74
MCRARY, WILLIAM	*DOCKET ONLY	471	GREENSBORO	04/14/74
MCRAY, WILLIAM	*DOCKET ONLY	545	GREENSBORO	04/14/74
MCREA, S.H.	WASHINGTON	285	ELIZABETH CITY	05/30/68
MCREE, WILLIAM N.	MECKLENBURG	472	WILMINGTON	12/31/68
MCTAYLOR, TARLTON	*DOCKET ONLY	548	NEW BERN	03/17/68
MEACHAM, THOMAS B.	MECKLENBURG	41	WILMINGTON	01/17/68
MEACHUM, LILES &	ANSON	136	WILMINGTON	03/12/68
MEADOWS, SIMEON	*DOCKET ONLY	798	NEW BERN	05/30/68
MEAN, WALKER	NEW HANOVER	292	WILMINGTON	05/30/68
MEBAM, CHARLES P., &		809	WILMINGTON	03/28/78
MEBANE, JOHN	*DOCKET ONLY	499	NEW BERN	03/07/68
MEBANE, JOHN A.	*DOCKET ONLY	499	NEW BERN	03/07/68
MEEKINS, J.C.	TYRRELL	221	ELIZABETH CITY	03/07/68
MELTON, DANIEL	RUTHERFORD	23	STATESVILLE	01/08/73
MELTON, WILLIAM	DAVIE	444	WILMINGTON	12/30/68
MELVIN, ARTHUR W.	BLADEN	872	WILMINGTON	08/30/78
MELVIN, DAVID	BLADEN	739	WILMINGTON	07/05/73
MELVIN, JAMES	BRUNSWICK	707	WILMINGTON	06/04/73
MELVIN, JAMES	BLADEN	738	WILMINGTON	07/05/73
MELVIN, JAMES MCK.	BLADEN	703	WILMINGTON	05/30/73
MELVIN, JOHN	BLADEN	729	WILMINGTON	06/27/73
MELVIN, JOSEPH	BLADEN	796	WILMINGTON	03/09/78
MELVIN, ROBERT P.	BLADEN	876	WILMINGTON	08/30/78
MELVIN, STEHPEN H.	SAMPSON	700	WILMINGTON	05/30/73
MENCER, F.	*DOCKET ONLY	181	NEW BERN	01/11/68
MENDENHALL, JAMES	*DOCKET ONLY	872	NEW BERN	05/07/68
MENDENHALT, CYRUS P.	GUILFORD	636	WILMINGTON	06/24/71
MENNINGER, HENRY	*DOCKET ONLY	873	NEW BERN	06/24/68
MENROW, CHRISTOPHER	CUMBERLAND	453	WILMINGTON	12/31/68
MERCER, JOSEPH	CURRITUCK	220	ELIZABETH CITY	03/07/68
MERIDETH, JAMES M	*DOCKET ONLY	231	GREENSBORO	05/12/73
MERONEY, WILLIAM A.	DAVIE	34	WILMINGTON	01/03/68
MERRILL, ANDREW J.	*DOCKET ONLY	1554	NEW BERN	01/10/74
MERRITT, GEORGE W.	*DOCKET ONLY	424	GREENSBORO	11/03/73
MERRITT, W. H.	*DOCKET ONLY	148	NEW BERN	12/31/67
MERRYMAN, PLEASANT	*DOCKET ONLY	74	NEW BERN	11/29/67
MERWIN, PHINEAS	*DOCKET ONLY	206	NEW BERN	01/21/68
METTS, JAY J.	NEW HANOVER	798	WILMINGTON	03/11/78
MEWBORN, LEVI A.	*DOCKET ONLY	1884	NEW BERN	07/02/78
MEYER, HELENA L	*DOCKET ONLY	1887	NEW BERN	05/14/78
MEYER, JULIUS	*DOCKET ONLY	1858	NEW BERN	03/19/78
MICKLE, ANDREW	*DOCKET ONLY	131	NEW BERN	12/28/67
MIDDLETON, DAVID W.	RICHMOND	421	WILMINGTON	12/30/68
MIDGETT, WILLIAM P.	*DOCKET ONLY	1055	NEW BERN	12/23/68
MIKEL, JOHN	*DOCKET ONLY	1145	NEW BERN	12/31/68
MILLER, ALEXANDER	*DOCKET ONLY	1007	NEW BERN	12/17/68
MILLER, ANDREW J.	*DOCKET ONLY	506	NEW BERN	03/09/68
MILLER, JACOB	ROWAN	298	STATESVILLE	05/27/78
MILLER, JAMES A.		119	ASHEVILLE	12/21/78
MILLER, JAMES P.	*DOCKET ONLY	162	GREENSBORO	04/22/73
MILLER, JESSE H.	*DOCKET ONLY	154	NEW BERN	01/02/68
MILLER, JOHN	*DOCKET ONLY	463	GREENSBORO	02/21/74
MILLER, LEWIS	*DOCKET ONLY	9	NEW BERN	08/23/67
MILLER, MICHAEL	ROWAN	468	WILMINGTON	12/31/68
MILLER, PHILIP A. &		583	WILMINGTON	10/19/70
MILLER, R.M.		583	WILMINGTON	07/18/70

NAME OF BANKRUPT	RESIDENCE	CASE NUMBER	CITY OF COURT	DATE FILED
MILLER, RILEY	*DOCKET ONLY	269	GREENSBORO	05/23/73
MILLER, STEPHEN	*DOCKET ONLY	1252	NEW BERN	12/31/68
MILLER, W. J. T.	CLEVELAND	229	STATESVILLE	08/01/73
MILLER, WILLIAM D.	*DOCKET ONLY	505	NEW BERN	03/09/67
MILLER, WILLIAM M.	*DOCKET ONLY	296	NEW BERN	02/10/68
MILLIAN, H.M. & SONS	CUMBERLAND	69	WILMINGTON	01/28/68
MILLS & GIBB		771	WILMINGTON	03/28/74
MILLS & MILLS	IREDELL	143	WILMINGTON	03/17/68
MILLS, GEORGE J.	POLK	253	STATESVILLE	01/24/74
MILLS, RICHARD W.	IREDELL	491	WILMINGTON	12/31/68
MILLS, W.M.	ROWAN	89	WILMINGTON	02/20/68
MILLS, ZOPHAN & R.		319	WILMINGTON	06/30/68
MIMS, JOHN W.	*DOCKET ONLY	715	NEW BERN	05/27/68
MINSHEW. BRYANT	*DOCKET ONLY	824	NEW BERN	05/20/68
MINSHEW, ISAAC	*DOCKET ONLY	1251	NEW BERN	12/31/68
MINSHEW, JOHN J.	*DOCKET ONLY	1250	NEW BERN	12/31/68
MINTER, WILLIAM L.	SURRY	247	WILMINGTON	05/29/68
MITCHELL, C. G.	*DOCKET ONLY	563	NEW BERN	03/19/68
MITCHELL, ELIAS	ROBESON	752	WILMINGTON	11/01/73
MITCHELL, HENRY D.	*DOCKET ONLY	1535	NEW BERN	11/26/73
MITCHELL, JAMES E.	BERTIE	194	ELIZABETH CITY	08/02/77
MITCHELL, JAMES E.	BERTIE	263	ELIZABETH CITY	04/19/74
MITCHELL, JESSE M.	*DOCKET ONLY	401	NEW BERN	02/28/68
MITCHELL, LEROY	*DOCKET ONLY	102	NEW BERN	12/12/67
MITCHELL, R.G.	CHOWAN	257	ELIZABETH CITY	05/20/68
MITCHELL, S.	RUTHERFORD	55	WILMINGTON	02/21/68
MITCHELL, SOLOMON W.	*DOCKET ONLY	1851	NEW BERN	11/24/77
MIZELL, ISAAC	BERTIE	473	ELIZABETH CITY	12/31/68
MIZELL, J.J.	BERTIE	294	ELIZABETH CITY	06/01/68
MIZELL, JONATHAN T.	*DOCKET ONLY	1305	NEW BERN	11/28/70
MOCK, A. J.	*DOCKET ONLY	584	GREENSBORO	01/01/78
MOCK, A. J. &	ROWAN	262	STATESVILLE	07/31/77
MOCK, A. J. (D/B/A/)	ROWAN	263	STATESVILLE	07/31/77
MONK, WILLIAM	*DOCKET ONLY	243	NEW BERN	01/31/68
MONROE, SHULTZ &	PHILADELPHIA	789	WILMINGTON	02/23/74
MONTFORT, WILLIAM J.	*DOCKET ONLY	803	NEW BERN	03/28/68
MONTGOMERY, C. G & C	*DOCKET ONLY	587	GREENSBORO	12/14/76
MOODY, CALVIN	WATAUGA	314	STATESVILLE	07/25/78
MOODY, GEORGE LEWIS	*DOCKET ONLY	970	NEW BERN	11/28/68
MOODY, JOHN M.	*DOCKET ONLY	681	NEW BERN	04/30/68
MOODY, JOHN M.	NORTHAMPTON	389	ELIZABETH CITY	03/04/68
MOON, EDMUND	*DOCKET ONLY	1066	NEW BERN	12/28/68
MOON, GEORGE J.	*DOCKET ONLY	1199	NEW BERN	12/30/68
MOON, HENRY	*DOCKET ONLY	841	NEW BERN	05/20/68
MOON, HENRY ALBERT	*DOCKET ONLY	471	NEW BERN	03/04/68
MOON, ISAAC C.	*DOCKET ONLY	720	NEW BERN	05/28/68
MOON, JAMES A	*DOCKET ONLY	883	NEW BERN	08/19/68
MOON, JAMES F.	*DOCKET ONLY	747	NEW BERN	03/04/68
MOON, JAMES R. H.	*DOCKET ONLY	1115	NEW BERN	12/29/68
MOON, JOHN A.	*DOCKET ONLY	188	GREENSBORO	04/30/73
MOON, JOHN N.	*DOCKET ONLY	1100	NEW BERN	12/29/68
MOON, RIGHT	*DOCKET ONLY	1472	NEW BERN	06/11/73
MOON, WILLIAM	*DOCKET ONLY	410	NEW BERN	02/28/68
MOON, WILLIAM	*DOCKET ONLY	1135	NEW BERN	12/30/68
MOONE, ANDREW	*DOCKET ONLY	222	NEW BERN	01/27/68
MOONE, ELI F.	BURKE	38	STATESVILLE	02/03/73
MOONE, R. R.	*DOCKET ONLY	219	NEW BERN	01/24/68
MOONE, REUBEN T.	*DOCKET ONLY	631	NEW BERN	04/08/68
MOORE & WAKEFIELD		575	WILMINGTON	04/21/70
MOORE, ALONZO	*DOCKET ONLY	462	GREENSBORO	02/19/74
MOORE, CHARLES (7)	HENDERSON	98	ASHEVILLE	01/11/73
MOORE, F. L	*DOCKET ONLY	382	GREENSBORO	07/15/73
MOORE, GODWIN C.	HERTFORD	837	ELIZABETH CITY	12/29/68
MOORE, JACOB	MCDOWELL	190	STATESVILLE	06/04/73
MOORE, JAMES E.	*DOCKET ONLY	265	GREENSBORO	05/22/73
MOORE, JAMES G.	*DOCKET ONLY	484	GREENSBORO	03/29/75

NAME OF BANKRUPT	RESIDENCE	CASE NUMBER	CITY OF COURT	DATE FILED
MOORE, JOAB L.	MACON	97	ASHEVILLE	09/23/74
MOORE, JOHN		631	WILMINGTON	06/01/71
MOORE, JOHN A.	*DOCKET ONLY	598	GREENSBORO	11/30/77
MOORE, JOHN R.	HALIFAX	500	ELIZABETH CITY	11/02/69
MOORE, JOHN T.	*DOCKET ONLY	344	GREENSBORO	06/14/73
MOORE, JOHN W.	HERTFORD	426	ELIZABETH CITY	12/23/68
MOORE, LEANDER	NEW HANOVER	727	WILMINGTON	06/23/73
MOORE, MAURICE H.	GASTON	17	STATESVILLE	12/20/72
MOORE, PITTEWAY		624	WILMINGTON	04/14/71
MOORE, R.R.	NEW HANOVER	870	WILMINGTON	08/30/78
MOORE, ROGER W.	*DOCKET ONLY	386	NEW BERN	02/29/68
MOORE, THOMAS	SAMPSON	601	WILMINGTON	11/18/70
MOORE, WILLIAM W.	MARTIN	574	ELIZABETH CITY	12/20/70
MOORMAN, JOHN T.	RICHMOND	23	WILMINGTON	12/18/67
MOOSE, DAVID W.	ALEXANDER	197	STATESVILLE	06/09/73
MOOSE, EXUM L.	*DOCKET ONLY	1673	NEW BERN	05/25/78
MOOSE, JACOB	ROWAN	38	WILMINGTON	01/13/68
MOOSE, MATTHIAS	*DOCKET ONLY	458	GREENSBORO	02/07/74
MORGAN, BUSH &		610	WILMINGTON	01/19/71
MORGAN, ELIJAH H.	*DOCKET ONLY	1672	NEW BERN	05/25/78
MORGAN, JAMES	*DOCKET ONLY	518	GREENSBORO	03/03/73
MORGAN, JAMES M.	*DOCKET ONLY	1347	NEW BERN	05/06/71
MORGAN, JONATHAN	BUNCOMBE	96	ASHEVILLE	05/31/73
MORGAN, SETH	PASQUOTANK	47	ELIZABETH CITY	11/22/67
MORGAN, WILEY	ROWAN	300	STATESVILLE	05/29/78
MORGAN, WILLIAM	BUNCOMBE	95	ASHEVILLE	06/14/77
MORGAN, WILLIAM M.	*DOCKET ONLY	845	NEW BERN	04/18/88
MORING, CHRISTOPHER	ROWAN	614	WILMINGTON	04/21/71
MORISSON, ANDREW C.	ALEXANDER	87	STATESVILLE	04/25/73
MORISSON, JOHN L.	ROWAN	143	STATESVILLE	05/21/73
MORPHY, SAMUEL	*DOCKET ONLY	58	NEW BERN	11/10/67
MORRIS, ISAAC E.	MCDOWELL	272	WILMINGTON	05/30/68
MORRIS, J.E.	MCDOWELL	173	WILMINGTON	04/11/68
MORRIS, JAMES J.	*DOCKET ONLY	1688	NEW BERN	08/03/78
MORRIS, LEWIS	*DOCKET ONLY	310	GREENSBORO	06/02/73
MORRIS, MORDECAI	PASQUOTANK	278	ELIZABETH CITY	06/29/68
MORRIS, ROBERT	*DOCKET ONLY	1339	NEW BERN	12/09/70
MORRIS, ROBERT F.	*DOCKET ONLY	473	NEW BERN	03/04/69
MORRISETT, JOHNSON	HALIFAX	503	ELIZABETH CITY	08/31/70
MORRISETT, JOSEPH L.	CURRITUCK	51	ELIZABETH CITY	11/20/67
MORRISETT, LEMUEL	CAMDEN	84	ELIZABETH CITY	12/18/67
MORRISETT, PHILIP E.	CAMDEN	71	ELIZABETH CITY	12/09/67
MORRISON, THOMAS	RUTHERFORD	179	STATESVILLE	06/04/73
MORRISSON, MURRDOCK	RICHMOND	145	WILMINGTON	02/07/68
MORRISSON, WILLIAM	MCDOWELL	323	STATESVILLE	08/27/78
MORROW, JASWELL	MECKLENBURG	608	WILMINGTON	01/11/71
MORROW, MALCOM	BLADEN	696	WILMINGTON	05/30/73
MORTON, DURANT A.	*DOCKET ONLY	1190	NEW BERN	12/30/69
MORTON, H.H.	*DOCKET ONLY	400	NEW BERN	02/26/68
MORTON, JOSEPH	*DOCKET ONLY	358	NEW BERN	02/24/68
MOSCO, JOHN H.	FORSYTH	223	WILMINGTON	05/23/68
MOSELEY, DANIEL H.	*DOCKET ONLY	291	NEW BERN	02/11/68
MOSELEY, F. M.	*DOCKET ONLY	1585	NEW BERN	06/19/74
MOSLEY, NATHAN J.	*DOCKET ONLY	1324	NEW BERN	02/03/71
MOSS, ADOLPHUS A. &	*DOCKET ONLY	717	NEW BERN	05/27/68
MOSS, JOHN R.	*DOCKET ONLY	709	NEW BERN	05/26/68
MOTLEY, JOHN B.	NORTHAMPTON	216	ELIZABETH CITY	03/06/68
MOVING, WILLIE	*DOCKET ONLY	959	NEW BERN	11/09/68
MOYE, M.	*DOCKET ONLY	925	NEW BERN	09/08/68
MULHOLLAND, H.	*DOCKET ONLY	84	NEW BERN	11/30/67
MULHOLLAND, PASCHAL	*DOCKET ONLY	83	NEW BERN	11/30/67
MULINX, J.M.	MONTGOMERY	287	WILMINGTON	05/30/68
MULINX, JONATHAN D.	*DOCKET ONLY	155	NEW BERN	01/02/67
MULLEN, JOSEPH SR.	PERQUIMANS	280	ELIZABETH CITY	05/29/68
MULLIS, C. P.	*DOCKET ONLY	297	GREENSBORO	05/26/73
MUNDAY, JESSE	*DOCKET ONLY	320	NEW BERN	02/21/68

NORTH CAROLINA BANKRUPTS - ACT OF 1867

NAME OF BANKRUPT	RESIDENCE	CASE NUMBER	CITY OF COURT	DATE FILED
MUNDAY, JOHN H.	*DOCKET ONLY	200	NEW BERN	01/17/68
MUNE, WILLIAM	*DOCKET ONLY	941	NEW BERN	09/21/68
MURCHISON, ALEX	HARNETT	646	WILMINGTON	11/06/71
MURFIE, G. R.	*DOCKET ONLY	854	NEW BERN	06/19/68
MURPHREY, D. A. &	*DOCKET ONLY	1417	NEW BERN	02/08/73
MURPHY, J. W. (115)	MCDOWELL	99	ASHEVILLE	06/02/73
MURPHY, JOHN S.	*DOCKET ONLY	618	GREENSBORO	04/27/78
MURPHY, MILTON	*DOCKET ONLY	294	NEW BERN	02/13/68
MURPHY, PATRICK		325	WILMINGTON	06/25/68
MURPHY, THOMAS K.	DUPLIN	690	WILMINGTON	05/23/73
MURPHY, W. H. (DR.)	*DOCKET ONLY	1273	NEW BERN	06/12/69
MURRAY, A.	*DOCKET ONLY	596	GREENSBORO	11/06/77
MURRAY, DECATER C.	*DOCKET ONLY	91	NEW BERN	11/04/67
MURRAY, FERRIS &		774	WILMINGTON	08/31/74
MURRAY, P. M.	*DOCKET ONLY	552	GREENSBORO	10/27/75
MURRAY, WILLIAM J.	*DOCKET ONLY	599	GREENSBORO	01/02/78
MURRAY, WILLIAM J.	*DOCKET ONLY	599	GREENSBORO	01/02/78
MURRILL, ELIJAH	*DOCKET ONLY	1198	NEW BERN	12/30/68
MURROW, ANDREW C.	*DOCKET ONLY	618	GREENSBORO	05/03/78
MUSE, HAYWOOD	MOORE	105	WILMINGTON	02/27/68
MUWBORN, LEMUEL J.	*DOCKET ONLY	1676	NEW BERN	06/14/78
MYER, CHARLES D.	NEW HANOVER	165	WILMINGTON	04/01/68
MYERS, ALBERT	ANSON	238	WILMINGTON	05/27/68
MYERS, T.B.	TYRRELL	357	ELIZABETH CITY	08/31/78
MYERS, WHITAKER	PERQUIMANS	527	ELIZABETH CITY	05/09/71
MYNICK, JOHN C.	*DOCKET ONLY	1153	NEW BERN	12/30/68
MYRICK, GEORGE W.	*DOCKET ONLY	882	NEW BERN	08/19/68
MYRICK, ROBERT A.	*DOCKET ONLY	930	NEW BERN	09/21/68
McEACHEN, R. M.	*DOCKET ONLY	351	GREENSBORO	06/16/73
McLAIN, R.A.	*DOCKET ONLY	366	GREENSBORO	06/30/73
McLEOD, JAMES	*DOCKET ONLY	408	GREENSBORO	08/27/73
McLLEVAIN, ALEXANDER	*DOCKET ONLY	407	GREENSBORO	08/25/73
NAIL, THOMAS B.	IREDELL	100	STATESVILLE	04/20/73
NALL, JOHN D.	MCDOWELL	305	STATESVILLE	06/11/78
NANCE, CLEMUEL	*DOCKET ONLY	311	GREENSBORO	06/02/73
NASH, ABRAHAM	ROWAN	393	WILMINGTON	12/28/68
NASH, EDMUND	STANLY	418	WILMINGTON	12/30/68
NASH, JAMES E.	*DOCKET ONLY	1356	NEW BERN	09/08/71
NASH, JOSEPH	*DOCKET ONLY	271	GREENSBORO	05/23/73
NASH, WHITSON F.	STANLY	190	WILMINGTON	04/14/68
NASH, WILLIAM	*DOCKET ONLY	214	GREENSBORO	05/08/73
NASON, GEORGE W.	*DOCKET ONLY	1570	NEW BERN	03/02/74
NATION, JOHN H.	*DOCKET ONLY	115	GREENSBORO	02/12/73
NATIONS, JAMES	*DOCKET ONLY	156	GREENSBORO	04/18/73
NAYLER, JOHN W.	DAVIE	21	STATESVILLE	01/06/73
NEAGLE & GALLANT	GASTON	352	WILMINGTON	12/04/68
NEAL, CHARLES E.	*DOCKET ONLY	1191	NEW BERN	12/30/68
NEAL, JOHN	*DOCKET ONLY	1102	NEW BERN	12/28/68
NEAL, JOSEPH W.	*DOCKET ONLY	564	NEW BERN	03/19/68
NEELY, ARTHUR	DAVIE	506	WILMINGTON	01/01/69
NEFF, JOSEPH H.	NEW HANOVER	806	WILMINGTON	02/02/77
NEIL, JOHN	*DOCKET ONLY	78	NEW BERN	11/30/67
NEILL, CHARLES L.	NEW HANOVER	837	WILMINGTON	06/21/78
NEILL, HECTOR M.	CUMBERLAND	456	WILMINGTON	12/31/68
NELLEY, DANIEL G.	*DOCKET ONLY	78	GREENSBORO	01/27/73
NELSON, ANDREW	UNION	407	WILMINGTON	12/28/68
NELSON, AUGUSTUS W.	*DOCKET ONLY	1609	NEW BERN	06/29/75
NELSON, AUGUSTUS W.	*DOCKET ONLY	1377	NEW BERN	02/14/72
NELSON, THOMAS E.	*DOCKET ONLY	996	NEW BERN	12/09/68
NEMLIN, OLIVER	*DOCKET ONLY	45	NEW BERN	11/06/67
NEMSON, SIMON	*DOCKET ONLY	1403	NEW BERN	12/20/72
NEVILL, CHARLES	*DOCKET ONLY	348	GREENSBORO	06/14/73
NEWBERRY, M.D.L.	TYRRELL	292	ELIZABETH CITY	11/22/75
NEWBURG, HENRY E.	DUPLIN	804	WILMINGTON	11/11/76
NEWBURG, WILLIAM M.	CUMBERLAND	6	WILMINGTON	10/01/67
NEWBY, WILLIAM	BERTIE	509	ELIZABETH CITY	10/07/70

NAME OF BANKRUPT	RESIDENCE	CASE NUMBER	CITY OF COURT	DATE FILED
NEWELL, GEORGE W.	CUMBERLAND	16	WILMINGTON	11/06/67
NEWELL, KEA &	DUPLIN	477	WILMINGTON	12/31/68
NEWGATE, T.C.	BUNCOMBE	296	WILMINGTON	05/30/68
NEWMAN, JOHN	HERTFORD	538	ELIZABETH CITY	11/07/71
NEWSOM, ALLEN	*DOCKET ONLY	450	GREENSBORO	01/04/74
NEWSOM, JEREMIAH V.	HALIFAX	398	ELIZABETH CITY	12/18/68
NEWSOM, THADDEUS J.	*DOCKET ONLY	512	GREENSBORO	01/21/76
NEWSON, F. J. &	*DOCKET ONLY	897	GREENSBORO	02/08/76
NEWSON, JOHN	*DOCKET ONLY	161	GREENSBORO	04/22/73
NEWSUM, JAMES W.	NORTHAMPTON	530	ELIZABETH CITY	07/31/71
NEWTON, JOHN T.	SAMPSON	686	WILMINGTON	05/21/73
NEWTON, NICHOLAS	ALEXANDER	520	WILMINGTON	01/01/69
NEWTON, W. B. F.	*DOCKET ONLY	1368	NEW BERN	11/23/71
NEWTON, WALTER	*DOCKET ONLY	1361	NEW BERN	10/14/71
NEWTON, WESLEY J.	*DOCKET ONLY	103	NEW BERN	12/12/67
NICHOLLS, JOHN	*DOCKET ONLY	1131	NEW BERN	12/30/68
NICHOLS, JOHN	*DOCKET ONLY	1662	NEW BERN	04/19/78
NICHOLS, PAUL	CUMBERLAND	728	WILMINGTON	05/24/73
NICHOLSEN, JOHN A.	NEW HANOVER	294	WILMINGTON	05/30/68
NICHOLSON, BLAKE B.	HALIFAX	117	ELIZABETH CITY	02/17/68
NICHOLSON, GIDEON W.	*DOCKET ONLY	1319	NEW BERN	01/16/71
NICHOLSON, JOHN M.	*DOCKET ONLY	403	GREENSBORO	08/21/73
NICHOLSON, WILLLIAM	*DOCKET ONLY	976	NEW BERN	12/05/68
NIXON, GEORGE W.	CAMDEN	349	ELIZABETH CITY	08/30/78
NIXON, HILL W.	NEW HANOVER	767	WILMINGTON	01/21/74
NIXON, THOMAS	PERQUIMANS	384	ELIZABETH CITY	11/23/68
NOE, SIMEON M.	CURRITUCK	144	ELIZABETH CITY	02/17/68
NOELL, WILLIAM	*DOCKET ONLY	799	NEW BERN	05/20/68
NORFLEET, M. W.	*DOCKET ONLY	646	NEW BERN	04/18/68
NORMAN, L. J.	*DOCKET ONLY	114	GREENSBORO	02/12/73
NORMAN, NEHEMIAH		25	ELIZABETH CITY	10/08/67
NORMAN, W. M.	*DOCKET ONLY	371	GREENSBORO	07/03/73
NORTHROP & CUMMINGS	NEW HANOVER	863	WILMINGTON	08/31/78
NOXON, W. P.	*DOCKET ONLY	158	GREENSBORO	04/18/73
NULL, JOHN	*DOCKET ONLY	235	GREENSBORO	05/12/73
NUTT, ERASMUS D.	*DOCKET ONLY	70	NEW BERN	11/29/67
NYE, GEROGE A. P.	ASHE	213	STATESVILLE	06/30/73
O'BRIAN, RANSON	*DOCKET ONLY	800	NEW BERN	05/30/68
O'BRIANT, SOLOMON	*DOCKET ONLY	1103	NEW BERN	12/28/68
O'BRYAN, ELISHA	*DOCKET ONLY	328	GREENSBORO	08/06/73
O'NEAL, W. P.	*DOCKET ONLY	1116	NEW BERN	12/29/68
O'NEALE, NATHAM B.	*DOCKET ONLY	648	NEW BERN	06/15/68
OAKES, MORTIMER	*DOCKET ONLY	558	GREENSBORO	05/02/78
OAKSMITH, APPLETON	*DOCKET ONLY	1640	NEW BERN	01/16/77
OATES, J.R.	YADKIN	585	WILMINGTON	09/25/70
OATES, W.S.A.	CLEVELAND	485	WILMINGTON	12/31/68
ODOM, NOAH R.	NORTHAMPTON	394	ELIZABETH CITY	12/11/68
OEWNBY, URIAH (68)	HENDERSON	109	ASHEVILLE	03/06/73
OGBUM, W. C. &	*DOCKET ONLY	565	GREENSBORO	08/04/76
OGLESBY, LEVI F.	*DOCKET ONLY	1307	NEW BERN	12/02/70
OLDHAM, ALLEN	*DOCKET ONLY	43	NEW BERN	10/30/67
OLDHAM, WESLEY	*DOCKET ONLY	93	NEW BERN	12/04/67
OLIVER, MONROE &	*DOCKET ONLY	517	NEW BERN	03/12/68
OLIVER, ROBERT F.	*DOCKET ONLY	503	GREENSBORO	09/18/75
OLIVER, WILLIAM H.	*DOCKET ONLY	1266	NEW BERN	12/31/68
OLIVER, WILLIAM N.	*DOCKET ONLY	1583	NEW BERN	05/12/74
ONTLAW, GRADY	DUPLIN	691	WILMINGTON	05/30/73
ORR, JOSEPH W.	HENDERSON	110	ASHEVILLE	09/27/73
OSBORN, JOB	*DOCKET ONLY	1647	NEW BERN	07/16/77
OSBORN, THOMAS M.	*DOCKET ONLY	1092	NEW BERN	12/29/68
OSBORNE, CALEB	ALLEGHANY	224	STATESVILLE	07/21/73
OSBOURN, DAVID M &	*DOCKET ONLY	40	NEW BERN	10/18/67
OUSBY, JAMES L.	HALIFAX	403	ELIZABETH CITY	10/29/68
OUTERND, A.O.	DUPLIN	30	WILMINGTON	11/27/67
OUTLAND, WILLIAM J.	*DOCKET ONLY	1222	NEW BERN	12/29/68
OUTLAW, GRADY	*DOCKET ONLY	1432	NEW BERN	05/13/73

NAME OF BANKRUPT	RESIDENCE	CASE NUMBER	CITY OF COURT	DATE FILED
OVERBEY, JOHN S.	*DOCKET ONLY	202	NEW BERN	01/17/68
OVERBY, DAVID (SR)	*DOCKET ONLY	540	NEW BERN	03/17/68
OVERBY, JOHN H.	*DOCKET ONLY	801	NEW BERN	05/30/68
OVERCASH, HENRY	ROWAN	296	STATESVILLE	05/23/78
OVERTON, EZEKIEL	MONTGOMERY	260	WILMINGTON	05/29/68
OVERTON, M.J.	CAMDEN	299	ELIZABETH CITY	03/16/77
OWEN, THOMAS M.	*DOCKET ONLY	494	GREENSBORO	06/07/75
OWENS, A.W.	WASHINGTON	288	ELIZABETH CITY	10/14/75
OWENS, ALEXANDER	CURRITUCK	253	ELIZABETH CITY	05/11/68
OWENS, H. L.	*DOCKET ONLY	599	NEW BERN	03/25/68
OWENS, N.E.	TYRRELL	295	ELIZABETH CITY	02/04/76
OWENS, PHILLIP	ROWAN	19	STATESVILLE	12/23/73
OWENS, WILSON	TYRRELL	172	ELIZABETH CITY	02/28/68
OXENDINE, JAMES	ROBESON	827	WILMINGTON	05/18/78
PAGE & SURLEY	CUMBERLAND	115	WILMINGTON	03/03/69
PAGE, ANDERSON	*DOCKET ONLY	884	NEW BERN	08/19/68
PAGE, BENTLEY W.	*DOCKET ONLY	173	GREENSBORO	04/25/73
PAGE, RUFUS H.	*DOCKET ONLY	1680	NEW BERN	06/12/78
PAGE, WILBUR C.	*DOCKET ONLY	613	NEW BERN	04/01/68
PAILIN, JOHN	PASQUOTANK	305	ELIZABETH CITY	03/11/76
PALMER, A. W.	*DOCKET ONLY	780	NEW BERN	08/17/68
PALMER, ALEX W.	*DOCKET ONLY	687	GREENSBORO	06/10/78
PALMER, HENRY C.	CAMDEN	89	ELIZABETH CITY	12/23/67
PALMER, HORACE	*DOCKET ONLY	1068	NEW BERN	12/26/68
PALMER, O. A.	*DOCKET ONLY	1010	NEW BERN	12/18/68
PALMER, O. A.	*DOCKET ONLY	123	GREENSBORO	02/25/73
PALMER, T. W.	CLEVELAND	246	STATESVILLE	12/18/73
PALMER, THOMAS	CAMDEN	46	ELIZABETH CITY	12/16/67
PALMER, JOHN JOSEPH	*DOCKET ONLY	1170	NEW BERN	12/31/68
PAPE, DAVID A.	HALIFAX	233	ELIZABETH CITY	03/18/68
PAPE, JAMES A.	HALIFAX	215	ELIZABETH CITY	03/06/68
PAPE, WILLIAM B.	HALIFAX	254	ELIZABETH CITY	05/19/68
PARAMONE, W. B.	*DOCKET ONLY	1649	NEW BERN	08/24/77
PARANONE, MAXWELL	*DOCKET ONLY	1655	NEW BERN	01/02/77
PARHAM & DUNN	*DOCKET ONLY	1827	NEW BERN	02/28/78
PARISH, D. C.	*DOCKET ONLY	897	NEW BERN	08/17/68
PARISH, GEORGE W.	CHOWAN	361	ELIZABETH CITY	08/12/68
PARISH, JAMES	*DOCKET ONLY	267	NEW BERN	02/07/68
PARISH, JAMES	*DOCKET ONLY	359	NEW BERN	02/24/68
PARK, ISAAC A.	*DOCKET ONLY	37	GREENSBORO	08/21/72
PARKER, D. &	HERTFORD	388	ELIZABETH CITY	11/19/68
PARKER, EDMOND J.	GATES	189	ELIZABETH CITY	02/28/68
PARKER, JAMES F.	STANLY	98	WILMINGTON	02/25/68
PARKER, JOHN R.	DAVIDSON	300	WILMINGTON	05/30/68
PARKER, JONATHAN W.	*DOCKET ONLY	516	NEW BERN	03/12/68
PARKER, NEWTON H.	*DOCKET ONLY	500	NEW BERN	03/07/68
PARKER, ROBERT	WILKES	851	WILMINGTON	08/15/78
PARKS, JOHN P.	IREDELL	302	WILMINGTON	05/30/68
PARKS, WASHINGTON	*DOCKET ONLY	113	GREENSBORO	02/08/73
PARNELL, THOMAS L.	*DOCKET ONLY	779	NEW BERN	08/23/68
PARRISH J. M. & C.	*DOCKET ONLY	1154	NEW BERN	12/30/68
PARRISH, RALPH	*DOCKET ONLY	103	GREENSBORO	02/08/73
PARROTT, BENJAMIN	*DOCKET ONLY	980	NEW BERN	12/08/68
PARSLEY, OSCAR G.	NEW HANOVER	861	WILMINGTON	08/27/78
PARSON, THOMAS J	NORTHAMPTON	499	ELIZABETH CITY	08/05/69
PARSONS, JOHN	WILKES	138	STATESVILLE	05/21/73
PARSONS, JOHN	WILKES	237	STATESVILLE	10/08/73
PARTIN, JOHN A.	*DOCKET ONLY	244	NEW BERN	01/31/68
PASCHAL, RICHARD B.	*DOCKET ONLY	479	NEW BERN	03/04/68
PATE, GABRIEL G.	COLUMBUS	747	WILMINGTON	08/01/73
PATE, JOHN W.	*DOCKET ONLY	932	NEW BERN	09/21/68
PATRICK, DAVID S.	*DOCKET ONLY	233	NEW BERN	01/31/68
PATRICK, HUGH L.	*DOCKET ONLY	449	NEW BERN	03/02/68
PATRICK, JOEL	*DOCKET ONLY	1313	NEW BERN	12/17/70
PATRICK, JOHN	*DOCKET ONLY	1581	NEW BERN	05/11/74
PATRICK, JOHN M.	*DOCKET ONLY	1254	NEW BERN	12/31/68

NAME OF BANKRUPT	RESIDENCE	CASE NUMBER	CITY OF COURT	DATE FILED
PATTEN, JAMES C.	*DOCKET ONLY	629	GREENSBORO	06/04/78
PATTEN, JOHN	BUNCOMBE	271	WILMINGTON	05/30/68
PATTEN, JOHN M.	BUNCOMBE	85	WILMINGTON	04/13/68
PATTERSON, GEORGE	*DOCKET ONLY	624	GREENSBORO	06/04/78
PATTERSON, JOHN I.	*DOCKET ONLY	242	GREENSBORO	05/13/73
PATTERSON, MOSES	*DOCKET ONLY	1659	NEW BERN	03/23/78
PATTERSON, STURNER	*DOCKET ONLY	295	NEW BERN	02/13/68
PATTERSON, WILLIAM	*DOCKET ONLY	682	GREENSBORO	08/31/78
PATTERSON, WILLIAM	ROBESON	426	WILMINGTON	12/30/68
PATTON, REUBEN E.	MCDOWELL	315	STATESVILLE	08/08/78
PAXTON, ELIZABETH B.	CHOWAN	638	ELIZABETH CITY	03/27/71
PAYLOR, WILLIAM	*DOCKET ONLY	669	GREENSBORO	07/01/77
PAYNE, HIRAM A.	*DOCKET ONLY	427	GREENSBORO	11/12/73
PAYSON, JONAS W.	LINCOLN	489	WILMINGTON	12/31/68
PEACE, ABNER	*DOCKET ONLY	477	NEW BERN	03/04/68
PEARCE, A. W.	*DOCKET ONLY	886	NEW BERN	06/19/68
PEARCE, BENJAMINE F.	CUMBERLAND	375	WILMINGTON	12/22/68
PEARCE, BLOUNT C.	*DOCKET ONLY	710	NEW BERN	05/26/68
PEARCE, JOHN A.	*DOCKET ONLY	327	NEW BERN	02/21/68
PEARCE, JOHN J.	*DOCKET ONLY	1420	NEW BERN	04/21/73
PEARCE, JOHNSON &	CUMBERLAND	13	WILMINGTON	10/28/67
PEARCE, PETER C.	CAMDEN	529	ELIZABETH CITY	08/10/71
PEARCE, PHILIP	*DOCKET ONLY	885	NEW BERN	06/19/68
PEARCE, RICKS M.	*DOCKET ONLY	1383	NEW BERN	09/21/72
PEARCE, WILLIAM H.	*DOCKET ONLY	11	NEW BERN	06/27/67
PEARSON, BENJAMIN O.	CHOWAN	478	ELIZABETH CITY	12/31/68
PEARSON, CHARLES H.	HALIFAX	136	ELIZABETH CITY	02/17/68
PEARSON, D.C.		639	WILMINGTON	06/21/71
PEARSON, ICHABOD	*DOCKET ONLY	1582	NEW BERN	02/06/74
PEARSON, WILLIAM A.	*DOCKET ONLY	656	NEW BERN	06/19/68
PEBBLES, M.F.	NORTHAMPTON	325	ELIZABETH CITY	02/27/78
PEEBLES, N.A.	DAVIE	68	STATESVILLE	03/05/73
PEEBLES, NICHOLAS	NORTHAMPTON	246	ELIZABETH CITY	11/27/73
PEED, JOSEPHUS	*DOCKET ONLY	1052	NEW BERN	12/23/68
PEED, WILLIAM	*DOCKET ONLY	1621	NEW BERN	02/09/78
PEELER, PETER	CLEVELAND	199	STATESVILLE	06/20/73
PEGRAM, JACOB F.	GASTON	172	WILMINGTON	04/08/68
PELL, ANDREW	CURRITUCK	112	ELIZABETH CITY	01/20/68
PELLETIER, EDWARD W.	*DOCKET ONLY	1573	NEW BERN	03/14/73
PELLETIER, JERIMIAH	*DOCKET ONLY	1085	NEW BERN	12/28/68
PELLETIER, RICHARD	*DOCKET ONLY	604	NEW BERN	03/28/68
PELLETIER, WILLIAM	*DOCKET ONLY	1101	NEW BERN	12/29/68
PELLTIER, JOHN W.	*DOCKET ONLY	1699	NEW BERN	08/26/78
PEMBERTON, JOHN A.	CUMBERLAND	601	WILMINGTON	09/27/76
PENDER, ROBERT H.	*DOCKET ONLY	721	NEW BERN	05/29/68
PENDER, WILLIAM D.	*DOCKET ONLY	1132	NEW BERN	12/30/68
PENDERGRASS, A. J.	*DOCKET ONLY	585	NEW BERN	03/19/68
PENDERGRASS, WESLEY	*DOCKET ONLY	541	NEW BERN	03/17/68
PENDLETON, A. J.	*DOCKET ONLY	1648	NEW BERN	07/24/77
PENDLETON, A.L.	PASQUOTANK	300	ELIZABETH CITY	02/02/77
PENDLETON, H.L.	PASQUOTANK	204	ELIZABETH CITY	03/02/68
PENDLETON, JOHN F.	CHOWAN	640	ELIZABETH CITY	05/19/68
PENDLETON, K.R.	PERQUIMANS	240	ELIZABETH CITY	10/21/73
PENDLETON, REUBEN	PASQUOTANK	330	ELIZABETH CITY	05/18/78
PENLAND, S.E.	BUNCOMBE	486	WILMINGTON	12/31/68
PENNEY, THOMAS S.	DAVIE	331	WILMINGTON	09/25/68
PENNINGTON, GEORGE	*DOCKET ONLY	542	NEW BERN	03/17/68
PENNINGTON, JOHHN R.	*DOCKET ONLY	675	GREENSBORO	08/31/78
PENNINGTON, JOHN S.	*DOCKET ONLY	147	GREENSBORO	04/16/73
PENTON, HENRY D.	CHOWAN	639	ELIZABETH CITY	06/05/68
PEPKIN, ISAAC	HERTFORD	471	ELIZABETH CITY	12/30/68
PEPKIN, WILLIS	*DOCKET ONLY	424	NEW BERN	02/29/68
PEPPER, WILLIAM R.	*DOCKET ONLY	1329	NEW BERN	03/02/71
PERINIX, GEORGE W.	*DOCKET ONLY	647	NEW BERN	04/18/68
PERKINS, CALVIN G.	*DOCKET ONLY	253	NEW BERN	02/03/68
PERKINS, NATHAN S.	CHOWAN	424	ELIZABETH CITY	12/28/68

NAME OF BANKRUPT	RESIDENCE	CASE NUMBER	CITY OF COURT	DATE FILED
PERRIN, HENRY R.	NEW HANOVER	118	WILMINGTON	03/02/69
PERRY, A. C.	*DOCKET ONLY	912	NEW BERN	08/22/68
PERRY, ALLEN C.	*DOCKET ONLY	360	NEW BERN	02/24/68
PERRY, BENJAMIN L.	*DOCKET ONLY	1723	NEW BERN	12/31/78
PERRY, CALVIN	*DOCKET ONLY	428	NEW BERN	02/29/68
PERRY, ELI H. E. F.	*DOCKET ONLY	651	NEW BERN	04/21/68
PERRY, ELIJAH B.	*DOCKET ONLY	933	NEW BERN	09/21/68
PERRY, JOHN W.	*DOCKET ONLY	1465	NEW BERN	06/05/73
PERRY, KADIR (CADIR)	PASQUOTANK	110	ELIZABETH CITY	01/20/68
PERRY, MASK P.	*DOCKET ONLY	478	NEW BERN	03/04/68
PERRY, ROBERT G.	*DOCKET ONLY	1504	NEW BERN	08/07/73
PERRY, SAMUEL B.	*DOCKET ONLY	379	GREENSBORO	07/11/73
PERRY, SOLOMON W.	*DOCKET ONLY	476	NEW BERN	03/04/68
PERRY, STEPHEN JONES	*DOCKET ONLY	666	GREENSBORO	08/29/78
PERRY, WILLIAM	CHOWAN	480	ELIZABETH CITY	12/31/68
PERRY, WILLIAM	PERQUIMANS	459	ELIZABETH CITY	12/30/68
PERRY, WILLIE B.	*DOCKET ONLY	475	NEW BERN	03/04/68
PERRYMAN, CHARLES M	*DOCKET ONLY	275	GREENSBORO	05/24/73
PESKINSON, ROBERT J.	*DOCKET ONLY	1450	NEW BERN	05/20/73
PETERS, HUGH	MECKLENBURG	549	WILMINGTON	06/01/69
PETERSON, EVERETT	SAMPSON	862	WILMINGTON	08/29/78
PETERSON, STEPHEN	SAMPSON	691	WILMINGTON	05/13/73
PETTISHALL, LUCINDA	*DOCKET ONLY	357	NEW BERN	02/24/68
PETTITT, BENJAMIN	*DOCKET ONLY	674	GREENSBORO	08/31/78
PETWAY, P. S.	*DOCKET ONLY	1253	NEW BERN	12/31/68
PFAFF, ISAAC	*DOCKET ONLY	325	GREENSBORO	06/06/73
PFAFF, PHILLIP N.	*DOCKET ONLY	341	GREENSBORO	06/13/73
PFOHL, VOYLES		829	WILMINGTON	05/13/71
PFOHL, AUGUSTUS F.,	*DOCKET ONLY	529	GREENSBORO	11/30/72
PHELPS, HERMAN M.	MECKLENBURG	545	WILMINGTON	02/23/69
PHELPS, THOMAS H.	*DOCKET ONLY	640	GREENSBORO	08/18/78
PHELPS, WILLIAM A.	*DOCKET ONLY	1488	NEW BERN	07/05/73
PHILIPS, JAMESS G.	FORSYTH	31	WILMINGTON	01/03/68
PHILLIPS, E.E.	ROWAN	293	STATESVILLE	05/21/78
PHILLIPS, JAMES	BLADEN	878	WILMINGTON	08/30/78
PHILLIPS, MARY E.C.	HALIFAX	268	ELIZABETH CITY	05/27/74
PHILPOTT, J. W.	*DOCKET ONLY	565	NEW BERN	03/19/68
PHIPPS, ROBERT	ASHE	216	STATESVILLE	07/03/73
PHIPS, ELIJAH	ASHE	264	STATESVILLE	01/18/74
PHYSIC, GEORGE	*DOCKET ONLY	1433	NEW BERN	05/14/73
PIDGEON, ROBERT H.	*DOCKET ONLY	691	NEW BERN	05/19/68
PIERCE, A. S.	*DOCKET ONLY	913	NEW BERN	08/22/68
PIERCE, ALAXANDER B.	HALIFAX	418	ELIZABETH CITY	12/23/68
PIERCE, F. & COMPANY		803	WILMINGTON	11/08/76
PIERCE, RICE B.	HALIFAX	536	ELIZABETH CITY	08/26/71
PIKE, JOEL	*DOCKET ONLY	380	GREENSBORO	07/11/73
PIKE, JONATHAN, T.	*DOCKET ONLY	1700	NEW BERN	08/26/78
PILKINTON, ANDREW J.	*DOCKET ONLY	373	NEW BERN	02/24/68
PINDER, RANSON	POLK	115	ASHEVILLE	05/29/78
PINNER, LEANDER &		578	WILMINGTON	06/06/70
PIPKIN, JOHN W.	HARNETT	862	WILMINGTON	08/31/78
PIPKIN, SAMUEL D.	HARNETT	101	WILMINGTON	02/25/68
PITMA, J. M. (96)	HENDERSON	113	ASHEVILLE	09/16/74
PITT, B.F.	BERTIE	293	ELIZABETH CITY	06/01/69
PITT, HENRY B.	*DOCKET ONLY	1021	NEW BERN	12/21/68
PITTEWAY & MOORE		824	WILMINGTON	04/14/71
PITTMAN, BEVERLY	*DOCKET ONLY	1011	NEW BERN	12/18/69
PITTMAN, GEORGE A.	*DOCKET ONLY	254	NEW BERN	02/04/68
PITTS, GEORGE A.	*DOCKET ONLY	1133	NEW BERN	12/29/68
PLANTON, REUBEN	CLEVELAND	156	STATESVILLE	05/23/73
PLEDGER, JOHN	PASQUOTANK	596	ELIZABETH CITY	06/21/73
PLEDGER, JOHN A.	TYRRELL	217	ELIZABETH CITY	06/02/73
POE, HASTEN	*DOCKET ONLY	302	GREENSBORO	05/29/73
POGUE, E. H.	*DOCKET ONLY	555	GREENSBORO	04/05/76
POINDEXTER, A.P	YADKIN	591	WILMINGTON	10/15/70
POLLACK, WILLIAM F.	*DOCKET ONLY	1163	NEW BERN	12/30/68

NAME OF BANKRUPT	RESIDENCE	CASE NUMBER	CITY OF COURT	DATE FILED
POND, BENJAMIN K.	*DOCKET ONLY	167	GREENSBORO	04/15/73
PONTON, JOHN H.	HALIFAX	215	ELIZABETH CITY	06/24/73
PONTON, JOHN H.	HALIFAX	301	ELIZABETH CITY	06/24/73
PONTON, MANGO T.	*DOCKET ONLY	890	NEW BERN	08/19/68
PONTON, WILLIAM H.	*DOCKET ONLY	600	NEW BERN	03/25/68
POOL, GEORGE	*DOCKET ONLY	1262	NEW BERN	01/16/69
POOL, S.B.	HERTFORD	196	ELIZABETH CITY	03/01/68
POOL, STEPHEN D.	*DOCKET ONLY	1267	NEW BERN	12/31/68
POOL, WILLIAM E.	*DOCKET ONLY	63	NEW BERN	11/23/67
POOL, WILLIAM G. MD.	PASQUOTANK	275	ELIZABETH CITY	04/06/75
POOLE, JOHN W.	PASQUOTANK	81	ELIZABETH CITY	12/16/67
POPE, FREDERICK S.	*DOCKET ONLY	129	GREENSBORO	03/04/73
POPE, HENRY	*DOCKET ONLY	852	NEW BERN	06/19/68
POPE, JACKOB R.	HALIFAX	183	ELIZABETH CITY	05/03/73
POPE, N. HENRY	HARNETT	497	WILMINGTON	12/31/68
POPPE, GEORGE A.A.		770	WILMINGTON	04/14/74
PORTER, WILLIAM H.	BLADEN	640	WILMINGTON	09/30/71
PORTIS, JOHN L.	*DOCKET ONLY	612	NEW BERN	04/01/68
POSEY, A. E. (18)	HENDERSON	114	ASHEVILLE	01/27/73
POTEET, JOHN W.	ROWAN	85	STATESVILLE	04/21/73
POTTER, JAMES C.	*DOCKET ONLY	697	NEW BERN	05/22/68
POTTER, NATHANIEL	*DOCKET ONLY	1498	NEW BERN	07/24/73
POTTER, SAMUEL F.	BRUNSWICK	844	WILMINGTON	07/29/78
POWELL, AMOS S.C.	SAMPSON	262	WILMINGTON	05/29/68
POWELL, E. M.	*DOCKET ONLY	133	GREENSBORO	03/11/73
POWELL, E. M. (DR.)	*DOCKET ONLY	1275	NEW BERN	08/12/69
POWELL, EDWARD J.	*DOCKET ONLY	170	GREENSBORO	04/25/73
POWELL, HARRISON F.	*DOCKET ONLY	230	GREENSBORO	05/12/73
POWELL, JOHN A.	*DOCKET ONLY	1492	NEW BERN	07/10/73
POWELL, JOHN C.	*DOCKET ONLY	1065	NEW BERN	12/26/68
POWELL, NELSON A.	CALDWELL	3	WILMINGTON	09/21/67
POWELL, ROBERT M.	COLUMBUS	745	WILMINGTON	08/02/73
POWELL, SIDNER A.	*DOCKET ONLY	519	GREENSBORO	03/03/73
POWELL, SIDNES A.	*DOCKET ONLY	1374	NEW BERN	01/25/78
POWELL, WILLIAM H.	*DOCKET ONLY	165	NEW BERN	01/07/68
POWERS, EDWARD P.	CUMBERLAND	813	WILMINGTON	04/24/78
POWERS, JESSE	BUNCOMBE	112	ASHEVILLE	01/30/73
POWERS, W.R.	BUNCOMBE	193	WILMINGTON	04/29/68
POYNER, JOHN S.	CURRITUCK	206	ELIZABETH CITY	03/02/68
POYNER, W.S.	CURRITUCK	138	ELIZABETH CITY	02/17/68
PRAATHER, J. F. &	*DOCKET ONLY	522	GREENSBORO	05/08/73
PRAG, MOSES	*DOCKET ONLY	551	NEW BERN	03/18/69
PRANCE, BLOUNT C.	*DOCKET ONLY	710	NEW BERN	05/26/68
PRATHER, THOMAS F.	*DOCKET ONLY	523	GREENSBORO	05/08/73
PRATHER, THOMAS F.		563	WILMINGTON	10/29/69
PRATHER, THOMAS F. &		562	WILMINGTON	10/29/69
PRODY, HAYWOOD	*DOCKET ONLY	82	GREENSBORO	01/28/73
PREVO, WILLIAM A.	*DOCKET ONLY	36	GREENSBORO	11/09/72
PRICE, H. M.	*DOCKET ONLY	626	GREENSBORO	04/14/77
PRICE, JOSIAH L.	HALIFAX	434	ELIZABETH CITY	12/16/68
PRICE, PATRICK H.	*DOCKET ONLY	292	GREENSBORO	05/28/73
PRICE, THOMAS	*DOCKET ONLY	402	NEW BERN	02/28/68
PRICE, THOMAS D.	*DOCKET ONLY	842	NEW BERN	05/30/68
PRICE, WILLIAM	CUMBERLAND	783	WILMINGTON	09/13/75
PRICE, WILLIAM A.	PASQUOTANK	28	ELIZABETH CITY	10/14/67
PRIDDY, FLEMMING	*DOCKET ONLY	260	GREENSBORO	05/20/73
PRIDGEON, ROBERT W.	*DOCKET ONLY	1522	NEW BERN	10/06/73
PRINCE, A. D.	*DOCKET ONLY	634	GREENSBORO	07/31/78
PRITCHARD, E.W.	PASQUOTANK	279	ELIZABETH CITY	05/29/68
PRITCHETT, JAMES		319	WILMINGTON	06/30/68
PRITCHETT, THOMAS	*DOCKET ONLY	331	NEW BERN	02/22/68
PRITCHETT, WEBB	*DOCKET ONLY	372	NEW BERN	02/24/68
PRITCHETT, WILLIAM	*DOCKET ONLY	501	NEW BERN	03/07/68
PRITCHETTE, JABEZ	PASQUOTANK	294	ELIZABETH CITY	01/20/76
PRIWETT, HIRAM	WILKES	69	STATESVILLE	03/17/73
PROSISE, THAD J.	*DOCKET ONLY	1018	NEW BERN	12/21/68

NORTH CAROLINA BANKRUPTS - ACT OF 1867

NAME OF BANKRUPT	RESIDENCE	CASE NUMBER	CITY OF COURT	DATE FILED
PRUYN, DAVID J.	*DOCKET ONLY	1267	NEW BERN	03/10/70
PUCCI, G. C.	*DOCKET ONLY	749	NEW BERN	05/29/68
PUCKEL, C. D.	*DOCKET ONLY	458	GREENSBORO	02/05/74
PUGH, JOHN W.	HALIFAX	305	ELIZABETH CITY	04/01/76
PULLEN, BLAKE B.	*DOCKET ONLY	934	NEW BERN	09/21/68
PULLEN, JAMES D.	*DOCKET ONLY	1547	NEW BERN	12/22/73
PULLY, WILLIAM H.	*DOCKET ONLY	802	NEW BERN	05/30/68
PURGEAN, JAMES	*DOCKET ONLY	358	NEW BERN	02/24/68
QUARLES, A. M.	HALIFAX	487	ELIZABETH CITY	12/27/68
QUINN, JOHN W.	GASTON	5	STATESVILLE	12/06/72
RADCLIFFE, JAMES D.	RICHMOND	398	WILMINGTON	12/26/68
RAIFORD, M. D.	*DOCKET ONLY	838	NEW BERN	05/30/68
RAINES, JASPER J.	*DOCKET ONLY	85	NEW BERN	11/23/67
RAINEY, F.P.	NORTHAMPTON	345	ELIZABETH CITY	08/27/78
RALEIGH NATIONAL	NEW HANOVER	587	WILMINGTON	02/21/70
RAMLEY, JAMES W.	*DOCKET ONLY	38	NEW BERN	10/24/68
RAMSEY, JAMES	ROWAN	287	WILMINGTON	05/30/68
RAMSEY, JAMES T.	*DOCKET ONLY	17	GREENSBORO	10/05/72
RAMSEY, WILLIAM J.	*DOCKET ONLY	1453	NEW BERN	05/17/73
RAMSEY, WILLIAM J.	*DOCKET ONLY	1512	NEW BERN	07/03/73
RAMSON, MAXWELL	CATAWBA	515	WILMINGTON	01/01/69
RAMSON, V. W.	CATAWBA	94	STATESVILLE	04/20/73
RAMSOUR, ALFRED		256	STATESVILLE	01/06/74
RANDALL, L.D.	CLEVELAND	152	STATESVILLE	05/23/73
RANDOLPH, CHARLES A.	*DOCKET ONLY	1298	NEW BERN	10/25/70
RANDOLPH, RACHEL	*DOCKET ONLY	405	GREENSBORO	08/23/73
RANDOLPHE, J.C.	HALIFAX	334	ELIZABETH CITY	08/14/78
RANKIN, ALBERT	*DOCKET ONLY	568	NEW BERN	03/19/68
RANKIN, JOHN C.	*DOCKET ONLY	502	NEW BERN	03/07/68
RANKIN, W. S.	*DOCKET ONLY	499	GREENSBORO	04/08/75
RANKIN, WILLIAM W.	*DOCKET ONLY	503	NEW BERN	03/07/68
RANSOM, MATT W.	NORTHAMPTON	495	ELIZABETH CITY	12/29/68
RAPER, J. J.	*DOCKET ONLY	101	GREENSBORO	02/05/73
RAPER, M. D.	*DOCKET ONLY	108	GREENSBORO	02/05/73
RASBERRY, ALEXANDER	*DOCKET ONLY	833	NEW BERN	05/30/68
RATLEDGE, GILLIAM	DAVIE	68	STATESVILLE	03/05/73
RAWLE, D. E. & A.	*DOCKET ONLY	601	GREENSBORO	02/13/78
RAWLE, D. E. & A.	*DOCKET ONLY	601	GREENSBORO	02/13/78
RAWLS, ISAIAH	*DOCKET ONLY	1213	NEW BERN	12/31/68
RAY, ARCHIBALD	CUMBERLAND	877	WILMINGTON	05/01/73
RAY, HENRY M.	*DOCKET ONLY	593	GREENSBORO	09/27/77
RAY, JAMES F.	ROWAN	347	WILMINGTON	11/25/68
RAY, JESSIE	ASHE	495	WILMINGTON	12/31/68
RAYLE, B. Y.	*DOCKET ONLY	443	GREENSBORO	12/20/73
RAYMOND, ALFRED	CLEVELAND	548	WILMINGTON	05/22/69
RAYNOR, N.J.	BERTIE	244	ELIZABETH CITY	12/02/73
REA, W.D.	CHOWAN	273	ELIZABETH CITY	01/18/75
READ, ROBERT H.	*DOCKET ONLY	781	NEW BERN	08/10/68
READING, SIDNEY	MECKLENBURG	269	WILMINGTON	05/30/68
REAMS, ALEXANDER	*DOCKET ONLY	480	NEW BERN	03/04/68
REAVIS, THOMAS	*DOCKET ONLY	245	NEW BERN	01/31/68
REDDICK, THOMAS D.	GATES	642	ELIZABETH CITY	12/30/68
REDWINE, WILLIAM A.	*DOCKET ONLY	77	GREENSBORO	01/28/73
REED, W.H.	GATES	271	ELIZABETH CITY	11/04/74
REEL, ISAAC A.	MCDOWELL	192	STATESVILLE	06/11/73
REESE, ANTHONY	YADKIN	442	WILMINGTON	12/30/68
REESE, WILLIAM	HENDERSON	533	WILMINGTON	01/06/69
REEVES, ALEXANDER	ASHE	223	STATESVILLE	07/16/73
REEVES, CHARLES	ASHE	212	STATESVILLE	06/30/73
REEVES, R.E., & M.	*DOCKET ONLY	619	GREENSBORO	05/06/78
REEVES, SAMUEL,	ROWAN	281	WILMINGTON	05/30/68
REGAN, ELI T.	ROBESON	212	WILMINGTON	05/15/68
REGAN, HUGH	ROBESON	730	WILMINGTON	08/27/73
REID, HORACE K.	HALIFAX	641	ELIZABETH CITY	03/15/73
REID, JOHN	MACON	227	WILMINGTON	05/25/68
RENIGER, GEORGE H.	*DOCKET ONLY	681	GREENSBORO	08/29/78

NAME OF BANKRUPT	RESIDENCE	CASE NUMBER	CITY OF COURT	DATE FILED
RENSHAW, NOBB F.	MECKLENBURG	149	WILMINGTON	03/17/68
RENSTREE, J.D. &	WILSON	356	WILMINGTON	12/09/68
RESPASS, JAMES T.	*DOCKET ONLY	850	NEW BERN	08/15/68
REYNOLDS BROTHERS	-	809	WILMINGTON	02/28/78
REYNOLDS, DAVID	HALIFAX	240	ELIZABETH CITY	04/08/68
REYNOLDS, JAMER	*DOCKET ONLY	510	GREENSBORO	12/17/75
REYNOLDS, R. S.	*DOCKET ONLY	637	GREENSBORO	08/17/78
REYNOLDS, W. P.	*DOCKET ONLY	507	GREENSBORO	11/27/75
RHEM, EDWARD H.	*DOCKET ONLY	1425	NEW BERN	04/30/73
RHEM, JOSEPH S.	*DOCKET ONLY	1099	NEW BERN	12/29/68
RHEW, NELSON	*DOCKET ONLY	978	NEW BERN	12/07/68
RHYM, CHRISTY	GASTON	160	WILMINGTON	03/26/68
RHYNE, EMANUEL	GASTON	93	STATESVILLE	04/20/73
RHYNE, GEORGE C.	GASTON	221	STATESVILLE	07/09/73
RHYNE, HENRY M.	GASTON	24	STATESVILLE	01/08/73
RHYNO, JONATHAN	GASTON	62	STATESVILLE	02/26/73
RICE, JOHN W.	*DOCKET ONLY	1364	NEW BERN	11/13/71
RICE, NICHLESON	*DOCKET ONLY	693	NEW BERN	05/19/68
RICE, REECE	*DOCKET ONLY	632	GREENSBORO	06/29/78
RICH, C.W.	DAVIE	883	WILMINGTON	04/01/72
RICHARDS, HENRY	*DOCKET ONLY	481	NEW BERN	03/04/68
RICHARDS, W.F.	HALIFAX	245	ELIZABETH CITY	12/05/73
RICHARDS, WILLIAM	GASTON	262	STATESVILLE	06/20/74
RICHARDSON, CLEMENT	*DOCKET ONLY	1513	NEW BERN	08/19/73
RICHARDSON, DEMPSEY	PASQUOTANK	405	ELIZABETH CITY	12/18/68
RICHARDSON, FELIX, &	NEW HANOVER	44	WILMINGTON	01/22/68
RICHARDSON, JACOB	PASQUOTANK	183	ELIZABETH CITY	02/28/68
RICHARDSON, JOHN A.	*DOCKET ONLY	1569	NEW BERN	03/02/74
RICHARDSON, MASON J.	*DOCKET ONLY	454	GREENSBORO	01/19/74
RICHARDSON, SAMUEL &	NEW HANOVER	44	WILMINGTON	01/22/68
RICHARDSON, SAMUEL	*DOCKET ONLY	210	NEW BERN	01/21/68
RICHARDSON, W. R.	*DOCKET ONLY	914	NEW BERN	08/22/68
RICHARDSON, WILLIAM	*DOCKET ONLY	1455	NEW BERN	05/27/73
RICHARDSON, WILLIAM	*DOCKET ONLY	365	GREENSBORO	06/30/73
RICHARDSON, WILLIAM	*DOCKET ONLY	88	GREENSBORO	01/12/73
RICHEY, GEORGE H.	ROWAN	159	STATESVILLE	05/23/73
RICKS, ROBERT F.	*DOCKET ONLY	1551	NEW BERN	01/03/74
RICKS, WILLIE B.	*DOCKET ONLY	614	NEW BERN	04/01/68
RIDDICK, CHARLES A.	PASQUOTANK	45	ELIZABETH CITY	11/20/67
RIDDICK, ELISHA N.	PERQUIMANS	155	ELIZABETH CITY	02/24/68
RIDDICK, THOMAS T.	PERQUIMANS	114	ELIZABETH CITY	01/22/68
RIDDICK, W.D.	PERQUIMANS	115	ELIZABETH CITY	01/22/68
RIDE, TIMOTHY	*DOCKET ONLY	1139	NEW BERN	12/30/68
RIDENHOUR, PHILLIP	*DOCKET ONLY	59	GREENSBORO	01/11/73
RIDGE, NOAH	*DOCKET ONLY	297	NEW BERN	02/10/68
RIDLEY, THOMAS		850	ELIZABETH CITY	09/03/68
RIGGAN, JACOB J.	*DOCKET ONLY	586	NEW BERN	03/19/68
RIGGINS, C.D.	UNION	206	WILMINGTON	05/14/68
RIGGSBEE, ASA S.	*DOCKET ONLY	355	GREENSBORO	06/20/73
RIGGSBEE, ATLAS J.	*DOCKET ONLY	413	GREENSBORO	09/08/73
RIGGSBEE, JOHN M.	*DOCKET ONLY	104	NEW BERN	12/13/67
RIGGSBEE, JOSEPH J.	*DOCKET ONLY	354	GREENSBORO	06/19/73
RIGGSBEE, ZIMRIE	*DOCKET ONLY	409	GREENSBORO	08/27/73
RIKE, ALFORD J.	*DOCKET ONLY	311	NEW BERN	02/19/68
RILEY, GEORGE	*DOCKET ONLY	54	GREENSBORO	01/07/73
RINGGOLD, JOSEPH	*DOCKET ONLY	252	NEW BERN	02/03/68
RINSMON, NORMAN	ROBESON	781	WILMINGTON	12/23/73
RINTELS, WITTKOWSKY	MCDOWELL	173	WILMINGTON	04/11/68
RINTELS, WITTKOWSKY	WILKES	174	WILMINGTON	04/11/68
RINTELS, WITTKOWSKY	WILKES	176	WILMINGTON	04/11/68
RINTELS, WITTKOWSKY		581	WILMINGTON	06/22/70
RITTER, THOMAS W.	*DOCKET ONLY	256	GREENSBORO	05/17/73
RITTERM WILLIAM D.	MOORE	121	WILMINGTON	03/07/68
RIVENBARK, DAVID J.	DUPLIN	414	WILMINGTON	12/29/68
RIVER, WARREN	CUMBERLAND	850	WILMINGTON	08/13/78
ROACH, THOMAS	*DOCKET ONLY	190	NEW BERN	01/14/68

NORTH CAROLINA BANKRUPTS - ACT OF 1867

NAME OF BANKRUPT	RESIDENCE	CASE NUMBER	CITY OF COURT	DATE FILED
ROAR, R. P.	WILKES	235	STATESVILLE	09/29/73
ROARK, R.	CLEVELAND	126	WILMINGTON	03/12/68
ROBBINS & FULGHRUM	*DOCKET ONLY	1200	NEW BERN	12/30/68
ROBBINS, ALAEXANDER	*DOCKET ONLY	190	GREENSBORO	04/01/73
ROBBINS, FRANKLIN C.	*DOCKET ONLY	196	GREENSBORO	05/02/73
ROBBINS, FREDRICK W.	*DOCKET ONLY	47	NEW BERN	11/07/67
ROBBINS, JESSE	*DOCKET ONLY	198	GREENSBORO	05/02/73
ROBBINS, MICHAEL	*DOCKET ONLY	179	GREENSBORO	04/28/73
ROBERSON, HENRY P.	*DOCKET ONLY	220	GREENSBORO	05/07/73
ROBERSON, JOHN J.	*DOCKET ONLY	124	NEW BERN	12/28/67
ROBERT, BARNWELL S.	*DOCKET ONLY	1148	NEW BERN	12/20/68
ROBERT, JAMES & JOHN	*DOCKET ONLY	731	NEW BERN	05/29/68
ROBERTS, A. J.	*DOCKET ONLY	1005	NEW BERN	12/18/68
ROBERTS, DANIEL	*DOCKET ONLY	279	GREENSBORO	05/24/73
ROBERTS, GEORGE W.	*DOCKET ONLY	277	GREENSBORO	05/24/77
ROBERTS, J. D. & J.	*DOCKET ONLY	1033	NEW BERN	12/23/68
ROBERTS, JAMES	*DOCKET ONLY	213	NEW BERN	01/22/68
ROBERTS, JEREMIAH H.	CUMBERLAND	633	WILMINGTON	06/06/71
ROBERTS, N.	*DOCKET ONLY	972	NEW BERN	11/30/68
ROBERTS, RUFUS	CLEVELAND	243	STATESVILLE	12/02/73
ROBERTS, T. A.	*DOCKET ONLY	1147	NEW BERN	12/31/68
ROBERTS, WILLIAM C.	*DOCKET ONLY	1003	NEW BERN	12/26/68
ROBERTS, WILLIAM H.	*DOCKET ONLY	403	NEW BERN	02/29/68
ROBERTS, WILLIAM P.	GATES	193	ELIZABETH CITY	02/28/68
ROBERTSON & BROTHERS	MARTIN	631	ELIZABETH CITY	10/11/69
ROBERTSON, AARON	*DOCKET ONLY	1029	NEW BERN	12/23/68
ROBERTSON, H.E.	DAVIE	61	STATESVILLE	02/24/73
ROBERTSON, JOHN E.	*DOCKET ONLY	474	GREENSBORO	06/02/74
ROBERTSON, THOMAS I.	*DOCKET ONLY	15	GREENSBORO	08/31/72
ROBERTSON, WILL G.	CURRITUCK	207	ELIZABETH CITY	03/02/69
ROBERTSON, WILLIAM	YADKIN	156	WILMINGTON	03/28/68
ROBESON, BARTRAM	BLADEN	873	WILMINGTON	02/12/73
ROBINSON, ALEX C.	MONTGOMERY	221	WILMINGTON	05/21/68
ROBINSON, CHARLES H.	NEW HANOVER	795	WILMINGTON	08/31/76
ROBINSON, JAMES B.	MECKLENBURG	94	WILMINGTON	02/28/68
ROBINSON, JAND D.	*DOCKET ONLY	1281	NEW BERN	12/23/68
ROBINSON, M. L.	HENDERSON	117	ASHEVILLE	05/06/73
ROBINSON, RICHARD B.	*DOCKET ONLY	1155	NEW BERN	12/30/68
ROBINSON, THOMPSON	GASTON	517	WILMINGTON	01/01/69
ROBINSON, WILLIAM	*DOCKET ONLY	1067	NEW BERN	12/26/68
ROBINSON, WILLIAM E.	*DOCKET ONLY	969	NEW BERN	12/15/68
ROBINSON, WILLIAM E.	DAVIDSON	214	WILMINGTON	05/18/68
ROBINSON, WILLOUGHBY	MARTIN	266	ELIZABETH CITY	05/30/68
RODGERS, CALVIN J.	*DOCKET ONLY	867	NEW BERN	08/19/68
RODWELL, WILLIAM B.	*DOCKET ONLY	615	NEW BERN	04/10/68
ROGERS & CHAMBERS, &	CUMBERLAND	183	WILMINGTON	04/15/68
ROGERS & ETHERIDGE		236	ELIZABETH CITY	09/27/73
ROGERS, ALLEN	*DOCKET ONLY	205	NEW BERN	01/20/68
ROGERS, DAVID R.	CHEROKEE	323	WILMINGTON	08/01/68
ROGERS, LEVI	*DOCKET ONLY	544	NEW BERN	03/17/68
ROGERS, SION H.	*DOCKET ONLY	1544	NEW BERN	12/17/73
ROGSTER, HORACE T.	*DOCKET ONLY	692	NEW BERN	05/19/68
ROLLINS, PINKNY	BUNCOMBE	118	ASHEVILLE	08/31/78
ROMAINE, WILLIAM H.	*DOCKET ONLY	232	NEW BERN	01/30/68
RONEY, BENJAMIN F.	*DOCKET ONLY	603	NEW BERN	05/30/68
ROP, JOSEPH W.	MECKLENBURG	207	WILMINGTON	05/14/68
ROPER, JAMES F., A.	*DOCKET ONLY	517	GREENSBORO	12/04/73
ROSE, ARCHIBALD	*DOCKET ONLY	543	NEW BERN	03/17/68
ROSEMAN, JAMES C.	ROWAN	1	WILMINGTON	07/10/67
ROSEMAN, JAMES C.	ROWAN	428	WILMINGTON	12/30/68
ROSENBAUM, MORRIS &	*DOCKET ONLY	1616	NEW BERN	12/06/75
ROSENTHAL, GUSTAVUS	NEW HANOVER	561	WILMINGTON	10/22/69
ROTHROCK, JOHN M.	*DOCKET ONLY	102	GREENSBORO	02/08/73
ROTHSCHILD, JACOB	*DOCKET ONLY	493	GREENSBORO	06/07/75
ROUGHTON, MCALLISTER	*DOCKET ONLY	699	NEW BERN	05/25/68
ROUNDTREE, F. M.	*DOCKET ONLY	1582	NEW BERN	05/11/74

NORTH CAROLINA BANKRUPTS - ACT OF 1867

NAME OF BANKRUPT	RESIDENCE	CASE NUMBER	CITY OF COURT	DATE FILED
ROUNDTREE, S. H	*DOCKET ONLY	1721	NEW BERN	08/30/78
ROUNDTREE, THOMAS	*DOCKET ONLY	760	NEW BERN	05/29/68
ROUSE, ABNER	*DOCKET ONLY	832	NEW BERN	05/30/68
ROUSE, BENJAMIN S.	*DOCKET ONLY	1076	NEW BERN	12/25/68
ROUSE, JOSHUA	*DOCKET ONLY	454	NEW BERN	03/02/68
ROUTH, MOSES	*DOCKET ONLY	252	GREENSBORO	05/19/73
ROWAN & BRITTON	CHEROKEE	198	WILMINGTON	05/06/68
ROWAN, I. H.	*DOCKET ONLY	464	GREENSBORO	02/23/74
ROWE, WILLIAM L.	UNION	191	WILMINGTON	04/24/68
ROWELL, JOHN C.	BRUNSWICK	735	WILMINGTON	07/03/73
ROWENS, THOMAS	*DOCKET ONLY	1545	NEW BERN	12/19/73
ROZIER, JAMES A.	ROBESON	425	WILMINGTON	12/30/68
ROZIER, REUBEN	ROBESON	756	WILMINGTON	11/20/73
ROZSTER, S. B.	*DOCKET ONLY	568	NEW BERN	03/17/68
RUDASIL, WILEY	CLEVELAND	237	WILMINGTON	05/27/68
RUDD, THOMAS L.	*DOCKET ONLY	172	GREENSBORO	04/25/73
RUDD, WILLIS A.	*DOCKET ONLY	419	GREENSBORO	10/06/73
RUDDICK, ELLSBERY W.	PERQUIMANS	152	ELIZABETH CITY	02/24/68
RULIFSON, J. M. &	*DOCKET ONLY	772	NEW BERN	05/30/68
RUMLEY, GILBERT	*DOCKET ONLY	1349	NEW BERN	06/23/71
RUPELL & ELLIS	NEW HANOVER	480	WILMINGTON	12/31/68
RUSH, A. G.	*DOCKET ONLY	74	GREENSBORO	01/27/73
RUSH, BENJAMIN	CUMBERLAND	240	WILMINGTON	05/27/68
RUSH, CALVIN H.	*DOCKET ONLY	248	GREENSBORO	05/14/73
RUSSELL, BURNAL	*DOCKET ONLY	1195	NEW BERN	12/31/68
RUSSELL, DANIEL W.	*DOCKET ONLY	1123	NEW BERN	12/30/68
RUSSELL, ELVY	GATES	402	ELIZABETH CITY	12/18/68
RUSSELL, F.H.	GATES	408	ELIZABETH CITY	12/17/68
RUSSELL, HENRY C.	*DOCKET ONLY	1588	NEW BERN	02/18/74
RUSSELL, JAMES E.	GATES	455	ELIZABETH CITY	12/29/68
RUSSELL, JOHN N.	BUNCOMBE	118	ASHEVILLE	08/29/78
RUSSELL, MAJOR	*DOCKET ONLY	1701	NEW BERN	08/26/78
RUSSELL, RICHARD A.	*DOCKET ONLY	1392	NEW BERN	09/21/72
RUSSELL, WILLIAM A.	*DOCKET ONLY	362	GREENSBORO	06/27/73
RYTHENBURG &	NEW HANOVER	246	WILMINGTON	05/29/68
RYTTENBERG, HENRY	NEW HANOVER	49	WILMINGTON	01/24/68
SADLER, BENJAMIN	*DOCKET ONLY	1517	NEW BERN	08/25/73
SADLER, D. G.	*DOCKET ONLY	1499	NEW BERN	07/20/73
SAIL, WILLIAM	WILKES	48	STATESVILLE	02/18/73
SAILS, MARTIN	*DOCKET ONLY	858	NEW BERN	11/08/68
SAIN, CASPER	DAVIE	509	WILMINGTON	01/01/69
SALE, JOHN D.	*DOCKET ONLY	1182	NEW BERN	12/31/68
SALE, ROBERT	WILKES	250	STATESVILLE	01/15/74
SALLER, I.& ET AL	MECKLENBURG	25	WILMINGTON	01/16/67
SALLER, ISAAC & ET	MECKLENBURG	25	WILMINGTON	10/16/67
SALLEY, L.O.	RUTHERFORD	52	WILMINGTON	01/20/68
SAMDERSON, EDWARD F.	*DOCKET ONLY	1025	NEW BERN	12/22/68
SAMPSON, GEORGE	*DOCKET ONLY	1303	NEW BERN	08/22/70
SAMPSON, HENRY	*DOCKET ONLY	589	WILMINGTON	09/24/70
SANDERLIN, CALAB	PASQUOTANK	392	ELIZABETH CITY	12/12/68
SANDERLIN, DORSEY	CAMDEN	49	ELIZABETH CITY	11/04/67
SANDERLIN, JAMES S.	CAMDEN	212	ELIZABETH CITY	10/18/67
SANDERLINE, MAXEY	PASQUOTANK	393	ELIZABETH CITY	12/12/68
SANDERLINE, W.W.	CAMDEN	275	ELIZABETH CITY	05/29/68
SANDERLINE, WILSON	CURRITUCK	33	ELIZABETH CITY	10/27/67
SANDERS, J. J.	*DOCKET ONLY	482	NEW BERN	03/04/68
SANDERS, P. C.	*DOCKET ONLY	449	GREENSBORO	01/12/74
SANDERS, WILLIAM P.	*DOCKET ONLY	304	NEW BERN	02/18/68
SANDERSON, W.F.	WASHINGTON	73	ELIZABETH CITY	10/03/67
SANE, JAMES S.	*DOCKET ONLY	656	NEW BERN	04/25/68
SANFORD, GREEN	*DOCKET ONLY	175	NEW BERN	01/09/68
SAPP, THOMAS H.	*DOCKET ONLY	652	GREENSBORO	08/27/78
SARGENT, EDWARD	BURKE	189	STATESVILLE	08/09/73
SARRATT, N. J.	CLEVELAND	201	STATESVILLE	06/20/73
SASSER, TIPPO H.	*DOCKET ONLY	1695	NEW BERN	08/23/78
SATTERFIELD, GREEN	*DOCKET ONLY	750	NEW BERN	05/29/68

NAME OF BANKRUPT	RESIDENCE	CASE NUMBER	CITY OF COURT	DATE FILED
SATTERFIELD, JOHN B.	CHOWAN	482	ELIZABETH CITY	12/28/68
SAULS, BENJAMIN B.	*DOCKET ONLY	985	NEW BERN	12/15/68
SAULS, HENRY J.	*DOCKET ONLY	1579	NEW BERN	05/05/74
SAUNDER, MILTON	*DOCKET ONLY	1283	NEW BERN	12/31/68
SAUNDERLINE, JOHN W.	CURRITUCK	72	ELIZABETH CITY	12/05/67
SAUNDERS, ALFRED	*DOCKET ONLY	227	NEW BERN	01/28/68
SAUNDERS, REUBEN	NORTHAMPTON	80	ELIZABETH CITY	02/17/68
SAVAGE, JOHN Y.	HALIFAX	518	ELIZABETH CITY	11/30/70
SAWYER, COSIEN L.	CAMDEN	187	ELIZABETH CITY	05/12/73
SAWYER, D.H.	CAMDEN	76	ELIZABETH CITY	12/16/67
SAWYER, FREDERICK	CAMDEN	247	ELIZABETH CITY	04/13/68
SAWYER, MALACHI	CAMDEN	159	ELIZABETH CITY	02/23/68
SAWYER, NATHAN G.	CAMDEN	156	ELIZABETH CITY	02/24/68
SAWYER, WILL W.	CAMDEN	200	ELIZABETH CITY	03/02/68
SCALES, JACKSON	*DOCKET ONLY	153	NEW BERN	01/02/68
SCALES, RICHARD H.	*DOCKET ONLY	1181	NEW BERN	12/31/68
SCARBOROUGH, JOHN R.	MONTGOMERY	163	WILMINGTON	04/02/68
SCARR, F. & COMPANY	*DOCKET ONLY	814	GREENSBORO	03/07/78
SCHLOPBERG, MAX	CUMBERLAND	790	WILMINGTON	01/10/78
SCHLOPBERG, MAX	CUMBERLAND	881	WILMINGTON	08/31/78
SCHMERIN, JOSEPH	*DOCKET ONLY	1684	NEW BERN	04/27/78
SCHONWALD, JAMES	NEW HANOVER	119	WILMINGTON	03/06/68
SCHOOLFIELD, DANIEL	*DOCKET ONLY	216	GREENSBORO	05/12/73
SCHUCK, JAMES W.	NEW HANOVER	763	WILMINGTON	12/30/73
SCOTT, A. W.	*DOCKET ONLY	414	GREENSBORO	09/09/73
SCOTT, ADDISON	CABARRUS	359	WILMINGTON	12/12/68
SCOTT, BRICE F.	*DOCKET ONLY	1192	NEW BERN	12/30/68
SCOTT, HARDY O.	*DOCKET ONLY	1626	NEW BERN	02/19/76
SCOTT, JACOB F.	*DOCKET ONLY	733	NEW BERN	06/02/68
SCOTT, JAMES A.	MCDOWELL	329	STATESVILLE	09/30/78
SCOTT, JAMES J.	*DOCKET ONLY	991	NEW BERN	12/15/68
SCOTT, JAMES M.	*DOCKET ONLY	827	NEW BERN	05/20/68
SCROGGS, ANDREW	CALDWELL	162	STATESVILLE	05/23/73
SCULL, WILLIAM	JACKSON	274	ELIZABETH CITY	10/07/74
SEALY, MOORE T.	ROBESON	785	WILMINGTON	01/17/74
SEARS, B. J.	*DOCKET ONLY	82	NEW BERN	11/30/67
SEARS, C.T.	CURRITUCK	324	ELIZABETH CITY	02/26/78
SEBILL, NICHOLAS H.	MARTIN	147	ELIZABETH CITY	02/17/68
SECHRIST, A.	*DOCKET ONLY	752	NEW BERN	05/29/68
SEIGLE, TEMPLETON &	IREDELL	0	WILMINGTON	10/10/67
SELBY, BENJAMIN M	*DOCKET ONLY	761	NEW BERN	05/29/68
SELBY, JERRMIAH R.	*DOCKET ONLY	1462	NEW BERN	06/03/73
SELBY, TALBERT H.	*DOCKET ONLY	1487	NEW BERN	07/03/73
SELLARS, WILLIAM B.	*DOCKET ONLY	802	GREENSBORO	02/15/78
SELLARS, WILLIAM B.	*DOCKET ONLY	802	GREENSBORO	02/15/78
SERGEANT, JAMES	*DOCKET ONLY	278	NEW BERN	02/08/68
SERGEANT, R. W.	*DOCKET ONLY	753	NEW BERN	05/29/68
SEVIN, EDWARD	BUNCOMBE	195	WILMINGTON	05/01/68
SEWALL, RICHARD B.	*DOCKET ONLY	1156	NEW BERN	12/30/68
SHAFER, HENRY S.	*DOCKET ONLY	395	GREENSBORO	07/31/73
SHAFFER, A.W.		322	WILMINGTON	07/18/68
SHAFFER, A.W.		583	WILMINGTON	07/18/70
SHAFFER, A.W.		637	WILMINGTON	08/05/71
SHANNON, WILLIAM	PASQUOTANK	22	ELIZABETH CITY	10/05/67
SHANNONHOUSE, JAMES	PERQUIMANS	502	ELIZABETH CITY	02/09/70
SHARMONHOUSE, B.J.	MECKLENBURG	250	ELIZABETH CITY	05/08/68
SHARP, WILLIAM	HERTFORD	229	ELIZABETH CITY	02/28/68
SHARPE, W. H.	*DOCKET ONLY	1722	NEW BERN	08/30/78
SHARPE, WILLIAM R.	DAVIE	230	STATESVILLE	08/01/73
SHATNELL, N.	RUTHERFORD	80	STATESVILLE	04/04/73
SHAW, DANIEL	*DOCKET ONLY	429	GREENSBORO	11/26/73
SHAW, DUNCAN	CUMBERLAND	819	WILMINGTON	05/02/78
SHAW, FINLY W.	*DOCKET ONLY	851	NEW BERN	06/16/68
SHAW, FRANK D., JR.	NEW HANOVER	482	WILMINGTON	12/31/68
SHAW, JOHN D.	LINCOLN	244	STATESVILLE	12/02/73
SHAW, JOSEPH B.	PASQUOTANK	50	ELIZABETH CITY	11/11/67

NAME OF BANKRUPT	RESIDENCE	CASE NUMBER	CITY OF COURT	DATE FILED
SHAW, P.P. & COMPANY		318	WILMINGTON	06/30/68
SHEEK, ALBERT	DAVIE	568	WILMINGTON	01/24/70
SHEEK, DANIEL L.	DAVIE	565	WILMINGTON	01/24/70
SHEEK, JACOB	DAVIE	120	STATESVILLE	05/12/73
SHEEK, RICHARD	*DOCKET ONLY	29	GREENSBORO	11/26/72
SHEETS, DAVID J.	ROWAN	65	STATESVILLE	03/03/73
SHELTON, G. M.	*DOCKET ONLY	383	GREENSBORO	07/15/73
SHEPARD, ABNER (18)	HENDERSON	120	ASHEVILLE	01/17/73
SHEPARD, ANDREW	*DOCKET ONLY	1228	NEW BERN	12/26/68
SHEPARD, GARDNER	ONSLOW	659	WILMINGTON	02/23/72
SHEPARD, W.B.	CHOWAN	289	ELIZABETH CITY	11/03/75
SHEPHARD, NIMROD	HENDERSON	124	ASHEVILLE	01/22/73
SHEPHERD, ANDREW J.	ONSLOW	408	WILMINGTON	12/26/68
SHEPHERD, JOHN T.	IREDELL	94	STATESVILLE	04/20/73
SHERARD, JOHN V.	*DOCKET ONLY	421	NEW BERN	02/29/68
SHERWOOD, SANIEL N.	*DOCKET ONLY	432	GREENSBORO	11/29/73
SHICKLAND, LEVI	*DOCKET ONLY	1694	NEW BERN	08/20/78
SHIELD, JOHN	*DOCKET ONLY	657	GREENSBORO	08/28/78
SHIELDS, CHARLES	HALIFAX	506	ELIZABETH CITY	11/04/70
SHIPHEND, WILLIAM R.	*DOCKET ONLY	171	NEW BERN	01/09/68
SHIPMAN, A. R. (57)	HENDERSON	123	ASHEVILLE	04/22/73
SHIPMAN, JOHN (58)	HENDERSON	131	ASHEVILLE	04/22/73
SHOEMAKER, EDWARD M.	MECKLENBURG	475	WILMINGTON	12/31/68
SHOFFNER, JACOB	*DOCKET ONLY	19	GREENSBORO	10/15/72
SHOFFNER, MARTIN	STANLY	218	WILMINGTON	05/21/68
SHORES, DAVID	YADKIN	619	WILMINGTON	03/01/71
SHREVES, ROBERT W.	*DOCKET ONLY	338	GREENSBORO	08/10/73
SHULL, PHILLIP A.	LINCOLN	151	STATESVILLE	05/23/73
SHULTZ & COMPANY,	PHILADELPHIA	769	WILMINGTON	02/23/74
SHULTZ, N. & CO.	*DOCKET ONLY	1643	NEW BERN	03/21/77
SHULTZ, N. & COMPANY	*DOCKET ONLY	1387	NEW BERN	05/01/72
SHULTZ, NATHAN	*DOCKET ONLY	1600	NEW BERN	02/11/75
SIKES, JOHN M.	COLUMBUS	853	WILMINGTON	08/19/78
SIKES, WILLIS & W.	*DOCKET ONLY	644	GREENSBORO	08/23/78
SILER, LUN F.	MACON	222	WILMINGTON	05/22/68
SILER, THADEUS	MACON	310	WILMINGTON	05/30/68
SILLS, A.J.	HALIFAX	173	ELIZABETH CITY	03/26/73
SILVERTHAN, JORDAN	*DOCKET ONLY	397	NEW BERN	02/29/68
SIMMOND, DAVID D.,	*DOCKET ONLY	491	NEW BERN	03/06/68
SIMMONS, GEORGE W.	*DOCKET ONLY	1001	NEW BERN	12/11/68
SIMMONS, POWELL H.	*DOCKET ONLY	843	NEW BERN	05/30/68
SIMMONS, SAMUEL S.	TYRRELL	211	ELIZABETH CITY	06/11/67
SIMMS, A. J.	*DOCKET ONLY	381	NEW BERN	02/29/68
SIMONTON, JULIUS	IREDELL	411	WILMINGTON	12/29/68
SIMPSON, J. HAWKINS	*DOCKET ONLY	178	GREENSBORO	04/29/73
SIMPSON, JAMES	*DOCKET ONLY	157	GREENSBORO	04/18/73
SIMPSON, ROBERT	*DOCKET ONLY	352	GREENSBORO	08/18/73
SIMPSON, ROBERT,		119	ASHEVILLE	12/21/79
SIMPSON, WILLIAM	UNION	373	WILMINGTON	12/19/68
SIMPSON, WILLIAM L.	*DOCKET ONLY	32	GREENSBORO	12/02/72
SINCLAIR, ALEX	MECKLENBURG	471	WILMINGTON	12/31/68
SINCLAIR, PETER J.	MECKLENBURG	11	WILMINGTON	10/26/67
SITTERSON, JOSEPH M.	MARTIN	224	ELIZABETH CITY	03/07/68
SKINNER, C.W., JR.	CHOWAN	19	ELIZABETH CITY	08/29/67
SKINNER, H.H.		36	ELIZABETH CITY	10/04/67
SKINNER, THOMAS E.	*DOCKET ONLY	22	NEW BERN	10/04/67
SKINNER, WILLIAM S.	*DOCKET ONLY	1617	NEW BERN	12/14/75
SKIRVEN, THOMAS B.		48	ELIZABETH CITY	11/04/67
SLAGLE, J.H.L.	BUNCOMBE	252	WILMINGTON	05/29/68
SLATE, JOHN	*DOCKET ONLY	349	GREENSBORO	06/14/73
SLATER, R. H.	*DOCKET ONLY	136	NEW BERN	12/26/67
SLAUGHTER, J. S.	*DOCKET ONLY	570	NEW BERN	03/19/68
SLOAN, JOHN L	ROWAN	11	STATESVILLE	12/02/72
SLOAN, JOHN, JAMES	*DOCKET ONLY	731	NEW BERN	05/26/68
SLOAN, SAMUEL A.	ROWAN	348	WILMINGTON	11/17/68
SLOAN, WILLIAM	*DOCKET ONLY	509	GREENSBORO	12/18/75

NORTH CAROLINA BANKRUPTS - ACT OF 1867

NAME OF BANKRUPT	RESIDENCE	CASE NUMBER	CITY OF COURT	DATE FILED
SLOOP, JACOB	ROWAN	306	STATESVILLE	06/29/78
SLOOP, MUMFORD S.M.	CABARRUS	162	WILMINGTON	03/31/68
SMALL, RICHARD W.	CHOWAN	283	ELIZABETH CITY	05/26/68
SMALL, WILLIAM	PERQUIMANS	464	ELIZABETH CITY	12/28/68
SMALLWOOD, EDWARD F.	*DOCKET ONLY	1411	NEW BERN	02/01/73
SMART, T. L. (127)	BUNCOMBE	127	ASHEVILLE	05/12/73
SMASH, JOHN (129)	BUNCOBME	129	ASHEVILLE	04/27/73
SMASINGEN, JOHN M.	*DOCKET ONLY	1384	NEW BERN	04/20/72
SMITH, A. B.	*DOCKET ONLY	477	GREENSBORO	06/22/74
SMITH, AGNES	CHOWAN	310	ELIZABETH CITY	03/31/76
SMITH, ANDERSON	*DOCKET ONLY	128	GREENSBORO	03/01/73
SMITH, ASA J.	*DOCKET ONLY	1413	NEW BERN	06/03/73
SMITH, B.N.	MECKLENBURG	664	WILMINGTON	04/04/72
SMITH, BENJAMIN C.	*DOCKET ONLY	1371	NEW BERN	01/06/72
SMITH, BENJAMIN D.	*DOCKET ONLY	666	NEW BERN	08/19/68
SMITH, BURNS	*DOCKET ONLY	1505	NEW BERN	08/08/73
SMITH, CASPER M.	*DOCKET ONLY	125	GREENSBORO	02/27/73
SMITH, CHARLES	*DOCKET ONLY	108	GREENSBORO	02/05/73
SMITH, CHARLES A.	*DOCKET ONLY	569	NEW BERN	03/19/68
SMITH, CHARLES C.	*DOCKET ONLY	1353	NEW BERN	07/31/71
SMITH, CHARLES S.	HALIFAX	185	ELIZABETH CITY	05/07/73
SMITH, CHARLEY E.	ANSON	123	WILMINGTON	03/12/68
SMITH, D.A. &		603	WILMINGTON	11/08/76
SMITH, DAVID	*DOCKET ONLY	974	NEW BERN	12/05/68
SMITH, EVERITT	NEW HANOVER	213	WILMINGTON	05/15/68
SMITH, FANNIE E.	*DOCKET ONLY	433	GREENSBORO	12/03/73
SMITH, FIELDS &	ROBESON	416	WILMINGTON	12/30/68
SMITH, FREDRICK J.	*DOCKET ONLY	605	GREENSBORO	05/03/78
SMITH, FREDRICK J.	*DOCKET ONLY	605	GREENSBORO	05/03/78
SMITH, HALDEN	DAVIE	54	STATESVILLE	02/18/73
SMITH, J. BRITON	*DOCKET ONLY	1357	NEW BERN	09/06/71
SMITH, J.C.	ANSON	462	WILMINGTON	12/31/68
SMITH, J.M.	*DOCKET ONLY	97	GREENSBORO	02/05/73
SMITH, JAMES	*DOCKET ONLY	498	GREENSBORO	07/13/75
SMITH, JAMES W.	*DOCKET ONLY	198	NEW BERN	01/17/68
SMITH, JANUS S.	*DOCKET ONLY	1412	NEW BERN	02/05/73
SMITH, JOHN	*DOCKET ONLY	131	GREENSBORO	03/06/73
SMITH, JOHN	RUTHERFORD	207	STATESVILLE	06/25/73
SMITH, JOHN P.	ROBESON	458	WILMINGTON	12/31/68
SMITH, JOHN W.	STANLY	339	WILMINGTON	11/06/68
SMITH, JOSEPH	GATES	462	ELIZABETH CITY	12/28/68
SMITH, JOSEPH E. W.	*DOCKET ONLY	215	GREENSBORO	05/09/73
SMITH, JOSEPH S.	BUNCOMBE	270	WILMINGTON	05/30/68
SMITH, JOSHUA B.	*DOCKET ONLY	1539	NEW BERN	12/06/73
SMITH, L. C.	*DOCKET ONLY	201	NEW BERN	01/17/68
SMITH, L.H.		576	WILMINGTON	04/22/70
SMITH, LEONARD H.	MECKLENBURG	291	WILMINGTON	05/30/68
SMITH, PHILIP S.	*DOCKET ONLY	546	NEW BERN	03/17/68
SMITH, SAMUEL B.	*DOCKET ONLY	1506	NEW BERN	08/08/73
SMITH, SAMUEL E.	GATES	251	ELIZABETH CITY	05/09/68
SMITH, STEPHEN H.	MECKLENBURG	148	WILMINGTON	03/17/68
SMITH, THOMAS	*DOCKET ONLY	211	NEW BERN	01/21/68
SMITH, W. F.	*DOCKET ONLY	696	GREENSBORO	07/29/78
SMITH, W. H.	*DOCKET ONLY	751	NEW BERN	05/29/68
SMITH, W.W.	*DOCKET ONLY	430	GREENSBORO	11/28/73
SMITH, W.W.		576	WILMINGTON	04/22/70
SMITH, WALTER	*DOCKET ONLY	1299	NEW BERN	11/01/70
SMITH, WILLIAM	NEW HANOVER	245	WILMINGTON	05/29/68
SMITH, WILLIAM	*DOCKET ONLY	14	NEW BERN	09/30/67
SMITH, WILLIAM C.	*DOCKET ONLY	207	GREENSBORO	05/06/73
SMITH, WILLIAM H.	ROWAN	432	WILMINGTON	12/30/68
SMITH, WILLIAM O.	DAVIDSON	305	WILMINGTON	05/30/68
SMITH, WINSLOW A.	LINCOLN	345	WILMINGTON	11/21/68
SMITHEY, DAVID L.	*DOCKET ONLY	323	GREENSBORO	06/03/73
SMITHWICK, JAMES R.	*DOCKET ONLY	1117	NEW BERN	12/29/68
SNIPES, FRANCES C.	*DOCKET ONLY	441	GREENSBORO	12/13/73

NORTH CAROLINA BANKRUPTS - ACT OF 1867

NAME OF BANKRUPT	RESIDENCE	CASE NUMBER	CITY OF COURT	DATE FILED
SNIPES, JAMES	*DOCKET ONLY	545	NEW BERN	03/17/68
SNIPES, ROBERT A.	*DOCKET ONLY	804	NEW BERN	05/30/68
SNIPES, SARAH M.	*DOCKET ONLY	440	GREENSBORO	12/13/73
SNIPES, WILLIAM	*DOCKET ONLY	24	NEW BERN	10/07/67
SNOW, HENRY	YADKIN	66	WILMINGTON	01/18/68
SNOW, HENRY A.	HALIFAX	435	ELIZABETH CITY	12/08/68
SNOW, SAMUEL W.	*DOCKET ONLY	577	GREENSBORO	04/05/77
SNOW, SUGAR	HALIFAX	433	ELIZABETH CITY	12/08/68
SOLOMAN, SIGMUND	NEW HANOVER	859	WILMINGTON	08/26/78
SOLOMAN, WILLIAM P.	HALIFAX	643	ELIZABETH CITY	12/29/69
SOLOMON, WILLIAM P.	HALIFAX	489	ELIZABETH CITY	12/30/68
SORRELL, LION	*DOCKET ONLY	183	NEW BERN	01/15/68
SOUTHER, NOAH	MCDOWELL	56	STATESVILLE	02/18/73
SOUTHERLAND, JOHN D.	DUPLIN	29	WILMINGTON	12/05/67
SOUTHWICH & WHEELOCK		580	WILMINGTON	06/07/70
SPARKS, JOSEPH	YADKIN	830	WILMINGTON	05/21/71
SPARROW, B.W.	MECKLENBURG	278	WILMINGTON	05/30/68
SPARROW, THOMAS G.	*DOCKET ONLY	718	NEW BERN	05/28/68
SPEAKS, JAMES	WILKES	182	STATESVILLE	06/04/73
SPEARS, NEWTON J.	YADKIN	84	WILMINGTON	04/13/68
SPEED, R.K.	PASQUOTANK	7	ELIZABETH CITY	08/05/67
SPEED, ROBERT A.	*DOCKET ONLY	1157	NEW BERN	12/30/69
SPEED, THOMAS	*DOCKET ONLY	1171	NEW BERN	12/31/69
SPEER, SYLVESTER F.	*DOCKET ONLY	682	GREENSBORO	08/29/78
SPEIER, JOHN F.	NEW HANOVER	814	WILMINGTON	04/26/78
SPEIGH, WILLIAM	*DOCKET ONLY	1602	NEW BERN	02/26/74
SPEIRS, WILLIAM J.	GATES	194	ELIZABETH CITY	02/28/68
SPELL, GASTON	SAMPSON	699	WILMINGTON	05/30/73
SPELMAN, JOHN	*DOCKET ONLY	1134	NEW BERN	12/30/69
SPENCE, ALMON	PASQUOTANK	94	ELIZABETH CITY	12/25/67
SPENCE, JAMES B.	CAMDEN	218	ELIZABETH CITY	03/07/68
SPENCE, MARK B.	CHOWAN	131	ELIZABETH CITY	02/04/68
SPENCER, ALEXANDER	*DOCKET ONLY	1623	NEW BERN	02/15/76
SPENCER, CAREY	CURRITUCK	202	ELIZABETH CITY	03/02/68
SPENCER, ISAAC	TYRRELL	255	ELIZABETH CITY	01/10/74
SPENCER, JOSEPH A.	CAMDEN	644	ELIZABETH CITY	08/08/72
SPENCER, NATHAN	*DOCKET ONLY	43	GREENSBORO	12/16/72
SPENCER, PETER P.	*DOCKET ONLY	678	NEW BERN	05/18/68
SPICER, SOLOMON S.	*DOCKET ONLY	280	NEW BERN	02/10/68
SPRAGIUS, MILDRYAH	*DOCKET ONLY	302	NEW BERN	02/17/68
SPRING, BURROUGHS	-	813	WILMINGTON	04/11/71
SPRINKLE, OBADIAH	WILKES	206	STATESVILLE	05/25/73
SPRIULL, S.R.	HALIFAX	199	ELIZABETH CITY	05/24/73
SPRUILL, JAMES S.	WASHINGTON	79	ELIZABETH CITY	11/17/68
SPRUILL, SAMUEL	BERTIE	421	ELIZABETH CITY	12/24/69
SPRUILL, T.C.	CHOWAN	345	ELIZABETH CITY	08/30/78
SPRUILL, WILLIAM R.	PASQUOTANK	278	ELIZABETH CITY	05/29/68
SPRY, EDMOND	CURRITUCK	208	ELIZABETH CITY	03/02/68
SPRY, JAMES C.	DAVIE	261	STATESVILLE	06/20/74
SQUIRE, JOHN W.	GASTON	554	ELIZABETH CITY	11/29/72
SQUIRES, NICHOLAS	CAMDEN	99	ELIZABETH CITY	12/30/67
STACEY, A.G.	MECKLENBURG	338	WILMINGTON	11/06/68
STADLEY, D.	HENDERSON	530	WILMINGTON	01/04/69
STALEY, ADAM	WILKES	170	STATESVILLE	05/20/73
STALEY, ENOCK	WILKES	294	STATESVILLE	10/21/78
STALEY, ESLY	WILKES	53	STATESVILLE	02/18/73
STALLINGS,	*DOCKET ONLY	618	NEW BERN	04/01/68
STAMPER, JOHN	ASHE	175	STATESVILLE	06/02/73
STAMPS, MILTON	*DOCKET ONLY	303	NEW BERN	02/17/68
STANALAND, JOSEPH	BRUNSWICK	728	WILMINGTON	06/21/73
STANFIELD, J. A.	*DOCKET ONLY	1265	NEW BERN	01/26/69
STANFORD, ALEX T.	DUPLIN	710	WILMINGTON	06/11/73
STANLEY, ISAAC H.	*DOCKET ONLY	81	GREENSBORO	01/15/73
STANTON, EPHRAIM M.	PASQUOTANK	139	ELIZABETH CITY	02/17/68
STANTON, GEORGE	RICHMOND	340	WILMINGTON	11/06/68
STANTON, JOHN	PASQUOTANK	111	ELIZABETH CITY	01/20/68

NORTH CAROLINA BANKRUPTS - ACT OF 1867

NAME OF BANKRUPT	RESIDENCE	CASE NUMBER	CITY OF COURT	DATE FILED
STARNES, JANE	*DOCKET ONLY	209	GREENSBORO	05/07/73
STARNPER, ELI C.	ASHE	494	WILMINGTON	12/31/68
STEADMAN, J. M.	*DOCKET ONLY	435	GREENSBORO	12/05/73
STEDMAN, JAMES	YADKIN	500	WILMINGTON	01/01/68
STEED, JOHN S.	*DOCKET ONLY	168	GREENSBORO	04/23/73
STEEL, J.J.C.	UNION	392	WILMINGTON	12/28/68
STEEL, J.J.C.	UNION	392	WILMINGTON	05/02/78
STEELE, GEORGE	*DOCKET ONLY	152	NEW BERN	01/02/68
STEELE, MANLIUS D.	MECKLENBURG	634	WILMINGTON	06/12/71
STEELE, WILLIAM L.	ROWAN	326	STATESVILLE	08/29/78
STEELMAN, JACKSON	YADKIN	512	WILMINGTON	01/01/69
STEELMAN, WILLIAM	*DOCKET ONLY	415	GREENSBORO	09/17/73
STEEP, J. M (99)	BUNCOMBE	122	ASHEVILLE	06/07/73
STEGER, WILLIAM	PASQUOTANK	304	ELIZABETH CITY	05/10/76
STEPHENS, THOMAS J.	*DOCKET ONLY	1338	NEW BERN	03/31/71
STEPHENSON, EXUM	NORTHAMPTON	362	ELIZABETH CITY	04/06/69
STEPHENSON, JOHN	*DOCKET ONLY	42	GREENSBORO	12/10/72
STEPHENSON, JOHN W.	IREDELL	116	STATESVILLE	05/10/73
STEPP, JAMES (30)	HENDERSON	125	ASHEVILLE	01/10/73
STEPP, JOHN	BUNCOMBE	126	ASHEVILLE	06/02/73
STEPP, JOSEPH	BUNCOMBE	87	WILMINGTON	02/17/68
STEPP, WILLIAM	BUNCOMBE	130	ASHEVILLE	05/29/73
STERLING, RICHARD	*DOCKET ONLY	404	NEW BERN	02/28/68
STERNBURGER, SOLOMAN	NEW HANOVER	811	WILMINGTON	04/04/78
STERNS, ANDREW J.	*DOCKET ONLY	58	GREENSBORO	01/13/73
STERNS, THOMAS	*DOCKET ONLY	604	GREENSBORO	04/29/78
STERNS, THOMAS	*DOCKET ONLY	604	GREENSBORO	04/29/78
STETSON, M.B.	MACON	62	WILMINGTON	02/03/68
STEUHOUSE & MCCAULY	*DOCKET ONLY	615	GREENSBORO	04/26/78
STEVENS, AMOS W. &	*DOCKET ONLY	188	NEW BERN	01/09/68
STEVENS, JOHN F.	CLEVELAND	105	STATESVILLE	05/02/73
STEVENSON, J.R.	PASQUOTANK	103	ELIZABETH CITY	01/02/68
STEVENSON, JAMES C.		773	WILMINGTON	07/22/74
STEVENSON, JAMES S.	HERTFORD	209	ELIZABETH CITY	03/02/68
STEVENSON, WILLIAM	*DOCKET ONLY	675	NEW BERN	05/15/68
STEWART, DANIEL	RICHMOND	399	WILMINGTON	12/26/68
STEWART, J. F.	CALDWELL	113	STATESVILLE	05/02/73
STEWART, J. J	ROWAN	299	STATESVILLE	05/29/78
STEWART, JAMES	UNION	142	WILMINGTON	03/12/68
STEWART, MOSES	*DOCKET ONLY	316	GREENSBORO	06/03/73
STEWART, ROBERT A.	CHATHAM	54	WILMINGTON	01/30/68
STEWART, ROBERT S.	*DOCKET ONLY	75	GREENSBORO	01/25/73
STEWART, SAMUEL A.	MECKLENBURG	158	WILMINGTON	03/28/68
STEWART, THOMAS J.	*DOCKET ONLY	1256	NEW BERN	12/31/68
STEWART, WILLIAM	*DOCKET ONLY	239	GREENSBORO	05/12/73
STICH, FREIDLANDER &		772	WILMINGTON	04/27/74
STILEY, BENJAMIN F.	*DOCKET ONLY	1638	NEW BERN	01/08/77
STILL, WILLIAM M.	MECKLENBURG	473	WILMINGTON	12/31/68
STILLEY, C.C.	*DOCKET ONLY	1322	NEW BERN	01/30/71
STILWELL, J.	UNION	69	WILMINGTON	01/16/68
STIMSON, JAMES P.	*DOCKET ONLY	473	GREENSBORO	04/24/74
STING, JOHN	*DOCKET ONLY	434	NEW BERN	03/02/68
STINSON, GEORGE W.	*DOCKET ONLY	13	GREENSBORO	08/16/72
STINSON, JAMES P.	*DOCKET ONLY	546	GREENSBORO	04/24/74
STINSON, ROBERT M.	*DOCKET ONLY	848	NEW BERN	04/18/69
STIPE, WILLIAM B.	*DOCKET ONLY	57	GREENSBORO	01/10/73
STIREWALT, PAUL	*DOCKET ONLY	138	GREENSBORO	03/19/73
STIREWALT, VALENTINE	CABARRUS	36	WILMINGTON	01/13/68
STITH, B. D.	*DOCKET ONLY	782	NEW BERN	05/29/68
STOCKS, WILLIAM A.	*DOCKET ONLY	861	NEW BERN	11/12/68
STOKELY, J.D.	PASQUOTANK	116	ELIZABETH CITY	01/24/68
STOKES, KINCHEN	*DOCKET ONLY	107	GREENSBORO	02/05/73
STOKES, THOMAS	*DOCKET ONLY	250	NEW BERN	01/31/68
STOKES, THOMAS J.	*DOCKET ONLY	1415	NEW BERN	02/08/73
STOMER, WILLIAM W.	SAMPSON	647	WILMINGTON	12/16/71
STONE, ABRAM	GASTON	147	STATESVILLE	05/23/73

NAME OF BANKRUPT	RESIDENCE	CASE NUMBER	CITY OF COURT	DATE FILED
STONE, C. P	*DOCKET ONLY	1118	NEW BERN	12/29/69
STONE, FRANCIS	*DOCKET ONLY	89	NEW BERN	12/04/67
STONE, H. J.	*DOCKET ONLY	85	NEW BERN	12/04/67
STONE, JOHN	*DOCKET ONLY	87	GREENSBORO	01/30/73
STONE, JOHN C.	*DOCKET ONLY	669	NEW BERN	06/22/68
STONE, JOHN C.	*DOCKET ONLY	960	NEW BERN	11/09/68
STONE, WASHINGTON	*DOCKET ONLY	938	NEW BERN	09/29/68
STOUT, JOB	*DOCKET ONLY	183	GREENSBORO	04/29/73
STOUT, JONATHAN	WILKES	203	STATESVILLE	06/20/73
STRAGHOM, CALVIN G.	*DOCKET ONLY	483	NEW BERN	03/04/68
STRANGE, FRENCH	CUMBERLAND	615	WILMINGTON	02/21/71
STRAUGHN, E. W.	*DOCKET ONLY	459	GREENSBORO	01/11/74
STRAYHORN, WILLIAM	*DOCKET ONLY	431	GREENSBORO	11/28/73
STREET, WILLIAM J.	*DOCKET ONLY	984	NEW BERN	12/15/68
STRICKLAND, B. C.	*DOCKET ONLY	1611	NEW BERN	07/10/75
STRICKLAND,	*DOCKET ONLY	309	NEW BERN	02/18/68
STRICKLAND, ELBERT	SAMPSON	817	WILMINGTON	05/01/78
STRICKLAND, JOHN W.	NORTHAMPTON	437	ELIZABETH CITY	11/18/68
STRICKLAND, MAJOR	DUPLIN	688	WILMINGTON	05/29/73
STRICKLAND, N. W.	*DOCKET ONLY	1475	NEW BERN	06/18/73
STRICKLAND, WILLIAM	*DOCKET ONLY	684	NEW BERN	05/19/68
STROMER, HENRY E.	*DOCKET ONLY	1255	NEW BERN	12/31/68
STRONG, WILLIAM R.	*DOCKET ONLY	273	GREENSBORO	05/24/73
STROUD, ALFRED P.	*DOCKET ONLY	145	NEW BERN	12/31/67
STROUD, HUDSON C. C.	*DOCKET ONLY	108	NEW BERN	12/16/67
STROUD, THOMAS J.	*DOCKET ONLY	393	GREENSBORO	07/28/73
STRUDWICK, FREDERICK	*DOCKET ONLY	782	NEW BERN	08/19/68
STRUOP, J.C.	GASTON	98	STATESVILLE	04/20/73
STRUT, SAMUEL R.	*DOCKET ONLY	429	NEW BERN	02/29/68
STUMPS, JAMES	*DOCKET ONLY	567	NEW BERN	03/19/68
STURDIVANT, EDMUND	ANSON	379	WILMINGTON	12/23/68
STYNON, W. K.	*DOCKET ONLY	330	NEW BERN	02/22/68
STYRON, WILLIAM S.	*DOCKET ONLY	298	NEW BERN	02/15/68
SUDDERTH, C. M.	CALDWELL	134	STATESVILLE	05/21/73
SUDDERTH, J. M.	CALDWELL	269	STATESVILLE	11/26/74
SUGG, M.R.	*DOCKET ONLY	39	NEW BERN	10/25/67
SUIT, JAMES R.	*DOCKET ONLY	1460	NEW BERN	05/26/73
SULLIVAN, JOSEPH W.	CLEVELAND	122	STATESVILLE	05/12/73
SUMME, ALBERT T.	BUNCOMBE	132	ASHEVILLE	01/03/74
SUMMER, MATTHEW	*DOCKET ONLY	227	GREENSBORO	05/12/73
SUMMER, MILLS	HERTFORD	450	ELIZABETH CITY	12/28/68
SUMMER, THOMAS J.	*DOCKET ONLY	2	NEW BERN	06/04/67
SUMMERY, JOHN	HENDERSON	121	ASHEVILLE	06/12/73
SUMMEY, JACOB (20)	HENDERSON	128	ASHEVILLE	01/27/73
SUMNER, THOMAS J.	ROWAN	274	STATESVILLE	06/25/75
SUMROW, ROBERT H.	CABARRUS	350	WILMINGTON	12/04/68
SURLEY, PAGE &	CUMBERLAND	115	WILMINGTON	03/03/68
SURRATT, W. M. & A.	ROWAN	266	STATESVILLE	02/16/76
SUTTON, F. M.	*DOCKET ONLY	620	NEW BERN	04/02/68
SUTTON, HUGH A.	*DOCKET ONLY	164	NEW BERN	01/06/68
SUTTON, JOHN F. J.	*DOCKET ONLY	998	NEW BERN	12/11/68
SUTTON, JOHN M.	*DOCKET ONLY	490	NEW BERN	03/05/68
SUTTON, SAMUEL	PERQUIMANS	467	ELIZABETH CITY	12/21/68
SUTTON, WILLIAM	*DOCKET ONLY	1009	NEW BERN	12/18/68
SUTTON, WILLIAM I.	*DOCKET ONLY	1599	NEW BERN	02/03/75
SWARINGER, GEORGE	STANLY	401	WILMINGTON	12/26/68
SWEANEY, H. C.	*DOCKET ONLY	605	NEW BERN	05/30/68
SWEANEY, JOEL	*DOCKET ONLY	571	NEW BERN	03/19/68
SWEARINGER, JOHN M.	*DOCKET ONLY	489	NEW BERN	03/05/68
SWIFT, JOSHUA S	WASHINGTON	21	ELIZABETH CITY	09/14/67
SWINDELL, ANSON M.	*DOCKET ONLY	1481	NEW BERN	06/24/73
SWINDELL, EDWARD J.	*DOCKET ONLY	1486	NEW BERN	07/03/73
SYKES, B.F.	TYRRELL	293	ELIZABETH CITY	12/22/75
SYKES, MADISON	*DOCKET ONLY	1610	NEW BERN	07/07/75
SYKES, WILLIAM R.	NORTHAMPTON	375	ELIZABETH CITY	09/02/68
SYSTTER, BENJAMIN F.	*DOCKET ONLY	1531	NEW BERN	11/11/73

NAME OF BANKRUPT	RESIDENCE	CASE NUMBER	CITY OF COURT	DATE FILED
TABER, ALLEN (34)	HENDERSON	133	ASHEVILLE	01/31/73
TABER, ALLEN P.	HENDERSON	135	ASHEVILLE	08/22/78
TAFT, ALLEN H.	*DOCKET ONLY	1257	NEW BERN	12/31/68
TALLEY, JAMES B.	*DOCKET ONLY	343	GREENSBORO	06/13/73
TANKARD, GEORGE R.	*DOCKET ONLY	1491	NEW BERN	07/10/73
TANKARD, OLIVER H.	*DOCKET ONLY	1490	NEW BERN	07/10/73
TANNER, WILLIAM A.	RUTHERFORD	220	STATESVILLE	07/09/73
TAPP, HENRY	*DOCKET ONLY	806	NEW BERN	05/30/68
TATE, JAMES T.	MECKLENBURG	273	STATESVILLE	08/20/75
TATE, WILLIAM J.	*DOCKET ONLY	273	GREENSBORO	05/23/73
TATEM, W.H.	CAMDEN	279	ELIZABETH CITY	04/21/75
TATUM & COMPANY,	PASQUOTANK	510	ELIZABETH CITY	11/08/70
TATUM, CALEB	CURRITUCK	180	ELIZABETH CITY	02/29/68
TATUM, J.C. &	CHOWAN	616	ELIZABETH CITY	03/25/70
TATUM, JOHN C.	CAMDEN	846	ELIZABETH CITY	09/16/73
TATUM, OSBORNE	IREDELL	8	STATESVILLE	10/09/68
TAYLOR, ARCHIBALD	*DOCKET ONLY	1276	NEW BERN	09/21/69
TAYLOR, B.F.	CURRITUCK	104	ELIZABETH CITY	01/10/68
TAYLOR, CHARLES H.	*DOCKET ONLY	764	NEW BERN	06/02/68
TAYLOR, CHARLES H.	*DOCKET ONLY	109	NEW BERN	12/17/67
TAYLOR, DANIEL A.	*DOCKET ONLY	246	NEW BERN	01/31/68
TAYLOR, DAVID T.	*DOCKET ONLY	847	NEW BERN	05/15/68
TAYLOR, JACKSON	*DOCKET ONLY	1690	NEW BERN	08/07/78
TAYLOR, JAMES J.	*DOCKET ONLY	725	NEW BERN	05/27/68
TAYLOR, JAMES W.	*DOCKET ONLY	1347	NEW BERN	06/02/71
TAYLOR, JOHN	*DOCKET ONLY	1615	NEW BERN	12/02/75
TAYLOR, JOHN	DAVIDSON	301	WILMINGTON	05/30/68
TAYLOR, JOHN A.	*DOCKET ONLY	1016	NEW BERN	12/19/68
TAYLOR, MATCHELL	CAMDEN	807	ELIZABETH CITY	12/28/69
TAYLOR, MATHEW	NEW HANOVER	235	WILMINGTON	05/26/68
TAYLOR, RICHARD, N.	*DOCKET ONLY	12	NEW BERN	10/16/67
TAYLOR, S.W.	CHOWAN	248	ELIZABETH CITY	12/18/73
TAYLOR, SABAN	*DOCKET ONLY	1172	NEW BERN	12/31/68
TAYLOR, TERREL W.	HENDERSON	137	ASHEVILLE	03/01/73
TAYLOR, TIECHAR	HENDERSON	136	ASHEVILLE	08/02/73
TAYLOR, WILLIAM (JR)	*DOCKET ONLY	553	GREENSBORO	01/10/77
TAYLOR, WILLIAM H.	*DOCKET ONLY	834	NEW BERN	05/30/68
TAYLOR, WILLIAM J.	NORTHAMPTON	830	ELIZABETH CITY	03/12/69
TEAGUE, ABRAM O. P.	*DOCKET ONLY	83	GREENSBORO	01/29/73
TEAGUE, CHARLES	*DOCKET ONLY	285	GREENSBORO	05/28/73
TEAGUE, D. P.	*DOCKET ONLY	159	GREENSBORO	04/21/73
TEAGUE, M. M.	MCDOWELL	287	STATESVILLE	04/18/78
TEAGUE, MOSES	*DOCKET ONLY	84	GREENSBORO	01/29/73
TEAGUE, SOLOMON	*DOCKET ONLY	23	GREENSBORO	11/08/72
TELFAIR, ALEXANDER	*DOCKET ONLY	817	NEW BERN	04/01/68
TELFAIR, OCTAVIUS W.	*DOCKET ONLY	382	NEW BERN	02/29/68
TEMPLETON & SIEGLE	IREDELL	7	WILMINGTON	10/14/67
TEMPLETON & SIELGE	IREDELL	8	WILMINGTON	10/14/67
TERRALL, S. W.	*DOCKET ONLY	110	NEW BERN	12/17/67
TERRELL, JAMES M.	*DOCKET ONLY	784	NEW BERN	08/19/68
TERRY, WILLIAM A.	*DOCKET ONLY	332	GREENSBORO	06/07/73
THAGARD, W. C.	*DOCKET ONLY	439	GREENSBORO	12/12/73
THAXTON, JOHN	*DOCKET ONLY	328	NEW BERN	02/21/68
THERMASON, NATHANIEL	CLEVELAND	437	WILMINGTON	12/30/68
THERN, D.C.	IREDELL	362	WILMINGTON	12/14/68
THIEN, PHIL	*DOCKET ONLY	1563	NEW BERN	06/02/74
THIGPEN, IRVIN	*DOCKET ONLY	257	NEW BERN	02/05/68
THOMAS, ALLEN	*DOCKET ONLY	476	GREENSBORO	08/20/74
THOMAS, EDWARD D.	*DOCKET ONLY	1354	NEW BERN	09/05/71
THOMAS, HARRY H.	*DOCKET ONLY	892	NEW BERN	08/19/68
THOMAS, HENRY E.	*DOCKET ONLY	305	NEW BERN	02/18/68
THOMAS, J. J. & C.A.	*DOCKET ONLY	982	NEW BERN	12/09/68
THOMAS, JAMES	*DOCKET ONLY	182	GREENSBORO	04/29/73
THOMAS, JAMES	*DOCKET ONLY	286	GREENSBORO	05/28/73
THOMAS, JOHN	*DOCKET ONLY	250	GREENSBORO	05/15/73
THOMAS, JOSEPH	WATAUGA	308	STATESVILLE	07/23/78

NAME OF BANKRUPT	RESIDENCE	CASE NUMBER	CITY OF COURT	DATE FILED
THOMAS, WEBB &	*DOCKET ONLY	491	GREENSBORO	04/17/75
THOMAS, WILLIAM C.	*DOCKET ONLY	438	GREENSBORO	12/12/73
THOMAS, WILLIAM Y.	*DOCKET ONLY	339	GREENSBORO	06/11/73
THOMASON, A.H.	YADKIN	498	WILMINGTON	01/01/68
THOMASON, MICAJAH	*DOCKET ONLY	247	NEW BERN	01/31/68
THOMPSON, ELIJAH	*DOCKET ONLY	411	NEW BERN	02/28/68
THOMPSON, GEORGE W.	HERTFORD	195	ELIZABETH CITY	03/01/68
THOMPSON, JASON	*DOCKET ONLY	81	GREENSBORO	01/28/73
THOMPSON, JOHN	CHOWAN	477	ELIZABETH CITY	12/31/68
THOMPSON, JOSEPH	ROBESON	753	WILMINGTON	10/23/73
THOMPSON, JOSEPH	*DOCKET ONLY	1295	NEW BERN	10/11/70
THOMPSON, JOSEPH S.	*DOCKET ONLY	19	NEW BERN	10/02/67
THOMPSON, NEWTON	*DOCKET ONLY	350	GREENSBORO	06/16/73
THOMPSON, WILLIAM B.	ROBESON	682	WILMINGTON	05/14/73
THOMPSON, ZADACK S.	*DOCKET ONLY	1223	NEW BERN	12/29/68
THORBUM, COOPER	*DOCKET ONLY	767	NEW BERN	07/15/68
THORN, D.C.	IREDELL	8	WILMINGTON	10/14/67
THORN, JOHN W.	*DOCKET ONLY	127	GREENSBORO	02/28/73
THORN, THEOPHILUS T.	*DOCKET ONLY	1088	NEW BERN	12/26/68
THORNE, E. D.	*DOCKET ONLY	1842	NEW BERN	02/09/77
THORNTON, J. C.	DAVIE	176	STATESVILLE	06/02/73
THORNTON, RICHARD W.	CUMBERLAND	818	WILMINGTON	05/02/78
THORTON, ALLEN G.	CUMBERLAND	183	WILMINGTON	04/15/68
THORTON, RICHARD		318	WILMINGTON	06/30/68
THROWEN, L	BERTIE	549	ELIZABETH CITY	02/03/73
THURSTON, JOHN A.	*DOCKET ONLY	915	NEW BERN	08/23/68
THURSTON, W. J. Y.	*DOCKET ONLY	863	NEW BERN	04/30/68
TIDDY, WILLIAN & R.	*DOCKET ONLY	534	GREENSBORO	02/16/76
TIFT, GRINWOLD &		317	WILMINGTON	06/22/68
TIGHMAN, ALEXANDER	*DOCKET ONLY	1698	NEW BERN	08/24/78
TILLERY, RICHARD C.	*DOCKET ONLY	1333	NEW BERN	03/18/71
TILLETT, ISAAC	CURRITUCK	401	ELIZABETH CITY	12/17/68
TILLEY & BROTHERS	HALIFAX	337	ELIZABETH CITY	08/23/78
TILLEY, ABNER J.	*DOCKET ONLY	358	GREENSBORO	06/24/73
TILLEY, H.L.	HALIFAX	337	ELIZABETH CITY	08/23/78
TILLEY, J.R	HALIFAX	328	ELIZABETH CITY	04/11/78
TILLEY, M.W.	HALIFAX	337	ELIZABETH CITY	08/23/78
TINGAN, A. H.	*DOCKET ONLY	193	NEW BERN	01/17/68
TINGAN, BENJAMIN T.	*DOCKET ONLY	150	NEW BERN	12/31/67
TINGER, J. P.	*DOCKET ONLY	572	NEW BERN	03/19/68
TIPPETS, SIMEON	*DOCKET ONLY	682	NEW BERN	04/30/68
TISDALE, EDWIN S.	*DOCKET ONLY	1493	NEW BERN	07/11/73
TISE, CHARLES	*DOCKET ONLY	154	GREENSBORO	04/15/73
TISE, ISAAC	*DOCKET ONLY	987	NEW BERN	12/15/68
TITUS & COMPANY,	CUMBERLAND	14	WILMINGTON	11/01/67
TOLAR, ROBERT	BLADEN	873	WILMINGTON	08/30/78
TOLAR, ROBERT	BLADEN	874	WILMINGTON	08/30/78
TOLAR, WILLIAM	ROBESON	785	WILMINGTON	12/05/75
TOLEN, NATHAN B.	*DOCKET ONLY	1405	NEW BERN	01/11/73
TOLSON, C.C.	*DOCKET ONLY	1311	NEW BERN	12/07/70
TOMBERLIN, REUBEN	*DOCKET ONLY	253	GREENSBORO	05/17/73
TOMLISON, WILLIAM	*DOCKET ONLY	763	NEW BERN	05/29/68
TOMS, NATHAN	PERQUIMANS	469	ELIZABETH CITY	12/22/68
TOOLY, A. J.	*DOCKET ONLY	1483	NEW BERN	06/26/73
TOW, THOMAS (80/81)	HENDERSON	134	ASHEVILLE	05/21/73
TOWE, JAMES	PERQUIMANS	412	ELIZABETH CITY	12/25/68
TOWE, WILLIAM	PASQUOTANK	203	ELIZABETH CITY	03/18/68
TOWN, J. M., JOHN L	*DOCKET ONLY	576	GREENSBORO	07/01/77
TOWNES, CHEATHAM &	*DOCKET ONLY	890	NEW BERN	08/19/68
TOWNES, JOSEPH	*DOCKET ONLY	889	NEW BERN	08/19/68
TOWNSEND, C.F.	HENDERSON	536	WILMINGTON	01/06/69
TOWNSEND, E. C.	*DOCKET ONLY	579	GREENSBORO	04/17/77
TOWNSEND, W.D.	RICHMOND	79	WILMINGTON	02/10/68
TRADER, JAMES M	HERTFORD	540	ELIZABETH CITY	04/19/72
TRADWELL, ADAM,	*DOCKET ONLY	726	NEW BERN	05/24/68
TRANSAW, WILLIAM B.	WILKES	50	STATESVILLE	02/18/73

NAME OF BANKRUPT	RESIDENCE	CASE NUMBER	CITY OF COURT	DATE FILED
TRENATHAN, WILLIAM	*DOCKET ONLY	258	NEW BERN	02/06/68
TRENTMAN, H. M.	IREDELL	137	STATESVILLE	05/27/73
TRIPLETT, NIMROD	WILKES	82	STATESVILLE	04/18/73
TROGDEN & COMPANY	*DOCKET ONLY	610	GREENSBORO	04/01/78
TROTT, S.S.	ROWAN	160	STATESVILLE	05/26/73
TROTT, WILSON	ROWAN	35	STATESVILLE	01/21/73
TROUTMAN, JOHN J.	IREDELL	135	STATESVILLE	05/21/73
TROY, WESLEY	CUMBERLAND	868	WILMINGTON	08/30/78
TRUEBLOOD, NATHAN	PASQUOTANK	185	ELIZABETH CITY	02/29/68
TRUITT, LEWIS	*DOCKET ONLY	251	GREENSBORO	05/15/73
TRUITT, SAMUEL S.	PERQUIMANS	217	ELIZABETH CITY	03/07/68
TUCKER, GEORGE W.	*DOCKET ONLY	591	GREENSBORO	07/09/77
TUCKER, JAMES M.	*DOCKET ONLY	228	NEW BERN	01/28/68
TUCKER, THOMAS A.	DAVIE	181	WILMINGTON	03/28/68
TUERENTINE, SAMUEL	*DOCKET ONLY	13	NEW BERN	09/17/67
TURINTINE, JOHN A.	*DOCKET ONLY	1218	NEW BERN	12/31/68
TURNBULL, JOHN R.	*DOCKET ONLY	1158	NEW BERN	12/29/68
TURNBULL, PETER J.	*DOCKET ONLY	547	NEW BERN	03/17/68
TURNER, ALEX	SAMPSON	821	WILMINGTON	05/06/78
TURNER, JOHN B.	*DOCKET ONLY	1434	NEW BERN	05/15/73
TURNER, THOMAS	SAMPSON	822	WILMINGTON	05/06/78
TURNER, THOMAS T.	*DOCKET ONLY	405	NEW BERN	02/28/68
TURNER, WILFRED &		593	WILMINGTON	10/19/70
TURNER, WILLIAM H.	NORTHAMPTON	374	ELIZABETH CITY	09/10/68
TURNER, WILLIAM J.	*DOCKET ONLY	450	NEW BERN	03/02/68
TURNSTALL, THOMAS R.	*DOCKET ONLY	361	NEW BERN	02/24/68
TURRENTINE, JAMES M.	*DOCKET ONLY	71	NEW BERN	11/28/67
TURRENTINE, JOHN A.	*DOCKET ONLY	1006	NEW BERN	12/17/68
TURRENTINE, MCRAE &		771	WILMINGTON	03/28/74
TURRENTINE, SAMUEL	*DOCKET ONLY	162	NEW BERN	01/03/68
TUTTLE, PETER	CAMDEN	119	ELIZABETH CITY	01/24/68
TUTTLE, SIDNEY	*DOCKET ONLY	458	NEW BERN	03/04/68
TWITTY, HENRY F.	*DOCKET ONLY	891	NEW BERN	08/19/68
TYNEE, JOHN P.	HALIFAX	428	ELIZABETH CITY	12/21/68
TYSON, BENJAMIN H.	*DOCKET ONLY	1604	NEW BERN	04/28/75
TYSON, JOSIAH	*DOCKET ONLY	785	NEW BERN	08/19/68
TYSON, O. A.	*DOCKET ONLY	146	GREENSBORO	04/10/73
UNDERWOOD, DAVID J.	CUMBERLAND	595	WILMINGTON	10/26/70
UNDERWOOD, DAVIDSON	STANLY	95	WILMINGTON	02/25/68
UNDERWOOD, JOSEPH B.	CUMBERLAND	102	WILMINGTON	02/25/68
UNDERWOOD, WILLIAM	UNION	139	WILMINGTON	03/12/68
UPCHURCH, ALVIN N.	*DOCKET ONLY	1514	NEW BERN	06/27/73
UPCHURCH, AMBROSE	*DOCKET ONLY	178	NEW BERN	01/09/68
UPCHURCH, RICHMOND	*DOCKET ONLY	1503	NEW BERN	06/07/73
UPCHURCH, RUFUS	*DOCKET ONLY	139	NEW BERN	12/28/67
UPCHURCH, SIMS	*DOCKET ONLY	32	NEW BERN	10/19/67
UPCHURCH, WILLIFORD	*DOCKET ONLY	20	NEW BERN	10/04/67
VALENTINE, DANIEL	HERTFORD	108	ELIZABETH CITY	01/11/68
VALLEY, ADRIAN		632	WILMINGTON	05/17/71
VAMEY, WILLIAM W	WILKES	64	STATESVILLE	03/03/73
VANCE, ROBERT B.	BUNCOMBE	564	WILMINGTON	12/06/69
VANDERFORD, THOMAS	ROWAN	280	STATESVILLE	02/09/77
VANDERGRIFT, C. L &	*DOCKET ONLY	578	GREENSBORO	04/13/77
VANN, CHARLES	HERTFORD	432	ELIZABETH CITY	12/23/68
VANN, JAMES	CUMBERLAND	823	WILMINGTON	05/09/78
VANN, VALENTINE	SAMPSON	720	WILMINGTON	06/11/73
VANN, WILLIAM	NORTHAMPTON	371	ELIZABETH CITY	09/12/68
VANOWENINGS, STACY	NEW HANOVER	481	WILMINGTON	12/31/68
VAUGHAN THOMAS J.	HALIFAX	518	ELIZABETH CITY	11/30/70
VAUGHAN, JAMES	*DOCKET ONLY	1159	NEW BERN	12/30/68
VAUGHN, JAMES M.	*DOCKET ONLY	118	GREENSBORO	02/12/73
VAUGHN, JOHN	*DOCKET ONLY	881	GREENSBORO	08/31/78
VAUGHN, JOSEPH J.	HERTFORD	271	ELIZABETH CITY	05/29/68
VAUGHN, THOMAS J.C.	HALIFAX	231	ELIZABETH CITY	03/18/68
VAUGHN, WYATT B.	STOKES	264	WILMINGTON	05/30/68
VEST, J. P.	*DOCKET ONLY	445	GREENSBORO	12/23/73

NORTH CAROLINA BANKRUPTS - ACT OF 1867

NAME OF BANKRUPT	RESIDENCE	CASE NUMBER	CITY OF COURT	DATE FILED
VEST, JOEL	*DOCKET ONLY	237	GREENSBORO	05/12/73
VICK, SAMUEL W. &		809	WILMINGTON	03/29/78
VICKERS, DAVID	*DOCKET ONLY	317	GREENSBORO	06/03/73
VINCENT, B.J.	NORTHAMPTON	346	ELIZABETH CITY	08/29/78
VINCENT, NATHANIEL	NEW HANOVER	376	WILMINGTON	12/22/68
VOGLER, ELIAS A. &	*DOCKET ONLY	529	GREENSBORO	11/30/72
VOGLES & PFOHL		629	WILMINGTON	05/13/71
VOGLES, MORTIMER N.		629	WILMINGTON	05/13/71
W.C.& R RAILROAD		708	WILMINGTON	05/05/73
WADDELL, FREDRICH		448	WILMINGTON	12/30/68
WADDELL, JOHN M.	*DOCKET ONLY	754	NEW BERN	05/29/68
WADDILL, MATHEW	*DOCKET ONLY	641	GREENSBORO	08/20/78
WADDILL, R. W.	*DOCKET ONLY	916	NEW BERN	09/22/68
WADE, CARTER	ASHE	164	STATESVILLE	05/26/73
WAGGONER, JOSEPH	*DOCKET ONLY	99	GREENSBORO	01/27/73
WAGGONER, SPENCER	FORSYTH	248	WILMINGTON	05/29/68
WAGNER, D. M.	IREDELL	169	STATESVILLE	05/29/74
WAGNER, GEORGE	*DOCKET ONLY	121	GREENSBORO	02/24/73
WAGONER, A. S.	*DOCKET ONLY	185	GREENSBORO	04/30/73
WAGONER, DANIEL W.	*DOCKET ONLY	96	GREENSBORO	02/05/73
WAKE, ROBERT F.,	*DOCKET ONLY	2	NEW BERN	06/04/67
WAKEFIELD, MOORE &		575	WILMINGTON	04/21/70
WALDO, JOHN T.	MARTIN	142	ELIZABETH CITY	02/17/68
WALFINDER, JOHN J.	*DOCKET ONLY	1636	NEW BERN	12/04/76
WALKER A. W.	*DOCKET ONLY	418	GREENSBORO	10/02/73
WALKER, A. M.	*DOCKET ONLY	531	GREENSBORO	01/20/74
WALKER, ABRAM	*DOCKET ONLY	412	NEW BERN	02/28/68
WALKER, ARTHUR M.	IREDELL	239	STATESVILLE	10/10/73
WALKER, B.C.	CURRITUCK	232	ELIZABETH CITY	08/15/73
WALKER, DITRION	*DOCKET ONLY	270	NEW BERN	02/08/68
WALKER, FREEMAN	*DOCKET ONLY	549	NEW BERN	03/17/68
WALKER, J. THOMPSON	*DOCKET ONLY	164	GREENSBORO	04/22/73
WALKER, JESSE	*DOCKET ONLY	574	NEW BERN	03/19/68
WALKER, JOHN	*DOCKET ONLY	340	GREENSBORO	06/12/73
WALKER, JOHN	ROBESON	605	WILMINGTON	11/28/70
WALKER, JOHN	CLEVELAND	118	STATESVILLE	05/12/73
WALKER, W. E.	*DOCKET ONLY	918	NEW BERN	08/22/68
WALKER, W.W.	TYRRELL	135	ELIZABETH CITY	02/17/68
WALKER, WILLIAM A.	*DOCKET ONLY	853	GREENSBORO	08/27/78
WALKER, WORREL P.	*DOCKET ONLY	382	NEW BERN	02/24/68
WALKER. E.F.	BURKE	9	WILMINGTON	10/13/67
WALL, H.	RUTHERFORD	247	STATESVILLE	12/20/73
WALL, PINKNEY	*DOCKET ONLY	12	GREENSBORO	08/19/72
WALL, ROBERT M.	STANLY	420	WILMINGTON	12/30/68
WALLACE, WILLIAM S.	MECKLENBURG	230	WILMINGTON	05/25/68
WALLACE, WILSON	*DOCKET ONLY	244	GREENSBORO	05/13/73
WALTENS, INERSON B.	*DOCKET ONLY	251	NEW BERN	01/31/68
WALTERS, WILLIAM F.	*DOCKET ONLY	044	NEW BERN	12/24/68
WALTON, EDWARD S.	*DOCKET ONLY	372	NEW BERN	01/18/72
WALTON, WILLIAM	BERTIE	230	ELIZABETH CITY	03/01/68
WARD & COMPANY	*DOCKET ONLY	624	NEW BERN	02/15/76
WARD, A. S.	*DOCKET ONLY	183	NEW BERN	12/31/68
WARD, EDWARD W.	*DOCKET ONLY	373	NEW BERN	01/20/72
WARD, ELDRIDGE	SAMPSON	858	WILMINGTON	08/26/78
WARD, FRANCIS B.	DAVIE	130	STATESVILLE	05/18/73
WARD, JOHN	*DOCKET ONLY	122	NEW BERN	12/29/67
WARD, RICHARD G.	*DOCKET ONLY	017	NEW BERN	12/26/68
WARD, W. P & E. W.	*DOCKET ONLY	634	NEW BERN	04/17/68
WARD, WDWARD W.	*DOCKET ONLY	372	NEW BERN	01/18/72
WARE, JAMES	CLEVELAND	434	WILMINGTON	12/30/68
WARE, JAMES M.	*DOCKET ONLY	535	GREENSBORO	02/17/78
WARE, W. P. &	*DOCKET ONLY	567	GREENSBORO	10/20/76
WARREN, AISLEY	NORTHAMPTON	172	ELIZABETH CITY	02/18/77
WARREN, JAMES	PASQUATANK	413	ELIZABETH CITY	12/24/68
WARREN, JOHN C.	SAMPSON	717	WILMINGTON	06/11/73
WARREN, JOHN Q.	*DOCKET ONLY	196	NEW BERN	12/31/68

NAME OF BANKRUPT	RESIDENCE	CASE NUMBER	CITY OF COURT	DATE FILED
WARREN, RICHARD D.	*DOCKET ONLY	1046	NEW BERN	12/22/68
WARREN, WILLIAM H.	*DOCKET ONLY	539	GREENSBORO	01/01/76
WARREN, WILLIAM H.	SAMPSON	825	WILMINGTON	05/10/78
WARWICK, JOHN B.	MECKLENBURG	120	WILMINGTON	03/07/68
WARWICK, WILLIAM	MECKLENBURG	157	WILMINGTON	03/28/68
WASBURNE, A. S.	*DOCKET ONLY	630	GREENSBORO	06/08/78
WASHINGTON NORTH	*DOCKET ONLY	632	NEW BERN	04/10/68
WASHINGTON, JAMES A.	*DOCKET ONLY	1125	NEW BERN	12/30/68
WATERS, JAMES	*DOCKET ONLY	979	NEW BERN	12/08/68
WATERS, WILLIAM	*DOCKET ONLY	999	NEW BERN	12/11/68
WATKINS, HENRY	*DOCKET ONLY	274	GREENSBORO	05/24/73
WATKINS, JOHN	*DOCKET ONLY	1464	NEW BERN	06/05/73
WATKINS, NATHANIEL	*DOCKET ONLY	1067	NEW BERN	12/28/68
WATKINS, W. H.	*DOCKET ONLY	607	GREENSBORO	05/01/78
WATSON, ALEX	ROBESON	205	WILMINGTON	05/11/68
WATSON, E. F.	*DOCKET ONLY	406	NEW BERN	02/28/68
WATSON, F. M.	*DOCKET ONLY	664	GREENSBORO	08/29/78
WATSON, HANNIBAL H.	*DOCKET ONLY	1376	NEW BERN	02/03/72
WATSON, JOHN H.	*DOCKET ONLY	36	NEW BERN	10/24/67
WATSON, JONES	*DOCKET ONLY	5	NEW BERN	07/23/67
WATSON, THOMAS B.	*DOCKET ONLY	1419	NEW BERN	03/08/73
WATSON, THOMAS C.	ROWAN	36	STATESVILLE	01/31/73
WATSON, WILLIAM F.	ROWAN	57	STATESVILLE	02/20/73
WATSON, WILLIAM H.	*DOCKET ONLY	936	NEW BERN	09/29/68
WATSON, WILLIAM M.	*DOCKET ONLY	732	NEW BERN	05/29/68
WATSON, WILLIAM M.	*DOCKET ONLY	1494	NEW BERN	07/16/73
WAY, L. F.	IREDELL	186	STATESVILLE	06/07/73
WEARTHERSBEE,	*DOCKET ONLY	378	NEW BERN	02/27/68
WEATHERINGTON, JERRY	*DOCKET ONLY	306	NEW BERN	02/18/68
WEATHERSBEE, R.E.	MARTIN	274	ELIZABETH CITY	05/29/68
WEATHERSBEE, WILLIS	HALIFAX	201	ELIZABETH CITY	05/24/73
WEAVER, H.B. &	BUNCOMBE	147	ASHEVILLE	08/17/73
WEAVER, JAMES A.	NORTHAMPTON	214	ELIZABETH CITY	03/09/68
WEAVER, JAMES D.	RUTHERFORD	57	WILMINGTON	01/20/68
WEAVER, JAMES G.	POLK	251	STATESVILLE	01/15/74
WEAVER, R.A.	NORTHAMPTON	227	ELIZABETH CITY	03/09/68
WEAVER, RICHARD T.	HERTFORD	436	ELIZABETH CITY	12/23/68
WEBB & THOMAS	*DOCKET ONLY	491	GREENSBORO	04/17/75
WEBB, JAMES	*DOCKET ONLY	484	NEW BERN	03/04/68
WEBB, SILAS	*DOCKET ONLY	17	NEW BERN	10/17/67
WEBB, THOMAS	*DOCKET ONLY	550	NEW BERN	03/17/68
WEBB, W. G.	*DOCKET ONLY	667	GREENSBORO	08/29/78
WEDDINGTON, WILLIAM	*DOCKET ONLY	119	GREENSBORO	02/14/73
WEEKS, DRURY	CHEROKEE	199	WILMINGTON	05/06/68
WEEKS, W.R.	SAMPSON	816	WILMINGTON	05/01/78
WEILL & DECOSTA		776	WILMINGTON	12/17/74
WEILL, ABRAHAM	NEW HANOVER	663	WILMINGTON	08/29/78
WEILL, BARBARA		758	WILMINGTON	12/15/73
WELBON, JOHN	WILKES	107	STATESVILLE	05/02/73
WELBORNE, E. M.	WILKES	83	STATESVILLE	04/17/73
WELLS, EDWARD	ROBESON	857	WILMINGTON	08/24/78
WELLS, J. S.	CLEVELAND	27	STATESVILLE	01/22/73
WELLS, JOHN	BUNCOMBE	140	ASHEVILLE	05/10/73
WERNYSS, WILLIAM P.	SAMPSON	832	WILMINGTON	05/28/78
WESCOTT, JOHN	DARE	270	ELIZABETH CITY	10/15/74
WEST, J. EDWIN	*DOCKET ONLY	635	NEW BERN	05/30/68
WEST, OWEN	DUPLIN	856	WILMINGTON	08/24/78
WEST, S. B.	*DOCKET ONLY	921	NEW BERN	08/29/68
WEST, W. R. (106)	BUNCOMBE	144	ASHEVILLE	06/12/73
WESTBROOK, JAMES B.	*DOCKET ONLY	652	NEW BERN	04/21/68
WESTBROOK, NATHAN B.	*DOCKET ONLY	1511	NEW BERN	08/15/73
WESTERN NORTH	*DOCKET ONLY	548	GREENSBORO	07/01/74
WESTRAY, WILLIAM M.	HALIFAX	407	ELIZABETH CITY	12/22/68
WESTWOOD, CHARLES W.	*DOCKET ONLY	673	NEW BERN	05/12/68
WHALELY, HIRAM	CUMBERLAND	259	WILMINGTON	05/29/68
WHALEY, JAMES	*DOCKET ONLY	1715	NEW BERN	08/29/78

NAME OF BANKRUPT	RESIDENCE	CASE NUMBER	CITY OF COURT	DATE FILED
WHALEY, JONATHAN	*DOCKET ONLY	589	NEW BERN	03/21/68
WHARTON, JESSE	*DOCKET ONLY	576	NEW BERN	03/19/68
WHARTON, T. GREEN	*DOCKET ONLY	1038	NEW BERN	12/23/68
WHEALTY, W.R.	MARTIN	440	ELIZABETH CITY	12/28/68
WHEELER, HENRY	*DOCKET ONLY	225	GREENSBORO	05/10/73
WHEELER, PINKNEY	*DOCKET ONLY	581	GREENSBORO	05/19/77
WHEELESS, LEMUEL	*DOCKET ONLY	1069	NEW BERN	12/22/68
WHEELOCK, SOUTHWICK		580	WILMINGTON	07/07/70
WHELLER, EZEKIEL	*DOCKET ONLY	420	GREENSBORO	10/06/73
WHIBLEY, L. R.	*DOCKET ONLY	1479	NEW BERN	06/24/73
WHITAKER, BENJAMIN	HALIFAX	513	ELIZABETH CITY	11/28/70
WHITAKER, GEORGE	HALIFAX	460	ELIZABETH CITY	12/29/68
WHITAKER, JOSHUA	BUNCOMBE	138	ASHEVILLE	06/05/73
WHITAKER, L.F.	CABARRUS	334	WILMINGTON	10/09/68
WHITAKER, MATT	*DOCKET ONLY	212	NEW BERN	01/22/68
WHITAKER, MONTGOMERY	HALIFAX	515	ELIZABETH CITY	10/21/70
WHITAKER, RICHARD H.	*DOCKET ONLY	1162	NEW BERN	12/30/68
WHITAKER, THOMAS G.	*DOCKET ONLY	1120	NEW BERN	12/30/68
WHITAKER, THOMAS J.	*DOCKET ONLY	1258	NEW BERN	12/31/88
WHITAKER, WILLIAM H.	*DOCKET ONLY	147	NEW BERN	12/31/67
WHITE, A.P.	PASQUOTANK	291	ELIZABETH CITY	06/01/68
WHITE, BENJAMIN F.	PASQUOTANK	14	ELIZABETH CITY	08/21/67
WHITE, D. L.	*DOCKET ONLY	486	NEW BERN	03/05/68
WHITE, DAVID P. L.	*DOCKET ONLY	495	GREENSBORO	06/26/75
WHITE, E.S.	WILSON	228	ELIZABETH CITY	03/09/68
WHITE, GEORGE D.	HALIFAX	247	ELIZABETH CITY	12/09/73
WHITE, HAYWOOD A.	*DOCKET ONLY	1020	NEW BERN	12/17/68
WHITE, HENRY	PERQUIMANS	363	ELIZABETH CITY	09/15/68
WHITE, J.C.	PERQUIMANS	175	ELIZABETH CITY	04/05/73
WHITE, JAMES B.	*DOCKET ONLY	31	NEW BERN	10/18/67
WHITE, JAMES F.	GASTON	89	STATESVILLE	04/30/73
WHITE, JAMES H.	GASTON	191	STATESVILLE	06/11/73
WHITE, JAMES M.	PASQUOTANK	107	ELIZABETH CITY	01/10/68
WHITE, JAMES P.	IREDELL	84	STATESVILLE	04/18/73
WHITE, JOSIAH E.	PERQUIMANS	651	ELIZABETH CITY	04/05/73
WHITE, JOSIAH P.	PASQUOTANK	113	ELIZABETH CITY	01/22/68
WHITE, MOSES A.	IREDELL	177	STATESVILLE	06/03/73
WHITE, NEEDHAM	*DOCKET ONLY	1048	NEW BERN	12/18/68
WHITE, PETER F.	CHOWAN	431	ELIZABETH CITY	12/29/68
WHITE, ROBINSON	PASQUOTANK	24	ELIZABETH CITY	10/07/67
WHITE, SAMUEL C.	*DOCKET ONLY	1312	NEW BERN	12/06/70
WHITE, STEPHEN A.	*DOCKET ONLY	812	NEW BERN	05/30/68
WHITE, THOMAS	*DOCKET ONLY	1387	NEW BERN	12/01/71
WHITE, W. W.	*DOCKET ONLY	855	GREENSBORO	08/27/78
WHITE, WATSON	CHOWAN	270	ELIZABETH CITY	05/28/68
WHITE, WILLIAM	*DOCKET ONLY	1510	NEW BERN	08/15/73
WHITE, WILLIAM	*DOCKET ONLY	587	NEW BERN	03/19/68
WHITE, WILLIAM H.	*DOCKET ONLY	363	NEW BERN	02/24/68
WHITE, WILLIAM R.	*DOCKET ONLY	485	NEW BERN	03/04/68
WHITEHAND, JOHN J.	DUPLIN	382	WILMINGTON	12/23/69
WHITEHEAD, A.J. M.	*DOCKET ONLY	896	NEW BERN	05/20/68
WHITEHEAD, JOSEPH	HALIFAX	222	ELIZABETH CITY	06/30/73
WHITEHEAD, WILLIE	DUPLIN	381	WILMINGTON	12/23/68
WHITEHURST, MILES	PASQUOTANK	260	ELIZABETH CITY	05/25/68
WHITESIDE, A. W.	HENDERSON	141	ASHEVILLE	04/18/73
WHITFIELD, GEORGE W.	*DOCKET ONLY	53	NEW BERN	11/14/67
WHITFIELD, JEFFERSON	*DOCKET ONLY	231	NEW BERN	01/30/68
WHITFIELD, WILLIAM	*DOCKET ONLY	935	NEW BERN	09/21/68
WHITFORD, NELSON	*DOCKET ONLY	771	NEW BERN	05/30/68
WHITFORD, WILLIAM C.	*DOCKET ONLY	1404	NEW BERN	01/04/73
WHITTED, JAMES Y.	*DOCKET ONLY	72	GREENSBORO	01/25/73
WHITLEY, JONAH	*DOCKET ONLY	1160	NEW BERN	12/30/68
WHITLEY, E. D.	*DOCKET ONLY	1122	NEW BERN	12/30/88
WHITLEY, H. S.	*DOCKET ONLY	1019	NEW BERN	12/21/68
WHITLEY, NEEDHAM J.	*DOCKET ONLY	1119	NEW BERN	12/30/68
WHITMIRE, ROBERT	HENDERSON	146	ASHEVILLE	06/02/73

NAME OF BANKRUPT	RESIDENCE	CASE NUMBER	CITY OF COURT	DATE FILED
WHITSON, JASON	MCDOWELL	333	STATESVILLE	09/02/95
WHITSON, JASON C.	MCDOWELL	490	WILMINGTON	12/31/69
WHITT, JAMES	*DOCKET ONLY	329	NEW BERN	02/21/68
WHITTAKER, JOEL D.	*DOCKET ONLY	1693	NEW BERN	08/20/73
WHITTED, WILLIAM D.	HENDERSON	644	WILMINGTON	11/11/71
WHITTY, ALFRED	*DOCKET ONLY	1260	NEW BERN	12/30/68
WHITTY, JOSEPH	*DOCKET ONLY	452	NEW BERN	02/29/68
WHITWORTH, FERRDALL	GASTON	159	WILMINGTON	03/28/68
WHORTON, ROBERT	*DOCKET ONLY	451	NEW BERN	03/02/68
WIGGINS, BRINKLEY	PASQUOTANK	67	ELIZABETH CITY	12/20/67
WILBON, JOHN F.O.	CHATHAM	125	WILMINGTON	03/12/68
WILBORN & CARMICHAEL	WILKES	176	WILMINGTON	04/11/68
WILBORNE &	WILKES	174	WILMINGTON	04/11/68
WILCOVER, A. & S.	NEW HANOVER	242	WILMINGTON	05/27/68
WILCOVER, S., A. &	NEW HANOVER	242	WILMINGTON	05/28/68
WILCOX, LITTLEBURG	HALIFAX	493	ELIZABETH CITY	12/27/68
WILFONG, CALVIN A.	CATAWBA	106	STATESVILLE	04/26/73
WILKENSON, BENJAMIN	*DOCKET ONLY	1104	NEW BERN	12/29/68
WILKENSON, J. D.	*DOCKET ONLY	279	NEW BERN	02/08/68
WILKERSON, DAVID S.	*DOCKET ONLY	1121	NEW BERN	12/30/68
WILKERSON, FULLER &	*DOCKET ONLY	11	GREENSBORO	11/04/72
WILKERSON, JOHN	*DOCKET ONLY	658	GREENSBORO	08/28/78
WILKERSON, JOHN C. &	*DOCKET ONLY	1283	NEW BERN	02/10/70
WILKES, JOSIAH H.	*DOCKET ONLY	1034	NEW BERN	12/23/68
WILKINS, SAMUEL	*DOCKET ONLY	700	GREENSBORO	06/05/72
WILKINS, SAMUEL	*DOCKET ONLY	703	GREENSBORO	/ /
WILKINS, SAMUEL	RUTHERFORD	24	WILMINGTON	10/20/67
WILKS, JOSIAH W.	*DOCKET ONLY	1035	NEW BERN	12/23/68
WILLARD BROTHERS		770	WILMINGTON	07/22/74
WILLARD BROTHERS		774	WILMINGTON	08/31/74
WILLARD BROTHERS		774	WILMINGTON	05/06/76
WILLIAM, JOHN W.	*DOCKET ONLY	304	GREENSBORO	05/29/73
WILLIAM, THOMAS	YANCEY	377	ELIZABETH CITY	08/21/68
WILLIAMS, A.J.		331	ELIZABETH CITY	05/28/78
WILLIAMS, ALFRED	HENDERSON	143	ASHEVILLE	02/19/73
WILLIAMS, ARCHIBALD	*DOCKET ONLY	281	NEW BERN	02/08/68
WILLIAMS, BLANEY	DUPLIN	376	WILMINGTON	12/22/68
WILLIAMS, BUCKNER D.	*DOCKET ONLY	975	NEW BERN	12/06/68
WILLIAMS, C. J. L.	*DOCKET ONLY	303	GREENSBORO	05/29/73
WILLIAMS, CASWELL	*DOCKET ONLY	1063	NEW BERN	12/26/68
WILLIAMS, CRAWFORD	YADKIN	597	WILMINGTON	10/31/70
WILLIAMS, DAVID	LINCOLN	153	STATESVILLE	05/23/73
WILLIAMS, DITRION	*DOCKET ONLY	575	NEW BERN	03/19/68
WILLIAMS, EDWARD	*DOCKET ONLY	1443	NEW BERN	05/21/73
WILLIAMS, EDWARD	DUPLIN	692	WILMINGTON	05/30/73
WILLIAMS, FRANCIS	IREDELL	263	STATESVILLE	06/26/74
WILLIAMS, G.A.	WASHINGTON	327	ELIZABETH CITY	04/02/78
WILLIAMS, GARRY	*DOCKET ONLY	1070	NEW BERN	12/26/68
WILLIAMS, GEORGE	SAMPSON	780	WILMINGTON	06/16/75
WILLIAMS, GEORGE W.	PASQUOTANK	120	ELIZABETH CITY	01/24/68
WILLIAMS, H.H.	*DOCKET ONLY	1467	NEW BERN	06/05/73
WILLIAMS, HENRY B.	MECKLENBURG	42	WILMINGTON	01/17/68
WILLIAMS, HENRY G.	*DOCKET ONLY	618	NEW BERN	04/01/68
WILLIAMS, HEZEKIAH	*DOCKET ONLY	1435	NEW BERN	05/16/73
WILLIAMS, HUBBARD	*DOCKET ONLY	306	GREENSBORO	05/29/73
WILLIAMS, HUBBARD	*DOCKET ONLY	305	GREENSBORO	05/29/73
WILLIAMS, ISAAC	CAMDEN	242	ELIZABETH CITY	04/25/68
WILLIAMS, JAMES	*DOCKET ONLY	990	NEW BERN	12/15/68
WILLIAMS, JAMES S.	UNION	51	WILMINGTON	01/24/68
WILLIAMS, JAMES T.	*DOCKET ONLY	1478	NEW BERN	06/24/73
WILLIAMS, JAMES W.	IREDELL	163	STATESVILLE	05/26/73
WILLIAMS, JOHN	*DOCKET ONLY	146	NEW BERN	12/31/67
WILLIAMS, JOHN A.	CUMBERLAND	671	WILMINGTON	10/26/72
WILLIAMS, JOHN A.	*DOCKET ONLY	994	NEW BERN	12/15/68
WILLIAMS, JOHN D.	*DOCKET ONLY	845	NEW BERN	06/15/68
WILLIAMS, JOHN L.	RUTHERFORD	130	WILMINGTON	03/12/68

NAME OF BANKRUPT	RESIDENCE	CASE NUMBER	CITY OF COURT	DATE FILED
WILLIAMS, JOHN R.	DAVIE	587	WILMINGTON	08/31/70
WILLIAMS, JONATHAN	DUPLIN	403	WILMINGTON	12/26/68
WILLIAMS, JOSEPH	YADKIN	187	WILMINGTON	04/03/68
WILLIAMS, LEWIS	*DOCKET ONLY	485	GREENSBORO	02/24/74
WILLIAMS, M. D. &	*DOCKET ONLY	68	NEW BERN	11/23/67
WILLIAMS, MUNFORD D.	*DOCKET ONLY	346	GREENSBORO	06/14/73
WILLIAMS, N.H.C.	DAVIDSON	304	WILMINGTON	05/30/68
WILLIAMS, NATHAMIEL	*DOCKET ONLY	105	NEW BERN	12/13/67
WILLIAMS, NICHOLAS	YADKIN	386	WILMINGTON	12/25/68
WILLIAMS, NICHOLS L.	YADKIN	185	WILMINGTON	04/16/68
WILLIAMS, OWEN	PASQUOTANK	121	ELIZABETH CITY	01/24/68
WILLIAMS, PETER S.	HERTFORD	537	ELIZABETH CITY	09/29/71
WILLIAMS, PLEASANTA	*DOCKET ONLY	375	GREENSBORO	07/05/73
WILLIAMS, R. D.	*DOCKET ONLY	413	NEW BERN	02/29/68
WILLIAMS, R. W.	*DOCKET ONLY	609	NEW BERN	05/30/68
WILLIAMS, ROBERT W.	*DOCKET ONLY	384	GREENSBORO	07/17/73
WILLIAMS, S. F. (5)	BUNCOMBE	142	ASHEVILLE	10/05/72
WILLIAMS, SAMUEL	*DOCKET ONLY	1436	NEW BERN	05/16/73
WILLIAMS, SAMUEL	PASQUOTANK	57	ELIZABETH CITY	11/18/67
WILLIAMS, SAMUEL A.	*DOCKET ONLY	1317	NEW BERN	01/04/71
WILLIAMS, T.B.	PASQUOTANK	100	ELIZABETH CITY	12/30/67
WILLIAMS, THOMAS	YADKIN	499	WILMINGTON	01/01/69
WILLIAMS, THOMAS	*DOCKET ONLY	1621	NEW BERN	02/08/76
WILLIAMS, THOMAS R.	*DOCKET ONLY	45	GREENSBORO	12/18/72
WILLIAMS, TURNER	HENDERSON	145	ASHEVILLE	01/06/73
WILLIAMS, W.K.A	MARTIN	186	ELIZABETH CITY	05/08/73
WILLIAMS, WILLIAM	PASQUOTANK	41	ELIZABETH CITY	11/18/67
WILLIAMS, WILLIAM	YADKIN	620	WILMINGTON	03/02/71
WILLIAMS, WILLIAM B.	*DOCKET ONLY	182	NEW BERN	01/13/68
WILLIAMS, WILLIAM	MARTIN	653	ELIZABETH CITY	04/19/73
WILLIAMS, WILLIAM R.	PASQUOTANK	545	ELIZABETH CITY	11/09/72
WILLIAMS, WILLIAM T.	HALIFAX	438	ELIZABETH CITY	12/27/68
WILLIAMS, J. J.	*DOCKET ONLY	90	NEW BERN	12/04/67
WILLIAMS, M. M.	*DOCKET ONLY	1224	NEW BERN	12/28/68
WILLIAMSOM, JAMES G	CLEVELAND	270	STATESVILLE	12/31/74
WILLIAMSON, GODFRY	MECKLENBURG	154	WILMINGTON	03/24/68
WILLIAMSON, JOHN T.	*DOCKET ONLY	29	NEW BERN	10/10/67
WILLIAMSTON &	EDGECOMBE	606	ELIZABETH CITY	05/01/72
WILLIFORD, ELIJAH	*DOCKET ONLY	118	NEW BERN	12/26/67
WILLIFORD, JOSEPH	*DOCKET ONLY	117	NEW BERN	12/26/67
WILLIS, ARMADA	*DOCKET ONLY	1441	NEW BERN	05/20/73
WILLIS, CHARLES	ROBESON	608	WILMINGTON	03/22/78
WILLIS, WILLIAM E.	*DOCKET ONLY	642	GREENSBORO	08/21/78
WILLLIAMS, NATHANIEL	*DOCKET ONLY	785	NEW BERN	08/19/68
WILLMOORE, JULIUS	MECKLENBURG	406	WILMINGTON	12/28/68
WILMINGTON BUILDING	NEW HANOVER	848	WILMINGTON	08/09/78
WILMINGTON SAVINGS	NEW HANOVER	750	WILMINGTON	09/27/73
WILSON, ARTHUR D.	SAMPSON	718	WILMINGTON	06/11/73
WILSON, FOSTER M.	BUNCOMBE	226	WILMINGTON	05/25/68
WILSON, HENRY J.	CURRITUCK	78	ELIZABETH CITY	12/16/67
WILSON, JOHN G.	HERTFORD	182	ELIZABETH CITY	04/25/73
WILSON, JOHN G.	HERTFORD	568	ELIZABETH CITY	04/23/73
WILSON, THOMAS	GASTON	159	WILMINGTON	03/18/68
WILSON, W.W.	DAVIE	510	WILMINGTON	01/01/69
WILSON, WILL G.	CURRITUCK	63	ELIZABETH CITY	11/24/67
WILSON, WILLIAM H.	*DOCKET ONLY	826	NEW BERN	05/30/68
WIMBERLY, JOSEPH W.	*DOCKET ONLY	61	NEW BERN	11/21/67
WIMBERLY, JOSPEH W.	*DOCKET ONLY	1574	NEW BERN	03/14/74
WIMSTEIN, LEVI &	*DOCKET ONLY	1632	NEW BERN	06/24/78
WINBORN, JOHN Q.	*DOCKET ONLY	1214	NEW BERN	12/31/68
WINBORN, WILLIAM B.	*DOCKET ONLY	1671	NEW BERN	05/23/78
WINBORNE, VAN B. &	*DOCKET ONLY	859	NEW BERN	05/30/68
WINCHESTER, P.M.	*DOCKET ONLY	1016	NEW BERN	12/19/68
WINCHESTER, W. G.	*DOCKET ONLY	85	GREENSBORO	01/18/73
WINDLEY, SAMUEL	*DOCKET ONLY	1537	NEW BERN	12/01/73
WINDLEY, WILLIAM B.	*DOCKET ONLY	944	NEW BERN	10/19/68

NORTH CAROLINA BANKRUPTS - ACT OF 1867

NAME OF BANKRUPT	RESIDENCE	CASE NUMBER	CITY OF COURT	DATE FILED
WINDSOR, WILLIAM F.	*DOCKET ONLY	361	GREENSBORO	06/26/73
WINSTEAD, EDWIN	*DOCKET ONLY	418	NEW BERN	02/29/68
WISE, M.M.	HERTFORD	165	ELIZABETH CITY	02/28/68
WISE, WILL B.	HERTFORD	129	ELIZABETH CITY	02/07/68
WISEMAN, ALEX (107)	HENDERSON	139	ASHEVILLE	06/03/73
WISEMAN, JESSE P.	ROWAN	648	WILMINGTON	12/28/71
WISEMAN, JOSIAH	MCDOWELL	205	STATESVILLE	06/25/73
WISHAST, ELI	ROBESON	731	WILMINGTON	06/27/73
WISWALL, HOWARD	*DOCKET ONLY	1656	NEW BERN	02/15/77
WITHERSPOON, ISAAC	ROWAN	358	WILMINGTON	12/10/68
WITHERSPOON, WILLIAM	ASHE	52	STATESVILLE	02/18/73
WITHERSPOON, WILLIAM	ASHE	257	STATESVILLE	03/30/74
WITTKOWSKY & RINTELS	MCDOWELL	173	WILMINGTON	04/11/68
WITTKOWSKY & RINTELS	WILKES	174	WILMINGTON	04/11/68
WITTKOWSKY & RINTELS	WILKES	176	WILMINGTON	04/11/68
WITTKOWSKY & RINTELS		581	WILMINGTON	07/22/70
WODDY, RUFFIN	*DOCKET ONLY	504	NEW BERN	03/07/68
WOLF, HILLIARD J.	*DOCKET ONLY	120	GREENSBORO	02/21/73
WOLFE, H.E.	WASHINGTON	213	ELIZABETH CITY	03/27/68
WOMACK, G. P.	*DOCKET ONLY	895	NEW BERN	08/15/68
WOMBLE, MIAL	*DOCKET ONLY	363	GREENSBORO	06/27/73
WOMMACK, ROSWELL A.	*DOCKET ONLY	1323	NEW BERN	01/31/71
WONTHAM, EDWARD W.	*DOCKET ONLY	870	NEW BERN	06/22/68
WOOD, DANIEL B.	ROWAN	42	STATESVILLE	02/05/73
WOOD, DEMPSEY (SR)	*DOCKET ONLY	1304	NEW BERN	11/25/70
WOOD, J.H.	HALIFAX	199	ELIZABETH CITY	05/12/73
WOOD, J.H., SR.	NORTHAMPTON	214	ELIZABETH CITY	06/18/73
WOOD, JAMES N.	*DOCKET ONLY	392	NEW BERN	02/29/68
WOOD, JOHN	DAVIE	63	STATESVILLE	02/28/73
WOOD, JOHN	DAVIE	63	STATESVILLE	02/28/73
WOOD, JOHN L.	PASQUOTANK	17	ELIZABETH CITY	08/25/67
WOOD, JOHNATHAN R	PASQUOTANK	654	ELIZABETH CITY	08/16/76
WOOD, M.L.	BERTIE	589	ELIZABETH CITY	06/02/73
WOOD, M.L.	BERTIE	210	ELIZABETH CITY	06/05/73
WOOD, ROBERT	NEW HANOVER	377	WILMINGTON	12/22/68
WOOD, SPIERS N.	*DOCKET ONLY	917	NEW BERN	08/22/68
WOOD, T.S.	ROWAN	505	WILMINGTON	01/01/69
WOOD, WILLIAM H.	*DOCKET ONLY	695	NEW BERN	05/19/68
WOOD, WILLIAM R.	HALIFAX	501	ELIZABETH CITY	11/20/69
WOODARD, STARKIE S.	NORTHAMPTON	379	ELIZABETH CITY	09/01/68
WOODARD, WILL W.	CHOWAN	192	ELIZABETH CITY	02/29/68
WOODARD, WILLIAM H.	*DOCKET ONLY	825	NEW BERN	05/30/68
WOODBURN, R. M.	*DOCKET ONLY	283	GREENSBORO	05/21/73
WOODING, JOHN E.	*DOCKET ONLY	649	NEW BERN	04/18/68
WOODROOF, BENJAMIN	NORTHAMPTON	603	ELIZABETH CITY	06/30/73
WOODROOF, BENJAMINE	NORTHAMPTON	225	ELIZABETH CITY	07/07/73
WOODS, HUGH	*DOCKET ONLY	451	GREENSBORO	01/13/74
WOODS, JAMES	*DOCKET ONLY	885	NEW BERN	05/02/68
WOODS, JOSEPH	*DOCKET ONLY	809	GREENSBORO	05/10/76
WOODSON, EDWARD C.	*DOCKET ONLY	1181	NEW BERN	12/30/68
WOODWARD, A.J.	CUMBERLAND	599	WILMINGTON	11/17/70
WOODWARD, DAVID	DUPLIN	723	WILMINGTON	06/13/73
WOODY, A. C.	*DOCKET ONLY	807	NEW BERN	05/30/68
WOODY, JAMES	*DOCKET ONLY	811	NEW BERN	05/30/68
WOODY, THOMAS	*DOCKET ONLY	808	NEW BERN	05/30/68
WOODY, JAMES D.	*DOCKET ONLY	573	NEW BERN	03/19/68
WOOLEN, DAVID	*DOCKET ONLY	296	NEW BERN	02/13/68
WOOLLARD, JEREMIAH	*DOCKET ONLY	1496	NEW BERN	07/31/73
WOOLLCOTT, WILLIAM	*DOCKET ONLY	414	NEW BERN	02/20/68
WOOLLIN, CHARLES W.		624	WILMINGTON	04/12/71
WOOLTON, JOHN F.	GASTON	233	STATESVILLE	09/18/73
WOOTEN, JOSIAH	*DOCKET ONLY	880	NEW BERN	05/20/68
WOOTEN, RICHARD S.	*DOCKET ONLY	879	NEW BERN	05/20/68
WORRELL, CYRUS	HERTFORD	177	ELIZABETH CITY	04/29/68
WORRELL, JOHN	HERTFORD	360	ELIZABETH CITY	10/19/68
WORSLEY, HENRY G.	*DOCKET ONLY	1091	NEW BERN	12/26/68

NORTH CAROLINA BANKRUPTS - ACT OF 1867

NAME OF BANKRUPT	RESIDENCE	CASE NUMBER	CITY OF COURT	DATE FILED
WORTH, DANIEL	*DOCKET ONLY	611	GREENSBORO	05/08/78
WORTHAM, GEORGE	*DOCKET ONLY	1719	NEW BERN	08/30/78
WRENN, W.W.	*DOCKET ONLY	414	NEW BERN	02/29/68
WRIGH, SAMUEL T.	*DOCKET ONLY	1258	NEW BERN	12/31/68
WRIGHT, DAVID L	*DOCKET ONLY	60	GREENSBORO	01/14/73
WRIGHT, GAMALIEL	CAMDEN	85	ELIZABETH CITY	12/18/67
WRIGHT, JAMES	*DOCKET ONLY	810	NEW BERN	05/30/68
WRIGHT, JOHN L	DAVIE	188	WILMINGTON	04/21/68
WRIGHT, L. P.	*DOCKET ONLY	453	NEW BERN	03/02/68
WRIGHT, S.P.	*DOCKET ONLY	952	NEW BERN	11/02/68
WRIGHT, THOMAS M.	*DOCKET ONLY	326	GREENSBORO	06/06/73
WRIGHT, WILLIAM N.	*DOCKET ONLY	1291	NEW BERN	08/08/70
WRIGHT, WILLIAM T.	*DOCKET ONLY	1227	NEW BERN	12/31/68
WRIGHTSEL, RILEY	*DOCKET ONLY	300	GREENSBORO	05/29/73
WYATT, WILLIAM H.	DAVIE	308	WILMINGTON	05/30/68
WYCHE, PERRY W.	*DOCKET ONLY	1519	NEW BERN	09/12/73
WYCHE, WILLIAM	NORTHAMPTON	430	ELIZABETH CITY	11/28/68
WYNNE, T.H.	CHOWAN	312	ELIZABETH CITY	05/18/68
WYNNE, WILLIAM B.	*DOCKET ONLY	940	NEW BERN	10/05/68
YANCEY, ELIZABETH	*DOCKET ONLY	33	NEW BERN	10/23/67
YARBROUGH, HENRY	*DOCKET ONLY	364	NEW BERN	02/24/68
YARBROUGH, MONROE	*DOCKET ONLY	577	NEW BERN	03/17/68
YATES, JESSE	WILKES	12	STATESVILLE	12/02/72
YELVERTON, ROBERT	*DOCKET ONLY	1084	NEW BERN	12/25/68
YELVESTON, B. D.	*DOCKET ONLY	1225	NEW BERN	12/29/68
YEOMANS, A. J.	*DOCKET ONLY	768	NEW BERN	06/02/68
YORK, A. J.	*DOCKET ONLY	5	GREENSBORO	07/10/78
YORK, LEANDER	*DOCKET ONLY	41	GREENSBORO	12/07/72
YOST, MARTIN	ROWAN	141	STATESVILLE	05/21/73
YOUNG, ARCHIBALD L.	ROWAN	290	STATESVILLE	05/02/78
YOUNG, GEORGE P.	*DOCKET ONLY	1385	NEW BERN	04/23/72
YOUNG, ISAAC J.	*DOCKET ONLY	1661	NEW BERN	04/17/78
YOUNG, ISHAM	*DOCKET ONLY	1577	NEW BERN	03/30/74
YOUNG, J.A.		635	WILMINGTON	06/15/71
YOUNG, JAMES	RUTHERFORD	60	WILMINGTON	01/21/68
YOUNG, JOHN	*DOCKET ONLY	56	GREENSBORO	01/09/73
YOUNG, JOHN A	MECKLENBURG	568	WILMINGTON	02/28/70
YOUNG, JOHN A	MECKLENBURG	609	WILMINGTON	01/16/71
YOUNG, JOHN A	MECKLENBURG	655	ELIZABETH CITY	11/26/72
YOUNG, MCNEELEY &	ROWAN	107	WILMINGTON	03/01/68
YOUNG, SAMUEL H.	*DOCKET ONLY	1667	NEW BERN	05/01/78
YOUNG, THOMAS W.	*DOCKET ONLY	100	NEW BERN	12/12/67
YOUNG, W.R.		578	WILMINGTON	05/08/70
ZIGLER, C. B.	*DOCKET ONLY	1095	NEW BERN	12/29/68
ZIMMERMAN, DANIEL	DAVIE	81	STATESVILLE	04/09/73
ZOELLERM EDWARD	*DOCKET ONLY	1079	NEW BERN	12/26/68

www.ingramcontent.com/pod-product-compliance
Lightning Source LLC
Chambersburg PA
CBHW030301030426
42336CB00009B/481